STRESS and the FAMILY

VOLUME II:
Coping With
Catastrophe

Edited by

Charles R. Figley &
Hamilton I. McCubbin

13745

BRUNNER/MAZEL, *Publishers* • New York

Library of Congress Cataloging in Publication Data

Main entry under title:

Stress and the family.

  Vol. 2 edited by Charles R. Figley & Hamilton I.
McCubbin.
  Includes bibliographies and indexes.
  Contents: v. 1. Coping with normative transitions
—v. 2. Coping with catastrophe.
  1. Family—Addresses, essays, lectures.
2. Stress (Psychology)—Addresses, essays, lectures.
I. McCubbin, Hamilton I. II. Figley, Charles R.,
1944-   . [DNLM: 1. Stress, Psychological.
2. Life change events. 3. Family. WM 172 S9136]

HQ734.S9735   1983   306.8'5   83-6048
ISBN 0-87630-321-1 (v. 1)
ISBN 0-87630-332-7 (v. 2)

Copyright © 1983 by Charles R. Figley & Hamilton I. McCubbin

Published by

BRUNNER/MAZEL, INC.
19 Union Square West
New York, N.Y. 10003

MANUFACTURED IN THE UNITED STATES OF AMERICA

Dedicated to

our family friends,
Reuben and Marion Hill,

and our families,
Marilyn and Jessica,
and
Marilyn, Todd, and Wendy and Laurie

Preface to the Series

As editors of this two-volume series, we are delighted to introduce the reader to a burgeoning area of research in the social sciences: family stress and coping. The books view the family as both producing and reacting to stress and attempt to identify the sources of stress from either inside or outside the family microsystem. Further, the volumes distinguish between sudden, unpredictable, and overwhelming catastrophic stress and the more "normal," gradual, and cumulative life stressors encountered over the life span. Moreover, the series brings into focus several rich perspectives which effectively integrate the hundreds of generalizations about the functional and dysfunctional methods family members use to cope with stress.

We hope that these volumes will be a unique contribution to the collection of publications already in print or in press by providing conceptual clarity and scholarly direction. This series represents an area of inquiry which has emerged quite recently, though early elements date back over a half-century. We build upon the important contributions of Reuben Hill, Hans Selye, Richard Lazarus, Mardi Horowitz, and many others in an attempt to synthesize the relevant research into an organized set of empirical generalizations. These are designed, among other things, to stimulate new hypotheses and innovations in research and intervention in this growing area.

Moreover, we hope that this series will help move the field of family studies forward by viewing family stress as a predictable aspect of family development and change over the life span. In this preface let us briefly discuss our purpose, beliefs, objectives, organizational structure, and how this nearly three-year enterprise was conceived and produced.

PURPOSE AND BELIEFS

The purpose of the series is to organize a compendium of empirically-based observations about the ways families produce, encounter, and cope with stress. The intended readers include students and professionals interested in understanding and helping people within the family context.

From the beginning we want our values known; by doing so we alert the reader to the presence of potential bias in our efforts to relate the facts as we find them. For instance, we believe that family members often know better than anyone else what is best for them and their family—better than clinicians, professors, advice column writers and other experts, for example. We also believe that the role of "helping" families is one of helping families attain goals, helping families experience the kind of life together they wish to have, though it may be different from what we wish for our own families. Finally, we believe that consulting with families is superior to directing them, and educating families is superior to indoctrinating them.

OBJECTIVES

In an effort to explicate the nature and consequences of stress for people living within families, we intend that our volumes reach five specific objectives:

(a) to clearly define and provide a framework for viewing the family system as both a stress absorber as well as a stress producer;

(b) to explicate the key concepts and variables associated with this framework;

(c) to identify the important areas of research inquiry which converge into the family stress area of study that facilitates the development of a discrete set of axioms toward which a theory of family stress can be built;

(d) to note the effective strategies of intervention by professionals to either mitigate or ameliorate the impairments of family stress; and

(e) to clearly identify the various sources of stress, stress reactions of family members, stress-coping resources, repertoire, and behaviors.

ORGANIZATIONAL STRUCTURE

The reader should be aware by now that *Stress and the Family* is divided into two volumes. The first volume, *Coping with Normative Transitions*, focuses on the everyday stressors families experience, especially those many transitions throughout the life cycle as family relationships change and family members grow and develop. The second volume, *Coping with Catastrophe*, focuses on the extraordinary stressors which strike families suddenly and often overwhelm the family's ability to cope. In each volume, chapters are organized into roughly two groups by the locus of family stressors: either from inside the family system (e.g., birth of a child, death in the family) or from outside the family system (e.g., economic inflation, unemployment).

A large collection of noted experts in various areas have been commissioned to write chapters which utilize the family stress framework to answer 10 questions:

1) What is the family stressor which is the focus of the chapter?
2) Why should there be an interest in this stressor?
3) What are some precepts/principles which make it easier to understand and appreciate the complexities and methods of coping with this stressor?
4) What are the elements of this stressor which are upsetting and require those affected to develop methods of coping?
5) What are the typical, dysfunctional methods individuals and families employ to deal with this source of stress?
6) What are the typical, functional methods of coping?
7) What are the resources available to the family system which are so effective in coping with the stressor?
8) What are some practical prescriptions for dealing with this stressor?
9) What are the effective methods employed by professionals and clinicians to help people and their families cope?
10) How can dysfunctional stress reactions be prevented?

Chapters 1, 10, and 15 in Volume I and Chapters 1 and 11 in Volume II, in addition to the introductions to the volumes, provide important conceptual clarity in an attempt to present an overview of the chapters that follow them. Definitions and discussions of critical concepts and synthesizing models and frameworks are found within these chapters.

HISTORY AND EMERGENCE OF THIS SERIES

To date, these two volumes are the first attempts to provide a textbook for students and professionals interested in a comprehensive understanding of stress and the family. Scholarly discussions of individual and family stress, however, have appeared in a wide range of behavioral, social, and medical publications for the past 60 years. Traditionally, these studies and clinical observations have been limited in scope, focusing on individuals exclusively or isolated circumstances of families in stressful situations. In addition, these previous works tend to underscore the dysfunctional and deleterious effects of stressful life events.

This two-volume series attempts to clarify the nature and processes of family adjustment to stress, with a deliberate and well-placed emphasis on family coping and support. The emergence of this series is due, in part, to the special chemistry which results in the collaboration between colleagues from different scholarly disciplines and interests. Figley is a family psychologist with special interests in how human beings react to traumatic events within the context of the family. McCubbin is a family psychologist with special interest in the family system's reactions to stress mediated by its members' coping responses and community supports. Together we share many basic assumptions about stress and the family, yet differ in our approach to many issues within this area. The former, for example, is more concerned about the clinical intervention implications and the latter more interested in the conceptualization and measurement issues.

Our collaboration dates back to 1975 when we served as co-panelists in a research symposium on the family readjustment problems of returning Vietnam veterans. We were each working in the same area, but within different contexts. Dr. McCubbin was Head of the Family Studies Branch of the Center for POW Studies at the Naval Health Research Center in San Diego. There he directed a major study of the impact of father absence and initial impact of his return among the families of prisoners of war and those missing in action during the Vietnam war. At the same time, Dr. Figley was studying the emotional upheavals associated with the war by studying Vietnam combat veterans and their families in his capacity as founder and director of the Consortium on Veteran Studies at Purdue University.

In 1976 we began to speculate together and separately about the stressors of separation and reunion associated with war, building upon the nearly 30 years of pioneering work of Reuben Hill. Less than four years later we, along with a dozen other colleagues, formed the Task Force on Families of Catastrophe to assist the U.S. State Department in efforts to care for the families of American personnel trapped in Iran between November, 1979, and January, 1981. At that time we applied what we had learned about the families affected by wars and other traumatic events. We became convinced that a textbook was needed which could pull together the family stress research literature not only to help policy makers and interventionists working with families in crisis, but for the field in general.

The first step in that direction was the 1980 Groves Conference on Marriage and the Family with the theme, "Stress and the Family." Dr. Figley served as program chair and Dr. McCubbin delivered the keynote address. It was from this conference, held in Gatlinburg, Tennessee in May, 1980, that many of the initial ideas and organizational structure of this series emerged. For example, many of the chapters contributed to both volumes (Chapters 2-5 and 12 in Volume I and Chapters 1, 4, 5, and 10 in Volume II) were presented in some form at this four-day seminal conference. Indeed, because of its conception within the Groves Conference and the importance of this society of family scholars and practitioners to future contributions to the social sciences, all royalties from the sale of these volumes are being donated to the Groves Foundation. These and other funds will enable the Groves Conference to continue to sponsor innovative and lively symposia each year, bringing together students of the family to consider the past and present and to speculate on the future as it has for nearly 50 years.

We hope that you enjoy the series and can begin soon to apply its lessons in whatever context is of importance to you.

Charles R. Figley
Hamilton I. McCubbin

Acknowledgments

The enterprise of scholarly inquiry can be an exciting and worthwhile venture, as the reader will discover in this volume. What is less obvious are the numerous individuals who have contributed so much of their time and talent to the creation of this volume.

As noted elsewhere, my collaboration with Hamilton McCubbin nearly spans a decade. We have become trusted friends and colleagues over the years, especially during the process of co-editing the two volumes in this series. His international stature as a family stress scholar is clearly evident throughout this volume and I am deeply indebted to him for his inspirational contributions as well as his editorial expertise.

The Groves Conference on Marriage and the Family deserves special acknowledgment. This society was the first to see the importance of the concept of stress and its relevance to the family and commissioned a national conference on the topic. Many of the chapters in this volume were conceived as a result of that conference.

It would have been nearly impossible to undertake and complete this massive project without the cooperation and assistance of so many at Purdue University. Dr. Norma Compton, Dean of the School of Consumer and Family Sciences, Dr. Billy R. Baumgardt, Director of the Agricultural Experiment Station, and Dr. Robert A. Lewis, Head of the Department of Child Development and Family Studies, provided critical administrative support and encouragement. The faculty of the Department of Child Development and Family Studies and the Child and Family Research Institute were extremely important in the development and completion of the project in various capacities: contributors, reviewers, or sources of encouragement. Also I appreciate the clerical help of Roberta Thayer, Karen Hinkley and Barbara Brecker, as well as the support with various tasks from my graduate students, Joan Jurich, Richard Kishur, and Sandra Burge. But the key person in the project who helped bring it to fruition was Vicki Hogancamp, who served at various times as conference coordinator for the conference on "Stress and the Family," editorial assistant, and co-author of one of the chapters in the series. Ms. Hogancamp's extraordinary skills and professionalism were clearly evident in her success at assisting the editors in critiquing, organizing, rewriting, editing, and typing a considerable portion of this volume.

We are also indebted to those who helped us read and review manuscripts, bringing to the task their special expertise on the various topics discussed in this book. Our thanks to Jan Allen, Arthur Blank, Veda Boyer, Bernard Bloom, Ann Wolbert Burgess, Michael Clapman, Richard Clayton, Barbara Dahl, Thomas Drabeck, Robert Fetsch, Richard Gelles, Harold Hackney, Donald Hartsough, James Huber, Anthony Jurich, Daniel Lonnquist, Phyllis Moen, Thomas Saarinen, Nancy Sederberg, Graham Spanier, M. Duncan Stanton, Dena Targ, Richard Venjohn and William Yarber. We would especially like to thank Laura Smart for her careful reading of the entire manuscript and her excellent suggestions on style and organization which improved the readability of this and the previous volume in the series.

I would also like to acknowledge several colleagues who were helpful to me during my sabbatical leave, enabling me to complete work on the series by providing resources of their respective institutions and the stimulation of their respective minds: Ann Wolbert Burgess, Boston University Medical School; Robert Rich, the Woodrow Wilson School of Public and International Affairs, Princeton University; and John Talbott, Payne-Whitney Clinic, Department of Psychiatry, Cornell Medical College.

Charles R. Figley
Purdue University

This volume would not have been possible were it not for the help of those who shared our commitment to understanding families under stress.

My co-editor, Charles Figley, has long been a colleague and friend, and a prime mover in this project. His skill as a scholar and an editor will long be appreciated by me.

We would not have been able to manage the challenge of integrating the various perspectives into a meaningful whole without the editorial work of Catherine Davidson at the University of Minnesota. Her patience, kindness, and thoroughness played a major part in smoothing out the rough edges and in giving the volume a touch of class. I would also like to thank Joan Patterson who took the time and offered her professional skills in reviewing several manuscripts.

I am very appreciative of the assistance given to us by key administrators at the University of Minnesota. I would like to thank Dr. Richard Sauer, Director, Agricultural Experiment Station, University of Minnesota, who gave this project the support it needed to see its way to completion. I would also like to acknowledge the continued support and patience of Dean Keith McFarland, and Associate Dean Signe Betsinger of the College of Home Economics at the University of Minnesota. Their encouragement was, as always, greatly appreciated.

Because this volume was prepared in part during a sabbatical leave, I would like to thank the University of Minnesota for allowing me this respite from academic and administrative duties and for continuing commitment to scholarship. I would also like to thank Gardner Lindzey, Director of the Center for Advanced Studies in the Behavioral Science at Stanford University for providing a nurturing setting to pursue the completion of this volume while serving as a summer scholar at the Center.

I am also indebted to the faculty and staff of the Department of Family Social Science, especially to Gloria Lawrence, Jane Schwanke, Todd McCubbin, Susan Rains-Johnson, Kay Lapour, Emma Haugan, Alida Malkus, and Dorothea Berggren for their assistance in manuscript preparation.

I am very grateful to those scholars who served as referees of the papers in this book. Their special expertise contributed greatly to the quality of scholarship. Our thanks to Professors Linda Budd, James Maddock, Jeylan Mortimer, Ronald Pitzer and Paul Rosenblatt of the University of Minnesota; Professor William Doherty of the University of Iowa; Professor Francille Firebaugh of Michigan State University; Professor Beatrice Paolucci of Ohio State University; and Professor Candyce Russell of Kansas State University. I would especially like to thank Professor Laura Smart of Northern Illinois University for her careful reading of the entire volume, and for her suggestions on style and organization, which improved the readability of the book.

Hamilton I. McCubbin
University of Minnesota

Contents

Contributors

Sandra K. Burge, M.S.
Doctoral student, Department of Child Development and Family Studies, Purdue University, West Lafayette, Indiana.

John F. Crosby, Ph.D.
Chairman, Department of Family Studies, University of Kentucky, Lexington.

Catherine L. Cyrus, M.S.
Doctoral Student, Department of Child Development and Family Studies, Purdue University, West Lafayette.

Charles R. Figley, Ph.D.
Professor and Director, Child and Family Research Institute, Purdue University, West Lafayette.

Thomas J. Glynn, Ph.D.
Psychological Sciences Branch, Division of Research, National Institute on Drug Abuse, Rockville, Maryland.

Vicki E. Hogancamp, B.A.
Assistant Director, Consortium on Veteran Studies, Purdue University, West Lafayette.

Edna J. Hunter, Ph.D.
Professor of Psychology, Director, Family Study Center, U.S. International University, San Diego, California.

Nancy L. Jose, Ph.D.
Assistant Professor, Department of Human Development and Family Relations, University of Kentucky, Lexington.

Hamilton I. McCubbin, Ph.D.
Professor and Head, Department of Family Social Science, University of Minnesota, St. Paul.

Marian P. Needle, Ph.D.
Office of International Programs, University of Minnesota, St. Paul.

Richard H. Needle, Ph.D., M.P.H.
Department of Family Social Science and School of Public Health, University of Minnesota, St. Paul.

Joan M. Patterson, M.S.
Doctoral Candidate and Research Associate, Department of Family Social Science, University of Minnesota, St. Paul.

Shirley M. Smith, M.A.
Assistant Dean of Academic Services, Purdue University, West Lafayette.

Douglas H. Sprenkle, Ph.D.
Associate Professor and Director of Research and Training for Family Therapy, Department of Child Development and Family Studies, Purdue University, West Lafayette.

Patricia Voydanoff, Ph.D.
Director of Research, Center for the Study of Family Development, University of Dayton, Dayton, Ohio.

Introduction

This second volume of *Stress and the Family* includes 11 chapters focusing on family stress emerging from the catastrophic events which impact families infrequently, but powerfully and without warning. As will be discussed throughout this volume, catastrophes are sudden, unexpected, frightening experiences for the individuals and families who survive them and for all the others who care about them.

In all, 15 scholars from five separate disciplines discuss nine catastrophes which could affect the family. Each chapter begins with a brief case study of a family struggling with the impact of a particular catastrophe. After discussing the case briefly and noting the pervasiveness and significance of the problem, each chapter 1) identifies and describes the primary sources of stress; 2) notes the characteristic ways families attempt to utilize their resources and cope with these stressors—both effectively and ineffectively; and 3) concludes with a discussion of how others—friends, professionals, or policymakers—can best help the family.

As will become evident, there are certain similarities in the ways families cope with catastrophes. In general, families utilize their inner strengths, pull together to confront the crisis—putting aside for a time petty squabbles—and draw upon outside resources among their kin and other social support networks. Some families, however, seem to fall apart when catastrophe strikes, as a water glass shattering after a sudden shift in temperature. These families cope ineffectively with the catastrophe and, depending on the extent of the crisis, recover more slowly, if at all.

As any experienced helper knows, s/he can only have limited impact on improving a family's situation, but a great deal of impact in disrupting it. Helping a family requires extremely sensitive judgments about when and when not to intervene and how much support, guidance, education, protection, or therapy to give. In most instances, a family will recover from a catastrophe, regardless of the quality of intervention.

We believe that to be effective in helping families affected by catastrophe the helper must understand the dynamics of family stress and coping, which are discussed thoroughly in this volume, so that

(a) the signs of stress and strain in the family can be detected;
(b) the functional and adaptive methods of family coping can be recognized and distinguished from dysfunctional and maladaptive methods;
(c) the family's progress from disorganization to crisis resolution can be detected; and
(d) the family's call for help can be recognized and provided.

The help provided can then be effectively evaluated and improved for families who request it again.

OVERVIEW OF THE CHAPTERS

Family reactions to crisis are both predictable and complex. The resources available to the family, both tangible and intangible, within and outside itself, are important to developing effective, functional coping methods, irrespective of the catastrophe or stressors.

Catastrophes

In Chapter 1 Charles Figley provides a blueprint for understanding the intricate patterns of individual and family reactions to catastrophes. He notes that a catastrophe is a classification of events which is associated with a wide gamut of stress-related consequences, affecting the individuals who survive them and those the survivors turn to for comfort—the family in particular and the social support system in general.

The central thesis of the chapter is that catastrophes affect not only individuals, but also the families within which the survivors reside and that, paradoxically, our membership in the family both exposes us to the catastrophes of other members and helps us to deal with those that affect us as individuals. In other words, our families—and other support systems for that matter—both treat us for and infect us with the effects of catastrophe. Specifically, the chapter has three major functions: 1) to define and discuss the significance of catastrophe and its crisis-inducing qualities; 2) to define and discuss several key concepts relevant to this discussion (e.g., trauma, victim, and survivor); and 3) to present a theoretical model which accounts for both immediate and long-term emotional reactions of both individuals and families associated with catastrophe.

Illness

Joan Patterson and Hamilton McCubbin, in Chapter 2, discuss the catastrophe of chronic illness in children and its impact on the family. They note how the family is fundamentally transformed by this catastrophe, straining its energy for coping. The authors point out that there are few existing guidelines for these families; most often they are left to fend for themselves. The authors discuss the sources of stress, which include concern about the welfare of the child, efforts to manage the demands of the illness (including both securing competent medical care and providing home treatment), and the pressures within the family associated with the illness.

Drug Abuse

Richard Needle, Thomas Glynn and Marian Needle (Chapter 3) have not only been involved in the research on adolescent drug abuse, but have also designed and administered drug treatment and prevention programs. In their chapter they note that teenage drug and alcohol use is widespread in this country, more than ever before in history. Indeed, drug *experimentation* by youthful family members would be a topic more appropriate for consideration in Volume I of *Stress and the Family;* and to a limited extent it is (see Volume I, Chapter 5). As the authors point out, families of teen drug *abusers* are, at least in the beginning, clearly experiencing catastrophic stress. The typical family reactions include some or all of the following: shock, fear, denial of the problem, rage and hostility toward the teen—even though the drug-abusing child may be close to death.

In reviewing the drug use literature, the authors note first the contributions of the family *to* adolescent drug abuse before proceeding to identify the impact of abuse *on* the family. They go on to present the primary sources of stress for these families, most of which are eventually able to mobilize their natural resources and, with the assistance of sources outside the family, help their children overcome the impairments and habits of substance abuse. Finally, the authors discuss the variations and effectiveness of professional intervention, emphasizing the importance of viewing and treating substance abuse as a *family* problem.

Abandonment

In contrast to the first two catastrophe chapters, which focus primarily on the child's disability, Chapter 4 by Douglas Sprenkle and Catherine Cyrus focuses on parents and the aftermath when one abandons and seeks a divorce from the other. The Academy Award-winning movie, *Kramer vs. Kramer*, for example provides an eloquent illustration of the issues and dynamics considered by this chapter: divorce, single parenthood, financial strains, and resentment toward the abandoning spouse are examples.

The authors first delineate the subjective experience of being emotionally abandoned—"dumped," as some have described it. The sources of stress for the abandoned spouse overlap considerably with the stressors of anyone experiencing a divorce, which has been discussed more fully in Volume I (cf., Chapter 7 by Ahrons); however, emotional abandonment includes additional stressors. The authors utilize the ABCX model of adaptation to family crisis (see Chapter 2) to conceptualize the abandonment experiences, and present a series of hypotheses. The latter portion of the chapter outlines the fundamentals of divorce therapy, which can help the client to revise self-destructive meanings attributed to the abandonment experience, and maximize resources so as to develop alternatives to the now-defunct marriage relationship.

Death

A substantial percentage of families is able to avoid the catastrophes of drug abuse, illness, and divorce; none can avoid death. As John Crosby and Nancy Jose point out in Chapter 5, death is nearly always ranked as one of life's most stressful events, with the death of a spouse *the* most stressful of all. After noting the specific sources of stress for the family, they discuss and contrast dysfunctional and functional methods of coping with death and grief. They note that family members who continue to avoid acknowledgment of the death, or conversely continue to obliterate the memory of the deceased, or inordinately idolize the deceased are in different ways resisting the critical and natural process of grieving. In contrast, the authors point out, the survivors who soon accept the facts and consequences of the death, the feelings associated with the deceased (e.g., guilt about relating to and surviving the deceased), and provide support and acceptance of other family members' reactions to the death will adapt to the death most effectively.

Unemployment

In contrast to the previous chapters which have focused on catastrophes which emerge from within the family, unemployment is most often imposed on the family from *outside* its boundaries. As Patricia Voydanoff (Chapter 6) points out, however, the impact is no less profound in many families, especially in those whose sole wage earner suddenly becomes jobless and is unable to find work soon.

Voydanoff identifies two major areas of stress—financial loss and role loss—for the family of the unemployed person. She goes on to note, however, that the family's definition of the event and family resources are important mediating factors in the overall impact of the catastrophe on the family.

Next, Voydanoff discusses the characteristic patterns by which these families of catastrophe cope—both in ineffective and effective ways. Adaptability and flexibility appear to be key factors. The latter part of the chapter focuses on the implications of the circumstances of families of unemployment in terms of policies (e.g., plant closing disclosures to allow sufficient time for families to prepare), practices by professionals (e.g., understanding of labor market dynamics, facilitating self-sufficiency and pride), and research (e.g., implications of the increase in *female* labor force participation and unemployment).

Rape

Perhaps the most intuitively frightening and traumatizing catastrophe is rape. Unlike the other crisis events noted above which impact the entire family, rape, as Sandra Burge notes in Chapter 7, is often kept secret from other family members because the victim fears blame and rejection. Yet, at the same time, she is unable to take advantage of what research has shown to be a significant resource: the emotional support of family and friends, which can help her work through the "rape trauma syndrome."

Burge points out that, because the crime is rape and thus involves sexual contact, many victims suffer from the "second rape" of societal disapproval and incredulity.

There is a thorough discussion of the methods families use in coping with the catastrophe. Dysfunctional methods include patronization, distraction, and protective silence. Functional methods include maintenance and utilization of quality family relationships, effective communication about the catastrophe and its impact, flexibility in re-covery, and taking advantage of external support services.

Disaster

Like unemployment, natural disasters can have a devastating impact, not only on the family and its members, but also on an entire community and its citizens. In Chapter 8, Shirley Smith notes the special trauma-producing nature of natural disasters, whose central elements make them so stressful. These elements produce a sense of danger, helpless-ness, destruction, disruption, and general loss. They are experienced to a greater or lesser degree, starting with warning (if any) of the impending danger, evacuation (if any), and the immediate and long-term adjust-ments to the impact of the disaster. Such an impact may include damage to the family's home, neighborhood, or the family wage earner(s)' place of employment. Smith points out that, at the very least, the family's routine is affected and the social and familial support network strained.

For many communities, as well as families, the impact of disasters is not always bad, at least in the long run. Many find now that such a challenge forced upon them by the natural disaster provides sufficient incentive to make a fresh start and try new methods and solutions to difficulties (such as restoring run-down housing, and creating a strong community spirit).

War

Chapter 9, by Vicki Hogancamp and Charles Figley, focuses on the immediate and long-term effects of war on the combatants who fought in it and the families to whom they returned. The particular souces of stress for the families during war center around separation and fear for the veteran's safety. In contrast to the stressors of the "family in wait-ing," homecoming and life thereafter pose much more complex and insidious pressures.

Though attempting to capture the experiences of most American war veteran families, the authors pay special attention to the latest group: those of the Vietnam era. For the returning veteran, his war experiences and the various changes in society and his family are stress-producing enough. In addition, he must contend with expectations to return to normal, the difficulties of finding employment, and any service-con-nected medical problems (including, for example, drug abuse and chem-ical poisoning). As with other survivors of traumatic events, the veteran's family is often the context within which he attempts to face and cope with these and other stressors. The authors note that denial and silence, anger, bitterness, and blame are common reactions to these stressors. If these reactions continue, however, the veteran and his family will be unable to deal effectively with the potentially chronic problems noted above. The authors go on to identify methods of coping which do lead to adaptation: understanding stress reactions, communication, flexibility, utilization of social support and community services, and a willingness to confront and view those elements of one's war experiences from a more constructive and positive perspective.

Captivity

One valuable lesson resulting from the recent international crisis surrounding American Embassy personnel held hostage in Iran was that the wives, parents, children, and other kin and friends of these captives were also held hostage, at least in spirit. The public became aware of the special stressors of the hostage families, similar to the ordeal of the families of prisoners of war. Chapter 10 by Edna Hunter places the families of the hostages within the broader context of captivity. She notes, for example, that although this catastrophe is similar to others (e.g., war, rape), captivity experiences for both the individual and family differ significantly in that they are most often both prolonged and indefinite. For the captive, she points out that important factors in assessing the stress include the duration, treatment, group support, and communications (letter, phone) with families.

The future and circumstances of the homecoming and process of reintegration are important sources of stress for the prisoner-hostage later. Some families cope well with both the separation and reintegration periods. Those who do not, according to Hunter, exhibit stagnation, self-induced isolation, blame and parental pressure/neglect. Those who do cope well tend to have been at least somewhat prepared for such a crisis, take a constructive/positive emotional stance, develop and utilize effective family communication, and are open to and utilize available interpersonal/social and professional support systems.

Looking to the Future

We, the editors, collaborate in Chapter 11 to provide closure not only to this volume, but also to the series. In the interest of preparing for the future we address the implications of our understanding about families and stress by focusing on four distinct areas: research, education, clinical treatment, and social policy. In the process of discussing these areas we meld in the various précis noted in the 25 other chapters in the two volumes.

A FINAL NOTE TO THE READER

As noted in the preface to *Stress and the Family*, our initial interest in this area of study emerged from our investigations of the immediate and long-term effects of the Vietnam war on the survivors and their families. What we discovered in this enterprise, beyond what we reported in voluminous technical reports and publications, both depressed and inspired us. War itself, as with other violent acts of man and nature, rarely results in progress; rather, it most often results in countless human tragedies which last a lifetime—lost lives, limbs, esteem, and confidence. This is the depressive nature of catastrophe; it hurts. As you read through the chapters which follow, we are sure that you will discover, as we have, the *inspiration* which accompanies catastrophes and their wake. Irrespective of the circumstances of the particular catastrophe, of the families it impacts, of the time and place it occurs, and of how long it lingers, the families of catastrophe survive. And more than simply surviving, most go on to lead happy and productive lives. Time does heal the wounds, but only to the extent that time is accompanied by other sources of strength which most families somehow find—and utilize effectively—in spite of the occasional well-intentioned, but unhelpful agencies, neighbors, friends, and relatives.

We hope that you will discover throughout this volume examples of how families spring back in rather characteristic ways to recover from life's most horrific events to resume their daily struggles and lifestyles. Knowing the process by which this occurs will help us—as either family members or as family professionals—facilitate, or at least not inhibit, the families of catastrophe in their struggle toward full recovery. But simply knowing that this process happens, has happened, and will continue to happen well beyond our own lifetimes gives us one additional measure of confidence in the vitality and power of the family.

STRESS
and the
FAMILY

VOLUME II:
Coping With
Catastrophe

CHAPTER

1

Catastrophes: An Overview of Family Reactions

CHARLES R. FIGLEY

The double doors of Community Hospital's emergency entrance swung open and Jose and Mary Allen rushed inside. Minutes ago they were phoned by the City Police Department and were informed that their 23-year-old daughter, Maria, had survived a head-on collision with another car. Maria's husband, Carl, who was driving her to the airport, was killed, along with the driver of the other car, which suddenly veered into their lane head-on. Jose and Mary went directly to the reception desk to ask how and when they would see their daughter; what was her condition? Mary was usually the calmer of the two but found herself screaming at the receptionist who wanted to know about insurance companies and home addresses. Those initial minutes in the emergency waiting room seemed like hours and the hours like days. Soon, though, they were joined by their two other daughters and several friends as the emergency medical team worked to save Maria's life. Just a week ago most of these same people had helped Jose and Mary celebrate their silver wedding anniversary. Everyone was so happy then. It seemed so long ago now.

*They waited three hours before receiving word that Maria would
survive and would probably recover fully over the next several
months. As they waited, there were several more emergency arrivals;
an assault, an industrial accident, and a near-drowning were the
worst of them. Each victim was accompanied by worried family and
friends. The Allens were not alone that night.*

*After more than a month Maria was released from the hospital to
complete her convalescence at her parent's home. Not only did her
family worry about Maria's physical condition, but they also worried
about her emotional condition. During her recovery she would
experience a collection of symptoms which would be clinically
diagnosed as "Post-traumatic Stress Disorder" (APA, 1980). This is
a common reaction among the victims of a wide variety of
catastrophic events which are emotionally upsetting. Maria's
symptoms included, for example, painful recollections of the accident
and initial experiences in the hospital; problems sleeping; moodiness;
emotional withdrawal; jumpiness; crying spells; and varying
amounts of depression associated with surviving when Carl did not.
During this recuperative period Maria's family would be a key factor
in her recovery from the emotional wounds of the accident as well
as the physical ones. Along the way she would discover, much to her
chagrin, that she was not the only one recovering from the emotional
wake of this catastrophe; so was her family.*

The story of the Allen family will unfold throughout this chapter. The
shock of the accident and the sudden and profound impact it had on
the lives of the victims—Maria *and* her family—exemplify the major
thesis of this chapter and those to follow: that the family is a critical ✓
support system to human beings during and following a traumatic event
and that the system and its members are affected in addition to the
victim, and sometimes to a greater degree. In order to lay the groundwork, this chapter will attempt to reach three objectives:

1) to define and discuss the significance of catastrophic events and
   their impact on human emotion and behavior;
2) to characterize the patterns of family reactions to catastrophic
   versus normative sources of stress; and
3) to characterize the functional versus the dysfunctional methods
   of families' coping with stress.

STRESS IS LIFE AND LIFE IS STRESS

The week prior to the accident, the Allen family celebrated an anniversary: Jose and Mary had been married 25 years. They were certainly years of pleasure and satisfaction, but they were also filled with anger, frustrations, disappointments, and several points of near breakup. The girls could recall the many marital squabbles lasting late into the night. But the youngest daughter, Ann, a senior in high school, reported that much of the tension was gone. Yet, there were other reasons now for her parents to be upset: Jose's job is pressure-packed since the housing market is way off and his income has dropped precipitously; Mary has returned to work as a nurse and is frustrated by the lack of time and energy to attend to household matters as she once did. Linda, the middle child and a sophomore in college, is forlorn over the recent breakup with Bob—they had planned to marry next year. Then there was the issue of the house: The parents wanted to sell it (it was too big for them now) and their children wanted them to keep it (the memories it held, they believed, were worth the extra expense). And, of course, Maria and her husband were very happy newlyweds, though they worried about keeping their jobs (the plant may close due to the economy).

No one can avoid the stress of life. Indeed, stress is not always negative; it is part of life. The complete *absence* of stress is as great a cause for concern as is too much. Stress is life and life is stress. What the Allens were recalling the week of the anniversary were the normative and environmental stressors discussed in detail in Volume I. Many of these are quite predictable and part of the natural growth and development of the family and its members through the life course. Often at some point in our lives, however, the individual and family developmental "rhythm" and routine may be jolted by an event occurring unexpectedly, off "schedule." These events and the pile-up of other normative stressors can cause the family to experience a crisis, under certain conditions. However, a catastrophe requires immediate attention and is, thus, synonymous with crisis.

CATASTROPHIC LIFE EXPERIENCES

At any time, anywhere, and under any circumstance we may be confronted with a catastrophe. A catastrophe is an event which is sudden, unexpected, often life-threatening (to us or someone we care deeply about), and due to the circumstances renders the survivors feeling an extreme sense of helplessness. With sufficient magnitude the event will 1) disrupt the lifestyle and routine of the survivors; 2) cause a sense of destruction, disruption, and loss; along with 3) a permanent and detailed memory of the event which may be recalled voluntarily or involuntarily (Burgess & Baldwin, 1981; Figley, 1978, 1979, 1982; Horowitz, 1979).

Victim Reactions

Figley (1979, 1982) has discussed the immediate and long-term consequences of catastrophe, drawing parallels, for example, among the emotional experiences of those who have survived war combat, being a prisoner of war, being a hostage of terrorists, being raped, or being a victim of a natural disaster. A simple model may be useful here to discuss the long-term impact of catastrophes as background for considering the role and impact of these catastrophic experiences in family life.

A Model of Catastrophic Experiences. There has been considerable speculation about how human beings behave in extreme emergency situations, such as passengers aboard a sinking ocean liner or disabled plane. How is it that some people stay calm, while others panic? What explains the sudden remembrances of a traumatic event which occurred a decade earlier, but which stimulates in the victim the same reactions as if it were happening again? Research reports have emerged over the last 40 years regarding, for example, soldiers in war (Figley, 1978; Grinker & Spiegel, 1945; Kalinowksy, 1950), flood victims (Bennet, 1970; Huerta & Horton, 1978), fire victims (Adler, 1943; Green, 1980), natural disaster victims (Chamberlain, 1980; Moore, 1958; Quarantelli & Dynes, 1977), terrorism (Ochberg, 1978), violence (Symonds, 1975), rape (Burgess & Holmstrom, 1979a and b; Katz & Mazur, 1979; Werner, 1972), and various other traumatic experiences (Horowitz, 1976; Janis, 1969; Lazarus, 1966). Except for Horowitz (1976, 1979), there is little discussion of both the lingering emotional impact of traumatic experiences *and* the *induction* of trauma during the event. The model presented below was developed for the purpose of illustration and discussion (see Figure 1). It helps us appreciate the immediate and long-term emotional consequences of a catastrophe for those who survive, as well as for the people who love and care for the survivor, particularly the family.

The diagram provides a schema of the interrelationship among 11 factors beginning with the catastrophic event and ending with emotional adjustment. In essence the model suggests a sequence of perceptions and reactions during and following a catastrophe. Catastrophic stress is not only a function of exposure to the catastrophe, but also a result of two additional factors. One is the coping ability the victim has prior to the event. Some researchers have found that previous experience with other catastrophes (especially similar ones), an internal locus of control, hardiness in adversity, and an ability to concentrate under pressure are coping mechanisms which reduce the amount of stress experienced during an emergency situation. Maria, for example, in the seconds surrounding the auto accident, was able to stay calm enough (rather than "freezing" in a helpless state) to both alert her husband to the oncoming car and help him direct the car away from its path.

Another set of factors which are associated with the amount of stress experienced by catastrophe victims during and just after a catastrophe includes several "situational parameters." These comprise sociality (the extent to which there was communication among fellow victims), ignominy (the degree to which the experience was degrading, humiliating, embarrassing), and a sense of helplessness (inability to influence or stop the situation, especially the danger). These three sets of factors—the catastrophic event or emergency, the victim's coping ability, and the situational context of the victim—account for the degree of intensity of the traumatic stress.

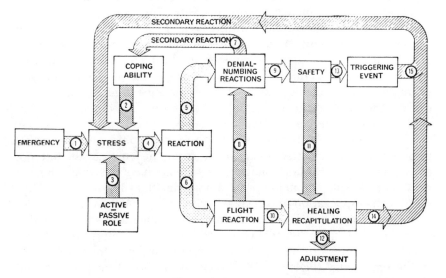

Figure 1. Long-term Stress Reactions

The victim's response during this acutely stressful time follows what Walter Cannon (1929), a pioneer stress researcher physiologist, identified as the "fight-or-flight" response. Subsequent research focusing on victims, cited above, tends to support this perspective. Caught in a catastrophic situation a small number of victims become panic-stricken and unable to function other than adopting a "flight reaction," except when fleeing (such as from a burning building) is the most appropriate response. Very frequently this reaction is accompanied by considerable emotional reactions on the part of the victim which attract the attention and assistance of others. This may result in (arrow 10) experiences of "healing recapitulation," whereby the victim is able to discuss his or her traumatic stress, after being removed from the catastrophe (such as a rape victim). Most often, however, during catastrophes which last over an extended period of time (war, captivity, blizzard), victims must somehow endure to cope with the continuing threat (arrows 5 through 8): to "fight" the catastrophe. This reaction, the "denial-numbing" response, was identified by Mardi Horowitz (1974, 1976) as a defensive coping mechanism that tends to remain with the victim long after the catastrophe ended. But as noted by others (Figley, 1978; Figley & Sprenkle, 1978), such a response is adaptable to surviving at the time. It is adaptable because the victim, caught in the catastrophe, either denies (or is incapable of perceiving) that the situation is as bad as it is or becomes numb to the stress (refusing to think about it). Both responses, the victim discovers, result in increased coping ability. The victim is becoming a "veteran" of the catastrophe, learning what it takes to survive—both in action and in thought. As a result there is a concomitant reduction in the amount of traumatic stress experienced during the catastrophe. This is why the initial period of any catastrophe is the most stressful and traumatic. Thus, during the period of the emergency (catastrophic event), the victim "circles" through a stress-reaction-denial/numbing-coping cycle to survive until the emergency is over.

The second facet of the model, the post-catastrophic (post-traumatic) period involves being *physically* away from the emergency, but not emotionally over it. Many catastrophe scholars have described this period as the "disillusionment phase" among disaster survivors (cf., Chapter 8), "disorganization and relapse" among rape victims (cf., Chapter 7) and periods of "relief and confusion, and avoidance" among combat veterans (cf., Chapter 9). It is within this period of "safety" (Horowitz, 1976) that victims are susceptible to powerful and painful recollections of the emergency (Figley, 1978, 1980b). Why? Based on research and clinical reports of thousands of victims of a wide variety of catastrophes, it is believed that victims attempt to cognitively *master* the impressions and memories of the catastrophe by answering such fundamental questions as:

1) What happened to me?
2) How did it happen?
3) Why me?
4) Why did I act as I did?
5) What will I do in another catastrophe?

When anything confronts us which is unexpected, we think about it enough until it becomes "expected" in the future.

Thus, following a catastrophe, victims ruminate about the series of events which entrapped them and search for these and other questions. As a result of their attempts to master the memories of the catastrophe, they may recall something that is especially troubling and so may trigger a secondary reaction (arrow 15) to the catastrophe. During this often brief episode victims may experience the same feelings and reactions which had occurred during the more troubling facets of the emergency. For Maria, for example, in an attempt to confront the questions above, she may suddenly recall those horror-filled seconds before the crash and become hysterical. During this episode, victims begin to cope much as they did during the emergency: experiencing the stress-reaction-denial/numbing-coping cycle. Victims may choose not to think about the events (i.e., denial-numbing) but may be "forced" to think about them by some situation, person, thing, or thought (i.e., triggering event) which startles victims into reminding them of the emergency. These have been referred to as flashbacks by several scholars and clinicians (cf., Figley, 1978).

The family has a central role to play at this point. Family members, perhaps more than any other group of people, can detect when the victim has not fully recovered emotionally from his or her ordeal (in contrast, for example, to clinicians, who are unable to distinguish between the victim's stress reactions and typical behavior). Moreover, the victim often feels more comfortable discussing his/her experience with family members. Thus, the family may be instrumental in promoting Healing Recapitulation (treating the "emotional wound" by extensive discussion) in order to help the victimized family member address and answer the questions of victims and reach Adjustment. Along the way, however, the victim (arrow 14) will experience several secondary reaction episodes.

It is important to recognize that with sufficient attention to the recovery process, the victim becomes a "survivor" (Figley, 1979). A survivor is able to take advantage of the skills developed as a result of his or her catastrophic experiences: the skills of survival; the confidence of mastering the stress during and following the catastrophe. A victim would say, for example, "I can't do it because of what I went through (during the catastrophe and its wake)!" In contrast, a survivor would say, "I *can* do it because of what I have survived!" This is consistent with research in experimental psychology in the area of learned helplessness (cf., Garber & Seligman, 1980), which suggests that animals and humans adapt by giving up, remaining a victim.

A Summary of the Victim's Response. According to the latest research on human response to extraordinary, sudden, and overwhelmingly stressful events, those caught in these catastrophes do not, as a rule, panic (Quarantelli & Dynes, 1977). Victims attempt to survive as best they can. The longer the ordeal, the greater the prospect of developing a strategy for survival, since the victim begins either to deny the direness of his or her situation or to become used to it. This survival behavior lasts beyond the length of the catastrophe, however, and over the months following the event the victim slowly regains his or her composure. The victim's initial and constant recollections of the event—and the accompanying hyper-alertness, sleeping problems, phobia, depression, and flashbacks—begin to fade. Usually, the more social support the victim receives during this period, providing him or her with an opportunity to talk about the experiences and with a sense of appreciation and respect, the faster the adjustment. Memories of the event may emerge at any time, even years following the catastrophe, as a result of some reminder. Again, the emotional support from others, including family members especially, is vital.

Families of Catastrophe

The focus of this volume is on the characteristic ways families and family members react to and resolve the effects of various types of catastrophes (crippling childhood illnesses, death, drug abuse, unemployment, rape, natural disasters, war, captivity). It is important to focus on the family in this context for three reasons. First, as noted in the previous section, the family provides critical support to the victim, thereby helping to prevent or abate the emotional and other (e.g., medical and economic) consequences of the catastrophe. Second, conversely, the family is a system which *induces* stress. Family members are affected by the upheavals of other family members, especially catastrophes. Third, family members may experience catastrophe simultaneously (such as in a tornado) and so give emotional support to each other as victims.

Social Support for the Victim. A review of the scientific literature confirms the existence of social support within the family system (Brown & Harris, 1978; Eaton, 1978; Kessler & Essex, in press; Lowenthal & Haven, 1968). Others have found that the absence of social support in combination with the occurrence of a catastrophic life event is associated with significant increases in symptoms of stress in contrast to the presence of social support (cf., Cobb, 1976; Dean & Lin, 1977; Mueller, 1980). A recent study attempting to develop a measure of social support (Burge & Figley, 1982) found that, among a diverse group of people, family members were cited most often as those one would turn to in times of need. In response to the question, "What do these people provide that you feel is helpful to you?", subjects noted five areas most frequently:

1) *Emotional Support,* or providing care, love, affection, comfort, sympathy, the sense that the supporter is on our side.
2) *Encouragement,* or a sense that the supporter makes us feel important; praises and compliments us fairly.
3) *Advice,* or help with solving problems; providing useful information, knows about where to go for help.
4) *Companionship,* or a social relationship; takes our thoughts off problems; fun to be with.
5) *Tangible Aid,* or helps with specific tasks such as lending money, providing transportation; helps with chores.

These findings are consistent with those of other researchers (cf., Hirsch, 1980) and explain why family members are so critical to victims of catastrophe. Maria, for example, would recover from her tragic accident much more quickly as a result of the support provided by her family in the forms noted above. Throughout this volume are concrete examples of how victims are helped by their families to recover from catastrophes which have occurred outside the context of the family, such as rape, war combat, and imprisonment. In contrast to these situations, we will also consider the costs and benefits of families becoming victims of catastrophe simultaneously through, for example, fire, natural disasters, unemployment, or death. For now, let us consider the costs to families who give support to their victimized members.

Secondary Traumatic Stress Reactions. Giving support to others is often not an altruistic act. We derive considerable pleasure from helping others. For example, we may feel appreciated, needed; we may have more confidence that when *we* are in need those we are supporting will become *our* supporters. This is certainly the case within the family system. Though some of us dispense support, encouragement, advice, companionship, and aid to our family members out of obligation (i.e., we would feel guilty otherwise), most of us give this support out of love and genuine caring. Sometimes, however, we become emotionally drained by it; we are adversely affected by our efforts. Indeed, simply being a member of a family and caring deeply about its members makes us emotionally vulnerable to the catastrophes which impact them. We, too, become "victims," because of our emotional connection with the victimized family member.

Figley (1982) has called this phenomenon "secondary catastrophic stress reactions," meaning that the empathic induction of a family member's experiences results in considerable emotional upset. This phenomenon is not unlike *couvade,* in which expectant fathers simulated the symptoms and experiences of their pregnant wives to the extent that their abdomens became swollen and they complained of diarrhea and vomiting in the absence of medical causes (cf. Rabkin & Struening, 1976). Psychosomatic medicine has reported similar phenomena: entire families developing various maladies which were directly associated with some family-centered upheaval, such as residential mobility (Mann, 1972) and divorce (Hetherington, Cox & Cox, 1976).

Over the months of her recovery, for example, Maria's parents would not only suffer from more psychosomatic illnesses, but also have bouts of sleeplessness about the condition of their daughter and the details of the accident; startle more easily while traveling in an automobile; seem preoccupied much of the time; be more forgetful than usual and more protective of their children. Thus, families of catastrophe are *victims* of catastrophe and require the same considerations by others that victims receive.

Family as Victim. When families experience a catastrophe together, there is obvious devastation to the intricate family system. The disruption of the routine life-style is most obvious. Various family rules, roles, and responsibilities will change because of the situation, although the basic lines of authority usually stay (see Chapter 8) for a detailed discussion). Family members may find it difficult to attend to another's problems related to the catastrophe, when they must deal with their own. Yet the experiences they share as a family are the very elements which tend to calm them during a catastrophe and also help them manage the memories and disruptions thereafter.

Catastrophe sociality is important not only *during* a catastrophe, but also *after* the catastrophe, when fellow survivors can help each other to understand and accept the catastrophe in the following ways: an information source (e.g., helping to answer the questions: What happened? Why did it happen? Why did I act as I did then and since? Will I be okay if it happens again?); as a peer or reference group to be able to evaluate adjustments in proper perspective (as a catastrophe survivor); and as role models (good or bad) for coping with the catastrophe.

In contrast to a family's attempts to help a member who, for example, survived a tornado in another state, family members who survived a tornado together may be more useful to each other. This may account for survivors of weather-related disasters—which most often impact entire families—having few long-lasting emotional problems (cf., Chapter 8).

Thus, family members should be viewed as victims, regardless of whether only one or all of them are victimized by a catastrophe. Probably due to the bonds of love and empathy among family members, when one member experiences the symptoms of catastrophic stress, others in the family experience catastrophic stress as well. The policy implications of this assertion will be discussed at the end of this chapter and in many chapters throughout this volume. For now it is important to discuss these families of catastrophe within the context of stress and coping and contrast the sources of stress from catastrophes with the stressors of everyday living, which was the focus of Volume I.

CATASTROPHIC FAMILY STRESSORS

It was pointed out and illustrated throughout Volume I of this series that family stress is generic: that the signs and symptoms of stress are the same irrespective of their sources. When family members experience stress, they may experience one or more of the following: elevations in tension, arguments, fighting among themselves, greater use of drugs, sleeplessness, headaches, colds, and other psychosomatic maladies. And throughout this and the previous volume contributors discuss various family situations (e.g., divorcing, single-parenthood, Black families) and note these and other symptoms of stress and the functional and dysfunctional methods families adopt to cope. What is characteristic of the chapters in this volume is that catastrophic family stressors are special and extraordinary. Apart from and in addition to the normative, developmental, and environmental stressors which all of us are exposed to as we live and age, catastrophe jolts us. As noted earlier, catastrophes are those profound events which make us feel out of control and helpless (though it may be only momentary), frighten us, overwhelm us, and for many years to come leave a lasting impression which we would much rather forget. It is important to review the special nature of catastrophic stressors in contrast to the normative stressors of family life. There are at least 11 characteristics of catastrophic stressors which differ from normative stressors. They are:

1) the amount of time one has to prepare;
2) previous experience with the stressor;
3) sources of guidance available to manage the stressor;
4) the extent to which others have experienced the stressor;
5) the amount of time in a "crisis" state;
6) the degree to which there is a sense of loss of control or help-lessness;
7) loss;
8) disruption and destruction;
9) danger experienced by people exposed to the stressor;
10) the quantity and quality of the emotional impact of the stressor; and
11) medical problems associated with exposure to the stressor.

Little or No Time To Prepare

A major characteristic of a catastrophe is its sudden onset, affording the victims little or no time to prepare. This was certainly the case for Maria and her family; an immediate response was required. This is in contrast to developmental transitions such as the birth of a child (Volume I, Chapter 4), parenthood during the teen years (Volume I, Chapter 5), and other normative stressors.

Since catastrophic events most often occur without any anticipation, the individual victim or family are prevented from planning and rehearsing a survival strategy. The exceptions, of course, are those families who practice evacuation methods in case of fire or some other catastrophe (e.g., tidal wave, earthquake), requiring that they leave their home immediately. Normative, developmental life events, however, are often viewed as important demarcation points associated with stress, which are anticipated by most.

Slight Previous Experience

Another characteristic about catastrophe which accounts for its stress-fulness is that it is a new experience for most who survive it. Indeed, repeated exposure to the same type of catastrophic event reduces the amount of stress. Frequent flood and coastal storm victims, for example, experience fewer symptoms of stress than new inhabitants. It is suggested that parenthood is on-the-job training: learning by doing, applying what has been learned in previous experiences. Maria and her family had no direct experiences with surviving an auto accident and were dealing with the horror of it all for the first—and, they hoped, last—time.

Few Sources of Guidance

Literally hundreds of books are written for the general public on marriage and family relationships; thousands of magazine and newspaper articles and columns are devoted to giving advice on coping with family life situations. Similarly, television, radio, and movies depict families in various situations which provide "lessons" for all of us in our own families. They deal with the stressors which most often impact the most people. However, sources of guidance are few in quality and number for families who must cope with the stress of sudden unemployment, abandonment, death, war, and other catastrophes.

Experienced by Few

The sources of guidance are so restricted for the families of catastrophe because so few experience catastrophe. In contrast, normative family stressors are often the topic of conversation at social gatherings. As Hunter (Chapter 10) points out, however, families of those held hostage or as prisoners of war believe that few if any know of their stress; they feel estranged from their neighbors and friends following, but especially during, captivity. Families of catastrophe are a small and elite group who are members not by choice but by circumstance, with limited access to others like them. This is why it is so important for families in similar situations to talk together for mutual support and guidance.

Interminable Time in Crisis

If crisis is synonymous with disruption (Burr, 1973), few normative family transitions last as long as a crisis, though collectively (i.e., pile-up effect) they may prolong this crisis period. In contrast, catastrophes may last days, months, and years. Maria and her family will require many months to recover from the weeks of intensive care in and out of the hospital, for example. There is a sense that the worst may not be over yet; there is an inability to relax and begin to recover from the shock.

Lack of Control/Helplessness

Associated with catastrophic stressors is a sense of being out of control and helpless. In contrast to normative life events, families caught in catastrophic situations are often unable to modulate the sources of stress, and are powerless to postpone or remove them. Carl's death and Maria's injuries were imposed upon them and the Allen family; they could do nothing to change these facts.

Sense of Loss

The Allen family, and especially Maria, experienced an overwhelming loss through the tragic death of Carl. Loss is a part of catastrophic stress even when someone does *not* die: a loss of innocence; a loss of time; a loss of a sense of invulnerability; a loss of a role or function. In contrast, normative, developmental changes most often result in something *gained:* life (i.e., birth), roles and responsibilities, skills, respect, or autonomy. Ultimately, though, there may also be some gain as a survivor of catastrophe (for example, self-assurance and emotional endurance), in spite of the upheaval.

Disruption and Destruction

Normative family transitions are disruptive, but in the wake of changes bring certain new roles, responsibilities, rules, and routines. They build and replace rather than destroy. Fundamental changes in the marital relationship, for example, have been traced to the transitions to parenthood (Figley, 1973). But catastrophes often leave deep and permanent changes. Significant disruption and destruction of a family's entire life-style is possible. Certainly the Allen family life, though fraught with the typical stressors impacting other families, was profoundly affected by the accident beyond anything they had ever known.

Dangerousness

The most significant facet of catastrophic stress, perhaps, is the degree of danger to one or more family members. Although some life transitions and accompanying stressors are dangerous (e.g., childbirth), the degree of threat is minimal. The threat of physical harm or death provokes the most intense of human reactions and leaves an emotional imprint, which often lasts a lifetime (Lifton, 1979). Thus, families are emotionally shaken by news that a family member is in danger, as in the case of the Allen family; or that a father is being held by terrorists as a hostage; or that a child could eventually die of a chronic illness without proper treatment.

Emotional Impact

. A growing body of scientific literature cited throughout this volume notes the emotional fallout of catastrophes which is both acute (e.g., sleeping disorders, depression) and chronic (e.g., social isolation, interpersonal conflict, distorted perceptions of self and others, phobia, paranoia, sexual dysfunction). This is in contrast with normative stressors, which are emotionally upsetting, but tend to be acute with limited duration. For example, the stressors experienced by the Allen family a week before the auto accident (such as loss of a love relationship, marital conflict) had varying effects on each of the members for a relatively brief period.

Medical Problems

Selye (1956, 1974, 1976a, b) and others (Ursin, Baade & Levine, 1978) have confirmed the stress-biophysiology connection. Worry makes us sick, literally. More specifically, researchers have attempted to quantify the medical risks of certain types of catastrophes (Dohrenwend & Dohrenwend, 1974). According to one group of researchers (Holmes & Rahe, 1967), for example, the highest health risk is the death of a spouse. Thus, it is clear that stress leaves an unmistakable imprint on the people affected. Headaches are, perhaps, the most frequently experienced stress-related medical problem, albeit minor. The problems of hypertension, heart disease, asthma, skin disorders, influenza, and other medical maladies are sometimes associated with the stress of normative life transitions. They are found much more frequently among the families of catastrophe.

In addition to these less obvious medical problems associated with surviving catastrophe are those which *directly* result from a catastrophe. Though physical and permanent psychological disabilities caused by catastrophes are hard to estimate, the obvious psychosocial implications are enormous. These impairments range from inability to earn an income to less severe limitations and inconveniences.

COPING WITH CATASTROPHE

Thus far we have discussed the special circumstances of catastrophes, and how individuals and families are affected by them in ways that are much more profound than other life stressors. Yet, returning to the theme of a generic family stress response, it is important that we discuss the characteristics which differentiate functional versus dysfunctional methods by which families cope with stress. For instance, is it possible for us to detect if the Allen family is coping with its special catastrophe in a functional versus a dysfunctional manner? If we can, it may be possible to provide specific guidance to families to help them through the more difficult times of their catastrophe.

There appear to be 11 universal characteristics which differentiate functional and dysfunctional coping:

1) ability to identify the stressor;
2) viewing the situation as a family problem, rather than merely a problem of one or two of its members;
3) adopting a solution-oriented approach to the problem, rather than simply blaming;
4) showing tolerance for other family members;
5) clear expression of commitment to and affection for other family members;
6) open and clear communication among members;
7) evidence of high family cohesion;
8) evidence of considerable role flexibility;
9) appropriate utilization of resources inside and outside the family;
10) lack of overt or covert physical violence; and
11) lack of substance abuse.

Let us consider each of these characteristics through the experiences of the Allen family.

The Case of the Allen Family

Over a six-month period following the accident, Maria recovered from her medical injuries which were considerable. She then returned to work on a part-time basis, remaining a resident of the Allen home for another two months until she was able to work full-time and move back to her apartment, which she had subleased during her convalescence. During this time the Allen family slowly regained their routine and life-style as they knew it prior to the catastrophic accident. Their management of the crisis provides an excellent case study of the functional methods of coping with catastrophic stress as outlined above.

The Allen family, throughout the months following the accident, placed their experiences and reactions in proper perspective by attributing much of their stress reactions to the catastrophe (#1) and viewing it not just as Maria's ordeal, but also the family's ordeal (#2). Thus, rather than blaming Maria for disruptions in the family, more attention was devoted to identifying and solving the problems emerging from the catastrophe (#3). Recognizing the extraordinary impact of the catastrophe on the entire family, the Allens were not only more tolerant of each other's behavior (#4), but also more liberal with their expressions of commitment and affection for one another (#5 & 7), sensing that such expressions would make the ordeal somewhat easier to endure. This was associated with frequent discussions about the special pressures on everyone and the importance of sharing individual perceptions and methods of coping (#6).

Although roles within the family were fairly stable prior to the catastrophe (e.g., Maria was surrogate parent to her younger sisters; father provided household maintenance work; mother and "baby" sister attended to family gatherings), responsibilities shifted during the crisis (#8), with Linda assuming many of Maria's previous roles. Although the Allens tended to be a rather independent and self-sufficient family, they not only drew upon the internal resources (e.g., religious, financial, housing, nurturance) of the family, but also were willing and able to seek and secure resources from outside (e.g., professional consultation from hospital staff; assistance from extended kin and friends for occasional meals, recreation, and companionship), which eased the strain of the catastrophe (#9). Finally, the Allens were able to resist the use of violence and substances such as drugs and alcohol to cope with the pressures of the catastrophe (#10 & #11).

CONCLUSION

Individuals and families have endured the catastrophes of life from the beginning of existence and have learned from their experiences how to cope more effectively with subsequent upheavals. Cultural and community supports emerged to protect and assist the victims of catastrophe. In modern America, for example, various agencies and organizations (such as the Red Cross) exist to provide aid to victims of disasters and other catastrophes. Despite this fact, our appreciation of the psychology of victims and their families has emerged only recently. With this recognition, past and present "relief" efforts may require considerable reconsideration. As the Allen family illustrates, for example, the family members may have suffered as much emotional pain as their daughter. They, too, are the victims of a catastrophe; they, too, deserve special attention and consideration. Their reactions are both predictable and manageable and those of us who are interested in the welfare and vitality of the family system must insure that the family of the victim, as well as the victim of catastrophe, receives adequate care for the reasons made obvious in this chapter.

The chapters which follow will focus on specific catastrophes which impact the family. We hope that this chapter will help you view each of these special "families of catastrophe" as not only unique, but also similar, in terms of the characteristic demands of family crisis in general and of catastrophe in particular.

Finally, as you read through these chapters, it will become obvious that the family is the single most important resource in dealing with catastrophic stress. By adequate attention to the health and vitality of the family system, victims of catastrophe may rely on a powerful stress-coping resource. And by supplemental consultation to families regarding the functional methods for coping with catastrophic stress, it is possible to care for the millions of victims of various traumatic events which occur yearly.

CHAPTER

2

Chronic Illness: Family Stress and Coping

JOAN M. PATTERSON and
HAMILTON I. McCUBBIN

Patti appears to be very much like other 14-year-olds starting ninth grade in a small high school in a rural midwestern town. She wants to be accepted by her peer group and carefully dresses to look older than her small size would suggest. She hopes this year to make the basketball team and participate in cross country track, even though in other years she had to drop out when she got sick.

Patti has cystic fibrosis (CF)—a genetically transmitted chronic illness which involves mucous obstruction of organ systems, such as the digestive and respiratory systems. This in turn affects height and weight gain and increases susceptibility to infections. Frequent hospitalizations due to complications and acute illness have been common for Patti. She was hospitalized twice last year. This creates a hardship for her family, especially her mother, who tries to stay with her at the metropolitan medical center 150 miles from home, despite the pull she feels to be at home attending to the needs of her husband and other two daughters, 16 and eight years old.

Indeed, the ongoing care and treatment for Patti have been a strain throughout the 13½ years since Patti was diagnosed to have CF. The continual requirement for between two and three hours of daily home therapy and treatment; the added financial burden of medical equipment, medications, and physician and hospital costs; the unrelenting need for regular exercise; the worry about possible complications, hospitalizations, and the prognosis of early death; the struggle to maintain a sense of normalcy in the face of special needs have all been sources of strain for Patti's parents and sisters. Her sisters sometimes wish their mother had more time for them, that they did not have to help out so much at home, and that their family could take vacations and go places and do things like other families.

Patti's mother, who had hoped to resume her career as an accountant, never returned to work after Patti's birth because of the home care demands. Besides, there really was no one she could hire to babysit a CF child and trust to do an adequate job. As a result, Patti's father has been the family's sole breadwinner. The normal financial burden of supporting five members plus the medical expenses have required him to work long hours and take on extra jobs which have isolated him from his family more than he likes and seem to contribute to increased conflict with his wife. He has helped out as much as possible with Patti's home therapies and treatment, realizing what a burden it is for his wife.

While friends and relatives have been helpful and a source of support, no one else in this small town has cystic fibrosis or can really understand what struggles Patti and her family undergo. The CF support group organized by the medical center is just too far away to attend regularly.

Patti, struggling for greater independence and her own identity, has recently become angry at her doctor for always pushing her to take her medications (about 60 pills per day), get a lot of exercise, and get her daily therapies. And she does not want to spend any more time in hospitals. She often does not take her pills and hides them to fool her mother. She resents her younger sister who is now almost as big as she is and gets to do a lot more things. Patti idolizes her older sister and longs for the day she might be as pretty and talented, have so many friends, and do so many fun things.

Patti's prognosis, however, includes a relatively short life expectancy. Despite the advances in early diagnosis and treatment for CF children, most do not live beyond their twenties. The ambiguity about Patti's life expectancy and if and when she could ever live independently are a particular source of strain for her parents as they try to plan their future. Her parents wonder if their active parenting career will be extended. Can Patti's mother ever resume her career? Will they be able to meet the continued financial burden or ever save for their retirement? Despite the hardships Patti's illness has engendered, the most difficult strain for the family is envisioning a future without Patti, knowing the prognosis of early death for CF children.

This case history illustrates some of the issues impacting on families with a chronically ill child. They experience an added set of strains and hardships, which interact with normative changes experienced by most families across the life cycle, all calling for continuous adaptation by the family. Social and behavioral scientists have a long history of working to identify and describe the difficulties, problems, and negative outcomes these families face. More recently, we have witnessed a concerted effort among scientists to examine how families, faced with the long-term care of a chronically ill child, are *able* to handle the financial, psychological, and interpersonal demands placed on them. This interest in families represents a major shift in emphasis away from the study of family *problems* and failures. Recently there has been a focus on the systematic assessment of how families cope with and adapt to a very difficult situation in an attempt to promote the health, well-being, and development of family members in the home. This chapter represents a continuation of this recent trend and integrates findings from our studies of families who have a handicapped or chronically ill child.

THE NATURE OF CHRONIC ILLNESS IN YOUNG CHILDREN

Our focus in this chapter will be on *chronic* illness, which has very different implications for the family than *acute* illness. In addition, our discussion will be centered around chronic illness in a *child* member rather than the illness of adults in the family. Finally, our discussion will center primarily on *parental* perceptions and responses as reflective of the family's adaptation to chronic illness, though child and sibling reactions are important and could be generalized from our discussion of parents.

Mattsson (1972) defines chronic illness as

a disorder with a protracted course which can be progressive and fatal, or associated with a relatively normal life span despite impaired physical and mental functioning. Such a disease frequently shows periods of acute exacerbations requiring intensive medical attention.

Chronic illness is an umbrella term for several disease entities such as cystic fibrosis, cerebral palsy, mylomeningocele, diabetes, and asthma. Although each disease has its own symptoms, etiology, treatment requirements, general prognosis, economic impact and implications for the extent of a child's participation in other social roles (Travis, 1976), there is also some commonality, particularly in terms of the impact on and coping by the family.

The family's central role in managing the chronically ill child's care and treatment throughout his or her lifetime is a primary factor distinguishing chronic illness from acute illness. In the case of acute illness, the person is usually hospitalized, and responsibility for care and treatment reside primarily with the physician and hospital staff. In contrast, the chronically ill child, living in the home environment, depends upon his or her family to take primary responsibility for care and treatment. Thus, as Travis (1976) has pointed out, the crux of the child's prognosis depends upon the family's ability to exert continuous effort in the child's behalf by securing competent medical care and following through with prescribed regimens.

The chronic illness never goes away. The child may become better or worse at times but always remains less than the normal healthy child—a situation which often produces recurrent grief (Wikler, 1981) for parents as the child moves through different developmental stages at a restricted level or different pace. The child's limitations have far-reaching impact on the whole family, affecting interpersonal relationships, where they live, finances, amount of free time, parental careers, etc.

The fact that a child has a chronic illness impacts other social systems he/she participates in, such as peer associations and school. Ultimately there is an interactive effect between these systems and the family and its members. The family usually has contact with many more professionals (e.g., social workers, psychologists or counselors), all of whom may help and support the family even while they scrutinize, create expectations, and give the family a sense of being judged.

SOURCES OF STRESS

If we consider Patti and her family along with observations reported in case studies and research studies regarding other chronic illnesses, we can summarize the hardships experienced by families who have a chronically ill child:

1) *Strained family relationships* often reflected in (a) overprotective-ness, jeopardizing the child's development of independence; (b) coalitions between the primary caretaker (usually mother) and the child, with other family members feeling left out; (c) scapegoating and blaming of the child or possibly blaming a parent believed to be genetically responsible; (d) overt or covert rejection of the child, which affects the child's physical and emotional development; (e) worry (possibly resentment) about extended parenting/caretaking responsibilities; (f) sibling competition for parental time and attention; (g) sibling comparisons and discrepancies regarding uneven physical, emotional, social, and intellectual development; and (h) an overall increase in intrafamily tension and conflict. These reactions will be discussed again within the context of dysfunctional coping.

2) *Modifications in family activities and goals,* such as (a) reduced flexibility in the use of leisure time and restricted options for family vacations; (b) less opportunity for both parents to pursue careers; and (c) worry and uncertainty about whether to have more children when the illness is related to genetic factors.

3) *The burden of increased tasks and time commitments,* such as providing special diets (diabetes, cystic fibrosis); extra cleaning of equipment or of the house (asthma); providing daily therapy or treatment; extra appointments to medical facilities, and hospitalizations resulting in family separations.

4) *Increased financial burden* due to medical specialist consultations, hospitalizations, medications, equipment needs, therapy, with variability of insurance coverage affecting direct costs to families.

5) *Need for housing adaptation* in terms of geographic proximity to adequate medical care, optimal climatic conditions for certain illnesses, and fitting the house with special features (e.g., ramp for wheelchairs).

6) *Social isolation* because of (a) friends' and/or relatives' reactions to and expectations regarding the chronically ill child; (b) family embarrassment when there are visible abnormalities; (c) limited mobility of the ill or handicapped child; (d) unavailability of adequate child care; (e) fear of accidents, or exposure to infections or conditions which might exacerbate the illness; and (f) limitations on social life as a result of the above factors.

7) *Medical concerns* related to (a) obtaining competent medical care; (b) understanding, clarifying, and verifying medical information; (c) the family's ability to follow through with prescribed home treatment; (d) the child's willingness to comply; (e) how to help the child endure or minimize pain; and (f) worry and uncertainty regarding the child's prognosis.

8) *Differences in school experiences* where special needs must be met in a regular school environment, special schools must be found, or education must occur in the home environment regularly or periodically—all of which require ongoing monitoring.

9) *Grieving* associated with developmental delays or abnormalities, restricted life opportunities for the child, and, for some illnesses, anticipation of an early or painful death.

Normative Family Demands

Chronically ill children share most of the characteristics and tasks of normal, healthy children. Over time, they develop, change, and grow. The normal developmental tasks of childhood, however, must be played out in a different context where the child's special needs or changing medical condition interact with the tasks, often exacerbating the demand and hardship on family members. These demands and needs experienced by families throughout life are highlighted in Table 1.

A Framework for Understanding Chronic Illness: The Double ABCX Model

Confronted with the ongoing stress of a chronically ill child plus additional life events and changes, some families actually appear to grow stronger and thrive. Other families grow weaker with repeated crises which, in some cases, lead to dissolution of the family system. In an effort to explain and understand this family variability in response to chronic illness and other stressors, we have advanced the Double ABCX Model of Family Stress (McCubbin & Patterson, 1983). This framework provides a way of viewing family efforts *over time* to adapt to multiple stressors through the use of various family resources and perceptual factors as the components for a coping process aimed at achieving family *balance*. The Double ABCX Model is presented in Figure 1.

How vulnerable families are to *crisis* (i.e., incapacitatedness in the family system) depends on the interaction of the *stressor* (a factor) with existing *resources* (b factor) and with family *perception* (c factor) (Hill, 1958). To illustrate these variables using Patti's family, one could define the initial stressor, factor "a," as the diagnosis of cystic fibrosis. Existing

Table 1

Responsibilities and Challenges in the Care of a Chronically Ill Child
Over Stages of the Family Life Cycle

Infancy (Birth-2 years)
  1. Initial Crisis—grieving
        Intensive medical services
        Diagnostic period
Pre-school (3-5 years)
  1. Ongoing medical/health monitoring
        Procurement of therapy services
        Prolonged dependency of child requiring added physical care
School Age (6-12 years)
  1. School programming
        Ongoing appraisal of child's development
  2. Establishment of members' roles in the family
        Dealing with sibling discrepancies re abilities
        Parents' instrumental and maintenance tasks
  3. Limited involvement in normal social engagements
Adolescent (13-20 years)
  1. Cognitive grasping of "permanence" with disability:
        Parental
        Child
  2. Identity, issues of child—"marginality"
  3. Increased physical size of child—impact on care
  4. More involved adaptive equipment—often necessitated by complications
  5. Sexuality issues
Young Adult (21)
  1. Discussion about guardianship issues relating to ongoing care of child
  2. Placement plans—depending upon feasibility of:
        employment
        self-care
        mobility
        leisure

Adapted from McCubbin, H.I., Nevin, R., Larsen, A., Comeau, J., Patterson, J.M., Cauble, E., & Striker, K. *Families coping with cerebral palsy.* St. Paul: Family Social Science, 1981.

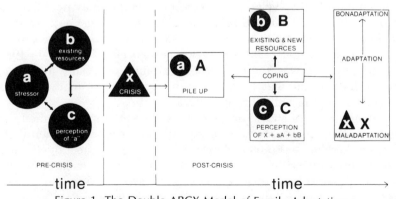

Figure 1. The Double ABCX Model of Family Adaptation

resources in that family, factor "b," included, for example: (a) flexibility in changing roles (Patti's mother stopped working; her father helped at home more) to take on new tasks and demands; and (b) the mutual emotional support Patti's parents found in each other to accept and learn to understand the illness. Their perception of the stressor event, factor "c," was that it was God's will and an opportunity to grow together through the challenge.

Sometimes, however, families faced with a diagnosis of chronic illness in a child are only able to define the event as catastrophic, and feel overwhelmed by the hardships. They may lack resources, such as agreement on family roles or emotional support for each other or adequate finances to cover the increased expenses. The result can be a crisis for a family, where family members become very disorganized, routines disintegrate, and family stability is threatened.

When families are observed over time, however, they usually recover from the crisis and achieve some level of adaptation. The Double ABCX Model suggests that *coping* is the central process describing families' efforts to adapt and achieve a new level of organization or balance in their system. Coping emerges out of the pile-up of demands on the family and involves an interaction of resources, perception, and behavioral responses.

Pile-up (aA). Families are seldom dealing with a single stressor like chronic illness. Rather, as Patti's family situation indicates, multiple changes and demands occur simultaneously. There are *normative changes,* like Patti starting a new school. There are *strains and hardships* associated with cystic fibrosis, like increased financial burdens, increased caretaking tasks, and increased marital or sibling conflict. These strains, which often emerge from another stressor like the diagnosis of cystic fibrosis, are often hard to resolve (e.g., increased conflict) or may not be resolvable (e.g., increased caretaking tasks). Thus they persist as a source of *chronic strain.* In our studies with families who have a child with cerebral palsy (McCubbin et al., 1981) or myelomeningocele (Nevin et al., 1981), we found that it was these persistent strains, especially intrafamily strains, that the families judged as most problematic in their overall struggles of coping with chronic illness.

Another source of strains and stressors were attempts to remedy the situation—the family's *efforts at coping* with their situation. When Patti's father worked longer hours and extra jobs in order to meet the financial burden, this isolated him from the family more and increased tension between him and his wife.

A fifth source contributing to the pile-up is *ambiguity.* Patti's parents, wanting at least four children, were unsure if they should have another child after her birth because CF is genetically transmitted by recessive genes. They deliberated for six years before having their youngest child. Families with chronically ill children also face considerable ambiguity surrounding the child's prognosis—how long he/she will live, inconsistent medical information regarding treatment, or how to plan their own parental careers, as was true for Patti's mother who did not know if or when to resume her career as an accountant.

Family adaptation in a chronic illness situation involves many stressors (i.e., events requiring change in the family system) and strains (demands and hardships often emerging from stressors) occurring simultaneously and all calling for attention. The size of this pile-up alone has multiple impacts on the family and its members. The health and well-being of the chronically ill child, a vulnerable member of the family system, can be affected by this pile-up. In our studies of cystic fibrotic children, we found a pile-up of life events and strains, particularly in the areas of intrafamily development and relationships, family management and decisions, and family finances had an adverse effect on the child's health as measured by a decline in the functioning of his/her respiratory system (Patterson & McCubbin, 1983). The pile-up of unresolved stressors and strains also contributes to undesirable characteristics in the family environment. Our studies revealed that families with a myelomeningocele child who had a pile-up of family life changes and strains were characterized by more conflict than families experiencing fewer life stressors and strains (Nevin et al., 1981).

Resources (bB). Resources are the psychological, social, interpersonal, and material characteristics of individual family members (e.g., ability to earn an income), of the family unit (e.g., flexibility, organization), and of the community (e.g., medical services, support groups) which are used to meet family demands and needs. When viewed over time and in response to a situation like the diagnosis of a child's chronic illness, there appear to be two general types of resources. The first are those *existing resources* already in the family's repertoire, which reduce their vulnerability to crisis. The second are those *new resources* which are strengthened or developed *in response* to new demands emerging out of the pile-up of stressors and strains. Patti's parents had to learn about cystic fibrosis and home treatment, find competent medical specialists, develop a tighter system of organization in the home to get the tasks done, and *find support* from friends and relatives as they grieved the reality of having a child with cystic fibrosis.

Families with chronically ill children exhibit wide variability in terms of the resources they have to work with and, even more importantly, in terms of their ability to find and use new resources needed to manage the multiple demands on their family. When families have insufficient resources, the needs and demands are not adequately met and this contributes to increased conflict in the family environment. From our studies of families who have a cerebral palsy child (McCubbin et al., 1981), we found less conflict in families who had the resources of (a) member self-esteem; (b) open, effective communication; (c) mutual assistance and support; (d) problem-solving abilities; (e) physical and emotional health; and (f) a sense of mastery over events they were experiencing.

Perception (cC). The cC factor of our model suggests two forms of perception. The first "c" is the family's definition of the stressor believed to have caused the crisis, i.e., the diagnosis of chronic illness. Families may see the illness as hopeless, shameful, overwhelming, or beyond their ability to manage. Or, in contrast, they may accept it and see it as a challenge. The second form of perception suggests that *over time* families engaged in a constructive effort to manage the stressor will redefine their *total situation*. This means taking into account not just the chronic illness and its hardships, but also other stressors. Moreover, it means surveying the resources they have and need, and ways to cope and manage so as to restore balance to their system and promote the social and emotional development of members of the family. Generally speaking, family efforts to redefine a situation as a "challenge," as an "opportunity for growth," or to "endow the situation with meaning" (Venters, 1980) appear to play a useful role in facilitating family coping and, eventually, adaptation (see Volume I, Chapter 10). Viewed in this way, the family's perception becomes a critical component of family coping.

COPING WITH CHRONIC ILLNESS

In addition to the family's perception of the crisis, coping includes both the *behavioral* responses of family members, as well as the responses of the family unit in an attempt to manage the situation. Moreover, coping is their ability to acquire and use the resources needed for family adaptation. These resources may be developed from within the family boundaries, such as cohesiveness by pulling together to meet the demands of home treatment for a chronically ill child. In addition, the family's resources may be acquired from outside the family, such as securing competent medical services in the community or social support from other families experiencing the same chronic illness.

Dysfunctional Coping

As already indicated, the chronic illness literature is replete with descriptive accounts of inadequate parental coping efforts and the consequent problems and failures experienced by families with chronically ill children. For example, some parents overprotect their child (Spock & Stedman, 1966), or one parent overprotects and forms a coalition with the child which excludes the other parent (Travis, 1976). Some parents withdraw from social involvement with others out of shame, embarrassment, or inability to find outside help (Meyer & Crothers, 1953). Other parents cope by denying the reality of the chronic illness and reject their child by withdrawing emotional support or ignoring his or her special physical needs.

Other parents not only display anger and resentment about the situation, but also direct their hostility toward the chronically ill child and/or toward each other. Blaming the other parent is not uncommon. Increased incidence of marital discord and divorce in these cases has been reported (Dodge, 1976).

These dysfunctional coping behaviors are often related to the way the family defines the chronic illness situation (e.g., a disaster, unfair and beyond the family's ability to manage). These families see themselves as victims, often of multiple life events, which they judge as unfair and beyond their control.

Functional Coping

Descriptive Reports. In the literature on chronic illness, several investigators have described helpful, positive coping behaviors of families confronted with a chronically ill child. Darling (1979), for example, observed parental "activism" which involved efforts to "normalize" the child's life, to initiate aggressive searches of services for the child, and in some cases, to bring about societal changes which would be more supportive of families with handicapped or chronically ill children.

Perceptual coping behavior, such as maintaining hope and attachment (Shere, 1957), optimism, faith and courage (Cardwell, 1956), and an altruistic view of the situation (Darling, 1979) have been reported as helpful to families. Chodoff, Friedman and Hamburg (1964) have pointed out that searching and finding some broad philosophical or religious framework to make the event of their child's illness comprehensible to them is a normal coping response used by parents of children with chronic illness.

Parental efforts to find sources of social support from the community for the child (Arnold, 1976) and for the whole family (Nevin, 1979) have been emphasized as an important coping behavior to relieve the emotional burden of living with chronic illness. Medical staff, including physicians, nurses, psychologists, and social workers, are one of the most important sources of support.

Empirical Studies of Parental Coping. As part of our research with families of chronically ill children, we have attempted to systematically assess the coping behaviors parents employ to successfully manage family life under these circumstances. This systematic assessment involved the use of a self-report questionnaire—Coping Health Inventory for Parents (CHIP) (McCubbin, McCubbin, Nevin & Cauble, 1979)—with over 500 families who have a child with cystic fibrosis, cerebral palsy, or myelomeningocele. Mothers and fathers filled out the questionnaire separately so we could assess whether they use different sytles of coping. Using this coping inventory, we have identified three coping patterns that parents use to manage family life when a child has a chronic illness. Each coping pattern is made up of several coping behaviors:

1) *Maintaining family integration, cooperation, and an optimistic definition of the situation.* Parents who use this coping pattern emphasize: (a) doing things together as a family unit; (b) strengthening family relationships; and (c) developing and maintaining a positive outlook on life in general and specifically when a member has a chronic illness.

2) *Maintaining social support, self-esteem, and psychological stability.* Parents who use this coping pattern try to: (a) maintain a sense of their own personal well-being through social relationships; (b) be involved in activities which have the potential of enhancing self esteem; and (c) manage psychological tensions and strains.

3) *Understanding the medical situation through communication with other parents and consultation with the medical staff.* Parents who use this pattern of coping develop relationships both with other parents who have a child with a similar illness and with the medical staff. They try to understand and master the medical

information needed to care for their chronically ill child and use the medical equipment in the home.

Parental Coping and the Family Environment. How does the use of these coping behaviors affect the way the family functions? Our findings (McCubbin, McCubbin, Patterson, Cauble, Wilson & Warwick, in press) revealed that while both parents use the coping patterns, the effects on the family are quite different. In Table 2, the significant associations between mother's and father's coping and characteristics of the family environment are summarized.

Mother's coping, directed at the maintenance of family integration, cooperation, and optimism; at maintaining social support, esteem, and emotional stability; and at understanding the medical aspects of the chronic illness, appears to focus on the interpersonal dimensions of family life—family cohesiveness and family expressiveness. Taken together, mother's three coping patterns play a major part in encouraging family members to be concerned, helpful, and supportive of each other and in encouraging members to act openly and to express their feelings directly.

Father's coping patterns appear to have a broader range of associations

Table 2
Parental Coping Patterns and Characteristics of Family Environment

	Characteristics of Family Environment	
	Interpersonal Relation-ship Dimensions	System Maintenance Dimensions
Parental Coping Patterns		
Mother's Coping I: Integration, Coop-eration & Optimism	+* Cohesiveness	
Mother's Coping II: Support, Esteem & Stability	+ Expressiveness	
Mother's Coping III: Medical Com-munication and Consultation	+ Cohesiveness	
Father's Coping I: Integration, Coop-eration & Optimism	+ Cohesiveness	+ Organization
Father's Coping II: Support, Esteem & Stability	+ Lack of conflict	
Father's Coping III: Medical Commu-nication & Consultation		+ Control

*+ = positive association with

with the major dimensions of family life. His efforts to maintain integration, cooperation, and optimism complement mother's coping efforts by facilitating family cohesiveness through concern, helpfulness, and support for each other. Through the use of this same coping pattern (Coping I), father also contributes to family interpersonal relationships by minimizing the open expression of anger and aggressive behavior which would otherwise contribute to conflictual family interactions.

In addition, father's coping patterns appear to support the system maintenance dimensions of family life. His coping efforts directed at family integration, cooperation, and optimism and at improving his understanding of the medical situation promote family structure, activities, and planning, while maintaining family organization with rigid rules and procedures.

This brief summary of findings regarding parental coping emphasizes that parents employ active efforts to manage the stress and hardships associated with having a chronically ill child, while at the same time coping with other normative life changes and sources of stress in the family. The negative consequences of these stressors are obvious, yet the same situation can also have positive consequences for overall family functioning. This adaptive family situation in turn promotes the physical, emotional, and social growth and development of all family members, including the chronically ill child. Clearly there are predictable demands on the parents' energy and emotions in caring for a chronically ill child at home. It is, therefore, important to recognize the need for parents to balance this concentrated care for the ill child with care for themselves as individuals and for the family as a whole. It is also important to underscore the importance of the father's role and the value of his coping efforts in maintaining family organization, reducing conflict, and promoting the child's health. Being aware that certain predictable patterns emerge over time within families with a chronically ill child is the first step in lessening the stressful consequences.

Seeking Intervention Assistance. Family crises should be an opportunity for family interventionists *to promote* family well-being. Not only can we make use of the community and its programs and services in support of families under stress, but also, perhaps more importantly, we can use the family situation as an opportunity to improve problem-solving skills, coping repertoire, and overall interpersonal relationships.

In the case of chronic illness, family patterns of managing life's situations are likely to be disturbed and family members are likely to face difficulties and changes for which they have no ready-made solutions.

The father, for example, may be angry with the wife's commitment to providing care to the ill child, and he therefore struggles with the dilemma of accepting the situation or attempting to change it to gain more attention for himself. So extensive may be the disruption of family routines and way of life that the family unit may not know where to begin rebuilding. And to the extent that the parents' sense of competence has been challenged, they may be uncertain about whether they are *capable* of improving the situation.

Intervention programs should promote the prevention of additional adverse effects of chronic illness and focus attention on current functioning and utilization of problem-solving concepts rather than retrospective emphasis in family history-taking (Compton & Gallaway, 1974; Hoff, 1978; Parad, 1966; Golan, 1978). To rely on the traditional counseling strategies of sorting out the family's "past," health professionals may ultimately sacrifice their vitally important opportunity to relate to the family's immediate and presenting problems and felt need. The parents' need to understand the medical situation, to manage the disturbing changes in family relationships, and to develop a range of coping strategies should be given priority.

Problem-solving strategies may include sharing information with families which provide order and explain the family's experiences and responses. Other sorts of information include reports of experiences of others in a similar situation, and descriptions of coping methods others may have used and found helpful.

One of the most useful forms of problem-solving appears to be the provision of social support (Cobb, 1976) to families of the chronically ill. Often these families find themselves in situations which leave them unsure whether their personal, material, or interpersonal resources are adequate to the demands being made on them. One form of support is offered by the "helper" (who may or may not be a professional) who is accepted as an ally by the members of the distressed family. Guided by the premise that the family unit is capable of helping itself, the "helper" offers encouragement and understanding as well as specific information which help family members to feel: (a) understood and appreciated (emotional support); (b) capable of managing life's hardships (esteem support); and (c) a sense of belonging to a larger group of persons/families who share their concerns (network support).

In summary, the fundamental strategies for prevention-oriented intervention (Rapoport, 1966a, Golan, 1978) which appear to be pertinent to the situation of working with families coping with a chronically ill child include:

(a) keeping an explicit focus on the present family crisis;
(b) helping families to gain a conscious grasp of the crisis in order to enhance purposeful problem-solving;
(c) helping parents to deal with and overcome doubts of adequacy and self-confidence;
(d) helping with interpersonal communication and assisting families in achieving a balance in individual growth and meeting family needs;
(e) offering basic information and education regarding the medical aspect of the problem;
(f) helping to develop social support;
(g) helping to master the medical procedures involved in home care of the chronically ill; and
(h) creating a bridge to community resources and opening the pathways of referral.

In the face of reduced funding for social service and medical-psychological services, we need to maintain our commitment to provide prevention-oriented services to families of chronically ill children. Such efforts, designed to provide families with information, are likely to increase their ability to cope with present and future demands.

3

Drug Abuse: Adolescent Addictions and the Family

RICHARD H. NEEDLE,

THOMAS J. GLYNN, and

MARIAN P. NEEDLE

Angela never thought of herself as a drug abuser. Neither did her parents, until they received a call from the police early one Sunday morning. At a slumber party Angela and her girlfriends decided to "experiment" with a mixture of booze and various types of barbiturates. Angela was unconscious when the police arrived to break up the loud party disturbing the neighbors. The ambulance arrived soon after that. The overdose nearly killed her.

To her parents, Angela was a typical 15-year-old girl—cute, popular, many friends, average grades, and a dependable babysitter for the neighborhood. The Sunday morning incident changed their perspective. They felt numb with disbelief at first; then frightened she might not survive the overdose; then enraged that she would "dare to do this" to them; and finally, suspicious of what else she had done in violation of their trust in her.

Slowly they would come to realize that it could have been much worse; she regretted the incident and would assure them she would not repeat such a thing again. Angela's parents would also discover that it was not the first time she had used drugs and alcohol, and that the pressures at home were at least partially to blame. The fact that her parents drank and used barbiturates excessively was not overlooked. Indeed, the Sunday morning incident may have been a blessing after all. What started as a near-fatal crisis turned out to be an opportunity for family self-examination and rejuvenation. They were lucky. Angela and her family are typical of many families of teenagers affected by the near epidemic of drug abuse in the United States. Did the family have any way of anticipating Angela's problems? What were the factors which led to her substance abuse? What were the drug abuse-related stressors for the family? What are some effective ways families cope with this problem?

America's youth are now abusing a wider variety of substances, more often, and beginning at a younger age than at any other time in our history (Petersen, 1980). For the families who face the frightening implications of their children's drug dependency, it is a lonely and difficult battle of catastrophic proportions. The catastrophe of adolescent drug abuse is the focus of this chapter. We will attempt to answer the questions posed above by first discussing the widespread problem of adolescent drug abuse. We will then note the role the family plays in the development, maintenance, and reduction of teen drug abuse, from the teen's perspective. From the family's perspective we will discuss the abuse as an additional source of stress within the family. We will also: 1) note the effective and ineffective ways families attempt to deal with the problem; 2) identify the family's own natural resources and those they may employ from outside—including programs for the education, treatment, and prevention of drug abuse; and 3) suggest some promising long-term solutions to this problem.

THE EPIDEMIC OF ADOLESCENT DRUG ABUSE

Although Angela and the majority of American adolescents are not substantially impaired by their drug use, some experts have warned that youthful substance abuse represents a major public health problem and that we are in danger of losing an entire generation to drugs (Pollin,

1981). Yet, in spite of these warnings, rates of use escalate. What is the basis of these concerns?

1) Nine percent of all high school seniors use marijuana on a daily basis (Johnston, Bachman & O'Malley, 1981).
2) Sixty percent of high school seniors have used marijuana at least once (Johnston et al., 1981).
3) Six percent of high school seniors use alcohol on a daily basis (Johnston et al., 1981).
4) Ninety-three percent of high school seniors have used alcohol at least once (Johnston et al., 1981).
5) Twelve percent of high school seniors use illicitly-obtained stimulants at least once a month (Johnston et al., 1981).
6) Over one-third of the marijuana-, PCP-, and over-the-counter analgesics-related visits to hospital emergency rooms made each year are by adolescents (National Institute on Drug Abuse, 1980).
7) Adolescents represent nearly a quarter of the yearly deaths attributed to the use of Quaaludes (National Institute on Drug Abuse, 1980).

Of course, Angela is more than a statistic to her family. Knowing that she is typical of other drug-abusing teens does not dampen the shock felt by her family.

DRUG ABUSE AS A FAMILY CATASTROPHE

Similar to major stressors, such as illness, death, or violence, realization that their teenager is a drug abuser is a catastrophic event to most families affected. Although the family tends to react quickly, the weeks and months following confirmation of the drug use and abuse are filled with anxiety and tension. Certainly the event and its wake may leave deep and permanent scars of memory for both teen and parents alike: Mistrust, resentment, and hostility are possible byproducts. The acute type of adolescent drug abuse is in sharp contrast with chronic drug abuse, characterized by more prolonged and routinized drug use. This latter type of abuse is often closely associated with deeply troubled teens and their families. In this chapter we are most concerned with the acute type or phase of drug dependency which strikes the family like a shock wave.

The case of Angela and her family briefly illustrates the typical family reactions to the realization of a teen member's drug abuse: shock, fear, denial of the problem, rage and hostility toward the teen—even though he or she may be close to death—the thought of punishment, gradual acceptance of the situation, followed by some form of recrimination. Eventually most families will come to realize that it is a family problem and not just a problem of one of their teenage family members.

FAMILIAL CONTRIBUTIONS TO ADOLESCENT DRUG ABUSE

There is a growing recognition (e.g., Harbin & Maziar, 1975; Glynn, 1981a; Seldin, 1972; Stanton, 1978, 1979a,b) that the family is clearly implicated in the initiation, maintenance, cessation, and prevention of drug use by one or more of its members. The fact that the role of the family in this behavior has only recently begun to be seriously considered is based not so much on the notion that families have changed but, rather, that patterns of drug use have changed.

Past research has focused primarily on individuals' abuse of harder drugs (opiate), often ignoring the role of the family (Clayton, 1979). Adolescents are among the heaviest users of non-opiate drugs, however, and because of the growing use rate became the target of increasing numbers of drug researchers. The progression to including families in the research focus and treatment was a logical one, since the drug-involved adolescent very often cited his or her drug use as a cause or effect of severe family stress.

What does recent research and treatment experience tell us about these families? Probably the most striking aspect of the drug-abusing family with a drug-abusing member is the resistance to precise labeling or predictable patterns of behavior. A wide array of variables such as the type of drug(s) used, measurable stress as the source or the result of drug use, sibling use, family communication patterns, parental modeling, occurrence of recent death or loss, or availability of community support systems may influence the incidence, prevalence, and patterns of use within a family; but there is rarely, if ever, a single cause for this behavior.

A Family Systems Perspective

There are a number of theoretical perspectives from which to view adolescent drug use in the context of the family. There are, nevertheless, a number of areas of agreement among clinicians and researchers. Probably the most significant trend in this field has been the increasing tendency to view drug use in the family from a systems perspective (Bateson, Jackson, Haley & Weakland, 1956; Haley, 1973; Jackson, 1957; Stanton, 1980a). Previously, for example, the cause or basis of an adolescent's drug use might have been said to be "family stress." The description of Angela's drug use, cited earlier, is a good example of this. While it would appear that her problems with drugs might stem from an unstable family situation and that if this were remedied, her drug problems might cease, analysis from a systems perspective would suggest that the situation may be more complex. It is possible that her drug use is only partially based on family problems stemming from stress and that, indeed, it is more the cause than effect of these problems. Perhaps, also, her drug use serves a function for the family, allowing family members to focus on this problem rather than on some of the more fundamental difficulties they may have.

Stanton and his colleagues (1978, 1980a,b), in their research on heroin addicts and their families, have suggested a model of intra-systemic dependency which has wide application to all types of drug abuse and family situations. In working with young, drug-abusing Vietnam veterans and their parents, Stanton noticed that the drug dependency was often used by the parents as an excuse to avoid their own problems, especially difficulties in their own marriage. Moreover, in order to solicit attention and subsequent care from the parents the abusing son would often regress to some form of anti-social or self-destructive behavior (e.g., lose his temper, take a drug overdose or commit a serious crime). The consequences of such acts were to shift the focus of attention toward the son and away from the parents and their relationship, often to the relief of all three! As Stanton (1980a) notes:

> . . . As the addict demonstrates increased competence, indicating the ability to function independently of the family—for example, by getting a job, getting married, enrolling in a drug treatment program, or detoxifying—the parents are left to deal with their still unresolved conflicts. At this point in the cycle, marital tension increases and the threat of separation arises. The addict then behaves in an attention-getting or self-destructive way, and the dysfunctional triadic cycle is again completed (p. 154).

Thus, Angela's parents may eventually come to view her drug dependency as a means of avoiding several fundamental problems within their marriage, and may even become dependent on Angela's problem as an escape from those problems on either a temporary or permanent basis.

Empirical Findings

While utilization of a systems perspective may be the most broadly accepted approach to understanding adolescent drug abuse in the context of the family, there are other more specific aspects of family behavior which research and treatment experience suggest may be found across many families with an adolescent drug-abuser. Examples of these are:

General Socialization of Youth. Glynn (1981b) has found that most effective family influences in children appear to be those which are developed prior to adolescence. Satisfactory relationships, general climate and emotional support within the family, and moderation in the use of alcohol are influences which appear to delay or diminish adolescent initiation into drug use. These parental influences on children developed over a long period of time. Attempts to make up for their absence (e.g., sharp increase in parental control) often lead to increased adolescent drug use.

Parental Influences on Adolescents. Generally parental use of drugs and alcohol are strong predictors of adolescent drug and alcohol use (Glynn, 1981b; Kandel, Kessler & Margulies, 1978; Smart & Fejer, 1972; Stanton, 1979b). Moreover, adolescent children who report a lack of closeness, support, and affection from their parents are more likely to begin to use drugs, and to maintain the abuse of drugs (Kandel, 1978; Stanton, 1979b).

Stanton (1979b), more specifically, has found that among families of opiate addicts (including, but not restricted to, adolescents) there appear to be generalized patterns of male and female users. In the families of male addicts, the mother is often involved in an indulgent, overprotective, overpermissive relationship with the addict, who is put in the position of a favored child and never treated as an adult. Fathers of male addicts, in contrast, are found to be detached, uninvolved, weak, or absent. Female addicts, on the other hand, report that their fathers are sexually aggressive though generally inept. Addicts of both sexes tend to maintain close ties to one or both parents up to and beyond the age of 30.

Other researchers have noted parental influence to be important in adolescent drug abuse but have devoted significantly less attention to the dynamics of the influence itself. Intergenerational relationships, especially parent-adolescent conflict, for example, have been associated with adolescent drug abuse (e.g., Freedman & Finnegan, 1976; Madanes, Dukes & Harbin, 1980; Noone & Reddig, 1976). Similar to Stanton (1979b), other researchers have noted the influence of drug use on parent-child overinvolvement, where the child is highly influenced by the parents (especially mother-son), and parental disengagement (especially father-family) patterns (e.g., Attardo, 1965; Cotroneo & Krasner, 1976; Kaufman, 1981, Zimmering, 1951). Other factors associated with drug abuse among adolescents include family communication and interaction patterns (Klagsbrun & Davis, 1977), family context and environment (Osterweis, Bush & Zuckerman, 1979), cultural disparity within families or between the family and the majority culture (e.g., Coleman, 1979; Vaillant, 1966), and experiences with death and loss of an intimate friend (Coleman, 1981; Coleman & Stanton, 1978; Stanton, 1977).

Finally, family stress events have been linked empirically with adolescent drug abuse. In a recent study, Duncan (1978) investigated the number and types of family-related stress events that preceded (within one year) the initiation of adolescent drug abuse. Table 1 lists, in their order of frequency, the types of stress events reported to occur significantly more often by a sample of adolescent drug abusers as opposed to a normal population of adolescents. In discussing these findings,

Table 1

Family Stress Events Reported During Year Preceding Onset of Adolescent Drug Abuse*

Stress Event	Percent of Drug-abusing Adolescents Reporting Stress Event (N = 31)
Increased arguments with parents	71
Change in financial status	58
Increased arguments between parents	42
Mother beginning to work	29
Hospitalization of parent	26
Change of father's occupation	23
Divorce of parents	19
Loss of job by parent	19
Marital separation of parents	16
Marriage of parent to stepparent	13
Third adult in family	13
Parent jailed	10
Death of sibling	6

* Adapted from Duncan, 1978.

Duncan notes that they support those approaches to understanding drug abuse which propose that this behavior is used to cope with excessive stress in the drug abuser's familial and social environment. Unfortunately, the use of drugs as a coping mechanism only adds to the family stress, producing further stress events which are again relieved by taking more drugs, thus creating a cycle which can maintain the drug-abusing behavior indefinitely.

These data, as well as those discussed earlier, make it evident that the drug-using experience of the adolescent family member is almost never an isolated one but rather a behavior with greater or lesser implications for the entire family system.

ABUSE-RELATED SOURCES OF STRESS FOR THE FAMILY

In considering Angela's family, it is impossible to know exactly which came first—the stress she experienced from the family or her drug abuse. In some ways it does not matter. What is important is what the family does about the realization that their adolescent member is abusing drugs. After reviewing the theoretical and empirical literature discussing the contribution of the family to teen drug abuse, our attention now focuses on the sources of stress associated with this news. Later we will note some of the ways families characteristically begin to cope with these stressors.

There appear to be six general categories of catastrophic-type stressors families face, at least initially, upon the realization that their youthful member is a drug abuser:

1) concern for the safety of the youth;
2) death;
3) guilt about parental responsibility for the abuse;
4) concern about the "spread" of abuse to younger siblings;
5) irritability over the residual effects of abuse; and
6) concern about the family's reputation and autonomy within the community.

Health and Safety of the Abuser

It is obvious from the case illustration that Angela's family's initial concern was for her health and safety. As noted earlier, scores of teenage deaths and disabling accidents are attributed to drug abuse. Research has shown, for example, that between 45 and 60 percent of all fatal crashes with a young driver are alcohol-related (NIAAA, 1981). The 10-to-19-year-old age group accounted for 21 percent of drug episode emergency room visits; nearly half (41%) of this group reported the reason for taking the substance was a suicide attempt or gesture (NIAAA, 1981).

Death

Confronting drug-using suicide attempts and/or death, almost always unexpected, challenges the family's ability to deal with the immediacy of the crisis: either hospitalization and/or long-term treatment for the individual who attempted suicide, or making funeral arrangements. Families must deal with the psychological implication of the death, the guilt that may arise as they attempt to explain the drug-using behavior, concern for younger perhaps non-drug-using siblings, time lost from work, absorbing funeral costs, informing family and friends, and dealing with insurance companies, schools, and others.

Guilt About Parental Responsibility

In addition to the guilt and rumination associated with drug-related disabilities, accidents, and deaths, parents invariably experience stress in connection with their sense of parental responsibility to provide guidance and protection for their children. This overall sense of obligation, together with clear knowledge about the child's drug abuse, cause considerable stress for the parent or older sibling. At the very least, parents of the drug-abusing adolescent often feel guilt and a sense of failure, even though the "abuse" was only an accident associated with experimenting with drugs. In its more extreme forms, however, parents' sense of responsibility may lead to rather punitive measures against the child, which may have potentially tragic consequences.

"Spread" of Abuse

In addition to the issues discussed above is the fear that drug abuse will be "contagious" within the family, spreading, for example, from the teen drug abuser to his or her younger siblings. Will Angela's younger brother begin to experiment with drugs now that it is clear that Angela has tried them? These and related concerns cause family members, especially parents, considerable distress and lead them to take preventive or overly harsh disciplinary measures, as will be noted later.

Irritability Over the Residual Effects of Abuse

Another source of stress for families is the general changes in the life-style of the adolescent. Jessor and Jessor (1977) have pointed out that drug abuse, especially the abuse of marijuana, is associated with a general shift in a wide constellation of behaviors of the teenage user. For some it is an entire life-style change. In other words the residual effects of drug abuse may be associated with shifts in the teen's need for independence, autonomy, and freedom (sometimes at the cost of academic achievement), decreased interest in religious, sports, and recreational activities, greater tolerance for deviance, and shifts in friends and social support systems. These shifts in behavior and life-style cause considerable concern and consternation for the parents and older siblings, independent of the drug-abusing behavior per se.

Threat of Community Sanctions

As noted earlier, families feel a sense of responsibility for their own members, as has been the case throughout history and in most human societies. Apart from the sources of stress noted above which are internal to either the individual (guilt) or family (conflict), or both, is a sense of duty and responsibility to the community. Angela's parents felt at least some degree of embarrassment as they dealt with hospital personnel, the law enforcement and criminal justice system, neighbors, and friends.

In more severe cases families must cope with much more overt and forceful sanctions resulting from an adolescent member's drug abuse: imprisonment, court-ordered treatment, and other forms of intervention. In each case the sanctions often result in considerable stress experienced by the entire family in various ways and degrees of severity.

FAMILY COPING

McCubbin and Patterson (1981b) advance the theory that family crises result from imbalances of family functioning—member-to-member and/or family-to-community relationships. Adaptation to crises reflects efforts to achieve balance in these relationships. Positive adaptation results in (a) the maintenance or strengthening of family integrity, (b) the continued promotion of both individual member and family development, and (c) a sense of control over environmental influences and maintenance of family independence. The negative end of the continuum is typified by a lack of balance in family functioning or managing to balance these relationships with a consequent deterioration in family integrity, curtailment or deterioration in member or family development, or a decline in family independence.

Dysfunctional Coping

The drug abuse episode and resulting hardships arising from the event require some response on the part of the family in order to maintain family functioning. The inability of some families to successfully contend with the threatening consequences of adolescent drug abuse and related piling up of other life stressors may reflect a fundamental pathology within the family system; these families are less able than others to manage various dimensions of family life. Yet, the lack of success in coping may not necessarily reflect the failure of the families but rather the societal and economic conditions in which they live and which prevent them from being more effective.

Frequently, the drug-abusing adolescent plays the role in the family system of distracting the parents from their own problems. When there are difficulties in the marital relationship, the drug-using adolescent is often *maintained* in his dependent role by parents (and siblings) who use his failure to prevent them from dealing with their own situation. Failure to seek therapy in such situations renders the entire family system dysfunctional and has the potential for affecting other children in the family as well.

In discussing dysfunctional patterns of coping, it is important to remember that ours is a society in which drugs are commonplace. Many adults, including parents of adolescents, are themselves drug users—to the point where drugs are a problem for them. Excessive use of prescription drugs for relaxation, tension release, sleep, to feel good or forget troubles may leave parents in a position where they are unable to be of help to their adolescent children when it comes to dealing with drug problems. In fact, the parents' drug problems may contribute toward augmenting the adolescents' problems.

Functional Coping

In contrast to families which cope poorly with the problem of adolescent drug abuse, those that function more effectively tend to be more balanced in two basic dimensions of family behavior—adaptability and cohesion (McCubbin & Olson, 1980). Adaptability refers to the "ability of a marital or family system to change its power structure, role relationships, relationship rules in response to situational and developmental stress." Cohesion may be defined as the "emotional bonding that family members have toward one another and the degree of individual autonomy they experience." Overall, those families which have a larger and more flexible range of responses are more effective. Positive communication skills, essential to effective problem-solving, are also more likely to be found in such families. The most viable family functioning allows individuals to experience a balance between independence and connectedness, stability and change, within their families.

The adaptability and cohesion potential of the family, together with their ability to communicate, will determine the impact of the adolescent's drug experience both on him/herself and the family. And, of course, the larger community and societal context play a significant role as well. Societal tolerance for experimentation and drug-using behavior varies over time and this in turn affects family response.

A major factor in the resolution of drug use problems in the family is the availability of social support, particularly that found in group settings such as drug counseling, religious organizations, psychological therapy, and community programs that include family-based counseling and education. It appears that a primary key to effective coping with stressful consequences lies in accessing information about available services and sharing experience in group settings with others who are experiencing similar situations. Identifying the problems and planning strategies to minimize the impact of the stress on the family, while working toward the resolution of underlying problem(s), are the goals of effective programs.

Adaptation to recurring life stresses associated with substance use problems also includes relying on family members' personal resources, the family system's internal resources, and social support from extrafamilial sources. By sharing responsibility for resolving substance use problems, some families are able to cope effectively without external therapy, particularly if they are able to obtain and make use of available information and resources. Other families in which substance use is a factor sometimes become involved in health care systems; this may produce stress within the family, but it eventually becomes a resource for helping the family with management of the crisis.

INTERVENTION PROGRAMS

It should be clear by now that: 1) adolescent drug abuse is a significant problem for society but especially for the families affected; 2) such abuse presents many stresses for the family to contend with; and 3) the methods families use to cope sometimes improve the situation, but frequently exacerbate the problem. Part of effective coping is the utilization of resources outside the family system, as well as those from within. The focus of this section is on intervention programs designed to help adolescent drug abusers and their families. The programs range from educationally-oriented prevention to long-term, in-depth family therapy. Each is designed for a particular family and situation and thus has significantly different goals and methods.

Several studies in more recent years have specifically focused on treating the adolescent drug abuser in the context of the family (e.g., Bartlett, 1975; Huberty, 1975; Kempler & MacKenna, 1975; Kovacs, 1975; Weingarten, 1980). Huberty, in particular, contends that the family is an essential aspect in the treatment of adolescent drug abuse. He believes this not only because the family may offer either support to the user or a clue as to what deeper problems may be the source of the drug abuse, but also because

> . . . failure to involve the family in treatment is almost certain to result in every family member—father and mother, brothers, and sisters—in some way sabotaging the efforts of the treatment staff (Huberty, 1975, p. 183).

Overview

Auerswald (1980) recently commented that if our country is serious about attacking the problems of drug abuse, the way to do it is to develop a system that will support and foster family life—not to develop drug abuse programs. Thus, programs unrelated to adolescent drug abuse which focus on enrichment and enhancement of familial interpersonal relationships—especially the parent-child and sibling relationships—would decrease the severity of problems such as drug abuse (cf., Guerney, 1976). Yet, families faced with the stress of drug abuse, especially when it directly results in anti-social behavior or personal risk to the abuser, require more immediate, problem-focused programs. Following is a brief description of some of these programs identified with the drug abuse problem.

Prevention Programs

The purpose of family-centered drug abuse prevention programs involves decreasing the vulnerability of the family system. This can be accomplished by 1) reducing or eliminating the problems that arise from inequities in education, health, housing, child care, and other human services; and 2) strengthening individual members, families, and social groups through the development of constructive coping skills to help them resist the stressors of modern society.

Needle and Carlaw (1981), for example, have developed such a program. The overall goal of the program is to help families enhance their ability to adopt positive health behaviors (e.g., diet, exercise, chemical intake) and to improve their ability to foster constructive coping strategies. The coping strategies reflect, they believe, both the internal adaptations to the stressor and active transactions with the community. The program teaches adolescent family members such skills as decision-making, assertiveness, and communication through group discussion, modeling, and behavioral rehearsal. The nature of stress in the teen's life—familial and non-familial—is discussed, with emphasis on the development of nonchemical coping skills. Adult family members are educated on current patterns of drug abuse, parental influence, peer group pressures, and the typical ways families handle the problem.

Ellis (1980), with a similar focus, combines a psychological and teaching approach in working with the adolescent and the family together. Through informally structured group training experiences, family members work through problems associated with the drug abuse problem. These often include, for example, family boundary issues (e.g., roles, responsibilities, friendships), decision-making, interpersonal communication, and values clarification. In contrast to more therapy-oriented programs, Ellis's "Family Intervention Model" is more prevention-oriented and educational in focus and content.

Family Therapy

Family therapy as a method of coping with a wide variety of problems has, in the past decade, emerged as a significant and separate mental health field (Olson, Sprenkle & Russell, 1980). The use of this therapeutic approach has also increased rapidly in helping families deal with drug abuse-related stress. The primary reason for this substantial growth is that thinking in the drug field has broadened to include viewing drug abuse within its interpersonal context, i.e., relative to other people who may be involved, such as parents, siblings, and peers (Stanton, 1979a). Family therapy outcome studies conducted thus far suggest that by focusing treatment upon drug use in the context of the entire family system, rather than solely upon the drug abuser him/ or herself, positive results may be achieved.

At this point in the development of the field, the most common therapeutic situation is one in which a drug-abusing family member is the identified patient and other members of the family participate in the therapy in order, as they perceive it, to help that individual deal with his or her drug use. In fact, as we have seen earlier, the participation of the rest of the family is crucial because the drug use of the identified patient is often only a manifestation of deeper and more serious family problems.

Use of this technique has increased to the point that Coleman and Davis (1978) were able to report that, on the basis of a national survey, 93 percent of drug programs across the country provide some type of family service or treatment to their clients and that 69 percent provide family therapy which includes the drug abuser. Further, when asked whether family treatment was important for the drug abuser's recovery process, over 95 percent of the drug programs replied that it was moderately or highly important.

Finally, Stanton's (1979a) review of family treatment approaches to drug abuse problems identified a wide-ranging array of types of therapy currently in use (e.g., marital treatment, group treatment for parents, concurrent treatment of parents and the identified patient, outpatient treatment with individual families, sibling-oriented treatment, multiple family therapy, and social network therapy). He cautions, however, that the clinical aspects of these techniques need to be more specific and clear, particularly with regard to how they best serve the family of the drug abuser, and that greater effort must be made in the area of accurately assessing the effectiveness of these treatments.

CONCLUSIONS AND FUTURE NEEDS

Our national goals for health promotion and disease prevention are focused on the major preventable health problems of different age groups—including adolescents and young adults. To improve the health and health habits of these groups requires policy and programmatic efforts at minimizing the most serious threats to their health—including violent death, accident, injury, and alcohol and drug abuse. The different threats to the health of children, youth, and adults are often characterized as the "new morbidity" for which environmental (e.g., social, physical, familial, and economic) and behavioral factors have been identified as causative or contributing. Alcohol and drug abuse behaviors are among these factors which increase the risk of accidents, suicide, and homicide and also contribute to such problems as poor school performance and family dysfunction (DHEW, 1979).

Families and peers greatly influence adolescent drug use, and families are impacted on by adolescent drug-using patterns. The stresses that arise during the adolescent years and the efforts of family members to minimize the consequences of the stress also affect drug-using behavior. Drug abuse is thought to arise in part from failed coping efforts; in families in which constructive coping resources and responses have been formed and continue to develop in order to meet the demands that arise from predictable and unpredictable stressors and crises, family members do not generally abuse drugs (Ellis, 1980). Auerswald (1980) has observed that well-organized, lovingly close families characterized by open communication and mutual respect may have members who briefly experiment with alcohol or marijuana but do not experience members who have serious, lasting drug habits.

Clearly, the family plays a role in influencing drug-using behavior and is affected by drug use of one or more of its members. The family must educate its members in the development of healthy coping styles, strengthened and supported by national efforts, including the health sector, individual citizens, neighborhood networks, self-help and mutual aid groups, schools, and governmental agencies. These efforts are necessary to accomplish our national health goals of health promotion and to reduce the misuse of alcohol and drugs.

4

Abandonment: The Stress of Sudden Divorce

DOUGLAS H. SPRENKLE and
CATHERINE L. CYRUS

Bob: My wife, Nancy, said she wanted to talk with me about something. I yawned and ambled into the living room, assuming it was about the bills or Saturday's bridge club. She said the marriage had died for her and that she wanted me out of the house as soon as possible. My God! I couldn't believe it! The next few days I alternated between being a zombie and a bundle of raging emotions. I also felt like someone had emblazoned some words on my forehead that everyone could read: "This man is a failure. His family dumped him." Everyone seemed to be pointing fingers at me and whispering, "Shame, how disgusting."

Because divorce is becoming an almost common, everyday occurrence, we have almost ceased to view it as a crisis. However, divorce can be a catastrophic event, especially if it is unwanted and unexpected. The stress associated with this particular form of divorce experience can be overwhelmingly painful and have far-reaching consequences, as noted in the illustration above.

This chapter attempts to focus on the unique circumstances of persons like Bob in an attempt to understand the stress of abandonment on the family.

There has been a great deal written about divorce in general during this past decade (cf., Price-Bonham & Balswick, 1980; see also Volume I, Chapter 7); however, very little has focused on different types of divorce. Although scholars have long recognized that one should not paint a uniform or monolithic picture of "marriage" or "family," only recently have researchers begun to discriminate between kinds of divorce. The pioneering work of Kressel et al. (1980) is one of the first attempts to generate descriptive categories which attack the myth that "a divorce is a divorce is a divorce" (Baker, 1981). In short, we are only now beginning to recognize that there are various types of divorce and each is associated with a particular set of stresses and challenges.

Of necessity, this chapter is somewhat speculative because there is no hard research data on individual and family reactions to unwanted and unexpected divorce (or any other type of divorce for that matter). In their comprehensive review of divorce research, Kitson and Raschke (1981) note that the largest body of divorce-related research has focused on the *causes or correlates* of divorce rather than on what happens during the separation and after divorce. Moreover, much of the research on the consequences of divorce has focused on harmful effects on physical and mental well-being (Bloom, Asher & White, 1978). Data which help us to *distinguish* between adequate and inadequate adjustment, and especially different patterns or ways of divorcing, are much less available. This chapter, therefore, will rely, in part, on data generated by clinical case studies, interviews, and a review of related literature on divorce adjustment that does not control for type of divorce. Such data are considered appropriate during the hypothesis-generating phase as opposed to the hypothesis-testing phase of exploration of a phenomenon (Kerlinger, 1973).

In Volume I (Chapter 7), Ahrons considers divorce as a normative, developmental change within many families. In contrast, this chapter focuses on divorce as a catastrophic source of stress, due to its often unwanted and unexpected nature. In 1980 the annual number of divorces was 1,182,000 (Monthly Vital Statistics Report, 1981). We can state with much more certainty the percentages of divorces that fall into the "unwanted" category as opposed to the "unexpected" category. A variety of studies (cf., Berman & Turk, 1981; White & Bloom, 1981) conclude that in only about 15% of all divorces do both partners *equally* desire the termination. Therefore, in the majority of divorces there is a partner who must adjust to a situation he or she does not want. Conversely, the percentage of divorces which are perceived as "unexpected" is simply not known.* However, based on discussions with marriage and divorce therapists nationwide, as well as a review of clinical literature, we suggest a disproportionate representation of the emotionally abandoned in therapists' caseloads. It is reasonable to conclude, therefore, that we are dealing with a problem that is common at least among persons seeking professional help.

In this chapter, we will discuss the following:

1) the meaning of emotional abandonment in the family and why it is so complex;
2) why this particular stressor is so painful, not only for the individuals involved, but also for their families and social networks;
3) what factors determine the level of stress experienced by emotionally abandoned spouses;
4) the methods, both constructive and destructive, used to cope with this stress;
5) interventions found to be useful with clients experiencing emotional abandonment;
6) the constructive potential of sudden divorce for the individual who survives; and
7) the gaps in our knowledge about this phenomenon and goals for future research.

SOURCES OF STRESS

Spanier and Thompson (1981) note that "few of the 2.4 million men and women who experience the breakup of a marriage each year get away without suffering some losses and upheaval" (p. 1). Ever since William Goode's (1956) classic study on divorce, the themes of change, stress, trauma, and disorganization have characterized the study of separation and divorce. Ahrons (Volume I, Chapter 7) provides an excellent

---

*Only one study was discovered which offered data on this dimension (Baker, 1981). Of all divorces occurring in a Central Indiana county during a six-month period in 1980-1981, 15% were perceived as sudden by at least one partner.

update. That separation and divorce are highly disruptive events is supported by the fact that Holmes and Rahe (1967) consider only the death of a spouse more traumatic in their widely recognized scale of stressful life events.

The breakup of brief childless marriages is often less stressful, particularly when the couple have led relatively separate lives anyway (Kressel & Deutsch, 1977); and some persons in intolerable marriages even experience relief at the time of separation and divorce (Spanier & Thompson, 1981), although such reactions are in the clear minority (Albrecht, 1980; Spanier & Casto, 1979; Weiss, 1975).

Some of the reasons that even "desired" and "expected" divorces are typically stressful include: 1) presence of children; 2) attachment to the former spouse; 3) perception of being a failure; 4) social rejection; 5) change in lifestyle and patterns; and 6) shifts in social support system.

Presence of Children

About 60% of divorces involve minor children. Virtually all parents worry about the effects of their divorce on the children and find matters related to custody, visitation, and child support particularly stressful (Hetherington, Cox & Cox, 1977; Wallerstein & Kelly, 1980). Although this chapter focuses primarily on the divorcing partners, the implications for their children may also be profound. In addition to the age of the children at this time of divorce, research (Bane, 1979; Black, 1959; Berman & Turk, 1981; Hetherington, Cox & Cox, 1976; Longfellow, 1979; Wallerstein & Kelly, 1980) suggests that there are six major variables which determine children's adjustment:

1) the quality of the nurturing relationship between the children and the custodial parent;
2) the quality of the relationship between the ex-spouses;
3) the psychological adjustment of the parents, especially the custodial parent;
4) a reliable relationship with the noncustodial parent;
5) financial resources; and
6) achievement by the children of a perceived and actual sense of control concerning the divorce situation.

Note that most of these variables interact with each other and that the child's adjustment is largely dependent upon others (primarily parents) who make up the relationship context in which the child exists.

Stress levels will be further heightened: when no age-appropriate explanation of the divorce is given to the children (Jacobson, 1978); when children create dysfunctional explanations such as "I caused Daddy or Mommy to leave," "I won't ever see Mommy or Daddy again," "If I love one, the other will hate me," and so forth (Wallerstein & Kelly, 1980); and when the child already has few resources in terms of self-esteem and coping skills (Wallerstein & Kelly, 1980). Naturally, these variables will be strongly influenced by the parents' own adjustment and cannot be assessed independently. We posit a strong positive correlation between the levels of stress of the parents (especially the custodial parent) and the children.

Attachment to Former Spouse

There is an emotional bonding process that occurs between mates that seems to die more slowly than love itself. This bonding process has some parallels with the attachment phenomenon described in the literature between infants and parents. Weiss, in his book *Marital Separation* (1975), writes extensively about the "erosion of love but the persistence of attachment" in divorce. For example, Bob—the husband in the opening case illustration—later said, "Even though our marriage was awful and Nancy dumped me, I want her back. I feel like the kid who is being deserted but wants his parents because they are the only parents he has. I know I should let go, but I just can't."

Perception of Being a Failure

Cultural norms about divorce, although more liberal than in past generations, still encourage people to think of themselves as failures if they do divorce (Hetherington et al., 1977). Despite society's growing acceptance of divorce, there are still sufficient negative stereotypes and sanctions existing for someone who is already feeling bad to seize upon. Divorce remains a very ambiguous status. People do not know whether to congratulate the newly divorced or to say they are sorry. The net effect is that quite often nothing is said, and in this vacuum the divorcé(e) makes interpretations consistent with his or her diminished self-esteem. As Bob put it, "Everytime I heard the minister mention marriage in a sermon, I was convinced he was admonishing me. Every time the secretaries at work gathered at the coffee pot, I was sure they were discussing me."

Social Rejection

Stress is experienced when the divorcé(e) anticipates negative reactions from children, friends, kin, church, and employer. Moreover, the perceived level of supportiveness one expects to receive from his/her social support network, as well as from the legal and helping professions, will affect the amount of stress experienced.

Change in Lifestyle

Divorce rapidly alters one's lifestyle in ways that would be stressful even if no divorce had occurred. Divorce typically entails a dramatic change in socioeconomic status, moving, changes in parental responsibilities, and assumption of different household responsibilities (Hetherington et al., 1976, 1977; Mendes, 1976; Goode, 1956; Glasser & Navarre, 1965; Bohannan, 1971; Brandwein et al., 1974; Berman & Turk, 1981). Many divorced men, for example, particularly those from marriages in which conventional sex roles have been maintained, initially experience considerable difficulty sustaining a household routine. Previously unemployed women are forced to work, and divorced fathers frequently expand their workload in order to increase their income to afford support payments.

Shifts in Social Support System

Changing friendship patterns also frequently accompany divorce. Divorcing persons tend to experience loss of support from their friendship networks and, as a result, often feel the anguish associated with social isolation (Brandwein et al., 1974; Berman & Turk, 1981; Goode, 1956; Miller, 1978; Raschke, 1974, 1977; Spanier & Casto, 1979). Hetherington, Cox & Cox (1977) reported that for only two months following divorce do married friends remain supportive and spend considerable time with their divorced friends. Thereafter, these contacts decline rapidly.

Friends and relatives will probably be equally caught off guard by the separation. Based on research concerning relatives' reactions to divorce, they will most likely show concern for both parties but eventually divorcing persons will increase contact with their own kin (consanguines) and decrease contact with their ex-spouse's families (affines) (Anspach, 1976; Booth, 1979). These same studies show that considerable anguish among close relatives is quite common. Grandparents—especially the parents of the noncustodial spouse—will worry about their access to the children. Friends will initially "rally around" the couple, or the individual with whom they were close prior to the separation, but later there will be a process of mutual withdrawal from these friends (Weiss, 1975). Co-workers will often wonder what to say and may be concerned about taking sides if they have a relationship with both parties to the divorce. The psychological and physical consequences of the divorce may also generate increased contact with physicians, clergy, and mental health workers (Bloom, Asher & White, 1978). For many divorcé(e)s, this event will expand their social network to include an attorney. In sum, the divorce will have a ripple effect with far-reaching consequences.

THE ABANDONMENT FACTOR

Although there is no empirical research on sudden divorce per se, there is a growing body of empirical evidence (Baker, 1981; Brown et al., 1980; Fisher, 1979; Goode, 1956; Spanier & Thompson, 1981) that clearly suggests that at the time of the divorce the pain is more acutely felt by the person who perceives him/herself as being emotionally abandoned. Utilizing his Divorce Adjustment Scale, Fisher (1979) found that after one year, the abandoned spouse attained a level of adjustment that the abandoner began with at the time of the overt break in the relationship. Fisher believes that the abandoner has experienced no less pain, but probably experienced more during the marriage or at least in the period prior to the decision to terminate the relationship.

Being Abandoned

It is important to note at the outset that the experience of being emotionally abandoned, while psychologically real, may not correspond with the actual facts of the marriage. Bob, for example, was actually involved in a process of "abandoning" his wife over a period of years prior to his "unexpected" divorce. Federico (1979) has written perceptively about the often unconscious or preconscious process whereby persons who perceive themselves as abandoned "provoke" this very behavior which now devastates them. In Bob's case he was simply unable to admit to himself that he wanted to be out of the marriage or at least was highly ambivalent about it. As he later confessed, he simply lacked the courage to end the relationship and really wanted to pass that responsibility to Nancy. "I'm really glad she blew the whistle on our relationship."

Some marriages even appear to be sustained by a process whereby the partners alternate between the roles of the abandoner and the abandoned (Federico, 1979). In these relationships a kind of quasi-intimacy is generated when there is a rejecting partner and a pursuer. Frequently these relationships experience dramatic flip-flops, expecially when the one doing the chasing finds some alternative attraction or simply gets tired and begins to exit from the marriage. At that point, the roles reverse. When Nancy announced the marriage was over, Bob suddenly was willing to do anything to save it. *Most abandoned mates, then, have probably been involved at some period during the marriage in some form of abandoning behavior.*

Just as the identification or labeling of the abandoner and the abandonee depends upon how one "punctuates" (Wazlawick, Beavin & Jackson, 1967) or divides the marital history, the person's perceptions of the "unexpectedness" of the divorce may be faulty as well. Frequently the abandoned mate has not seen or has chosen not to see a variety of clues that his/her partner was leaving or would leave the relationship if certain changes were not made. In Bob's case, the only factor truly "sudden" about his divorce was his rapid self-realization that Nancy was serious about her frustration with the relationship. However, it is important to emphasize that psychological or *perceived* suddenness is more significant than actual suddenness, which is probably quite rare.

Compounding the sources of stress accompanying divorce in general is a variety of acute problems associated with abandonment—specifically self-esteem, helplessness, circumstances of the separation, unpreparedness, and the concomitant impact on the children.

Reduced Self-esteem

Based on our clinical experiences the abandonee rarely escapes a sense of rejection, which is accompanied by a massive blow to his or her self-esteem. Just as those experiencing natural disasters feel their lives are being threatened by wind, water, or fire, abandonees often feel their very lives are in danger. The threat, however, is more that of psychic annihilation. To the degree that love builds up, rejection tears down; and to the extent that one's identity is propped up by the social scaffolding of marriage, it becomes threatened as one experiences the scaffolding crumbling with nothing to replace it. With sudden divorce, one's sense of identity is smashed.

Although often unconscious, people being abandoned make self-statements about their own worth or about their ability to cope during this time of trauma. For example, the following self-statements about being abandoned will magnify the stress level:

"I must be awful."
"God is punishing me."
"I am inherently rejectable."
"I have lost everything."
"I have no power or control over my life."

Self-esteem will be further damaged if the divorce involves the existence of third parties. Seeing one's spouse with one's own "replacement" frequently engenders feelings of worthlessness. In contrast, however, some abandonees are more traumatized when there is no one else. Being left for no one intensifies an already low self-concept.

Circumstances of the Abandonment

The manner in which the separation is carried out and the amount of hostility and anger displayed by the spouses increases the level of stress for the abandonee. One client, for example, came home one evening to find garbage strewn all over the kitchen and a not-too-cryptic note saying: "Thanks for messing up my life." Similarly, Hunt (1980) has described a man who came home one night and found his apartment literally stripped of all furniture, paintings, appliances, and even the curtain rods. When he opened the door to his balcony, to his amazement he discovered his wife had thrown his clothes over the railing and into the alley two stories below.

Loss Factor

The separation will be more stressful if the person generally evaluated his or her marriage favorably. The literature on marital quality (Lewis & Spanier, 1979) suggests that satisfaction with one's marriage is related to one's perception of the balance of rewards and tensions in that relationship. If tensions greatly exceed rewards, then the loss of the marriage will be less stressful (Spanier & Thompson, 1981).

Additional Catastrophes

As previously mentioned, even under the best of circumstances, divorce precipitates a considerable number of life changes which are stressful. The separation and divorce will be more stressful if other life crises exist. For example, only several weeks after he and his wife separated, one client had his house totally destroyed by a flood. Until that point the man was functioning at least marginally. Following the flood he was unable to work and was hospitalized in a psychiatric facility.

Sense of Helplessness

Marital abandonment precipitates the feeling of utter helplessness or the absence of fate control. One is presented with a bitter fait accompli and there is absolutely nothing that can be done. When Bob was first seen in therapy, one of his major frustrations was that Nancy was totally indifferent to his desire to work on the marriage. Although he desperately wanted to win her back and would have been willing to do "virtually anything," she was unresponsive. Indeed, the pursuit behaviors of the abandonee frequently drive the abandoner further away.

Unpreparedness

The experience of marital abandonment is unique and therefore the abandonee typically has no practice in coping with similar events. Persons who initiate divorce or move into the process more slowly have the opportunity to cultivate coping strategies or to develop support systems—luxuries usually unavailable to the abandonee. Men are more likely in these circumstances to have underdeveloped social networks, whereas women are more likely to have underdeveloped vocational or professional networks (Kitson & Raschke, 1981).

Impact on the Children

Since a reasonable explanation of separation, preferably prior to its occurrence is also related to good adjustment (Jacobson, 1978), the stress for children is compounded by a sudden divorce. If the custodial parent is devastated, the ex-spouses are hostile, one parent is simply not available, financial resources are minimal, and the children's context is generally chaotic, they will probably experience considerable pain unless they are remarkably resilient or their pre-separation life contained an abusive parent who is now gone (Wallerstein & Kelly, 1980).

Children will also suddenly be faced with numerous structural changes as a result of the divorce. Wallerstein and Kelly report that ". . . divorce becomes real for most children when one parent moves out of the home" (1979, p. 469); thus, the onset of sudden divorce generally precipitates the very event most feared by the children. Structurally, the family will change from a two-parent to a one-parent system. This may involve geographical moves resulting in changes in school, friends, and familiar territory. Other people may also begin moving in and out of the child's life, such as extended kin, child-care professionals, and lovers of the divorcing parents. There will probably be less contact with the noncustodial parent, and that parent will probably be seen in a different locale than the child's home.

RESOURCES

Personal Resources and Attributes

Stress is also increased when people have few personal resources, such as an attractive appearance, age (youth), social skills, and psychological coping skills. There are both direct and indirect benefits from having these resources. Being relatively young may, for example, directly affect one's ability to attract an alternative source of intimacy. Being young may also indirectly affect one's capacity to adapt to change, since old patterns are not as firmly established. Most studies relating age and divorce adjustment have found that older individuals, and older women in particular, do experience more distress (Kitson & Raschke, 1981).

Psychological coping skills, in turn, depend upon such psychological variables as self-concept, flexibility, and tolerance for change. Psychological characteristics previously demonstrated to positively affect divorce adjustment include, for example, nontraditional and/or egalitarian gender role attitudes in women, high tolerance for change, and lower dogmatism. Higher self-esteem also seems to be correlated with better adjustment (Fisher, 1979; Kitson & Raschke, 1981).

Financial

The stress level is affected by the socioeconomic resources of the individual, including salary and job satisfaction. There is considerable empirical evidence that actual amount of income and stability of income is related to divorce adjustment in general (Kitson & Raschke, 1981), and it is reasonable that these same factors will facilitate adjustment to sudden divorce. The more independent individuals are economically, the lower their stress level will be, other things being equal. These resources also increase a person's sense of fate control and diminish feelings of powerlessness.

Familial Support

The *actual* level of supportiveness experienced by the divorcing person from children, kin, friends, church, and employers affects the degree of stress experienced. Previously, attention was given to the perception that the individual had concerning the amount of support he or she anticipated receiving in contrast to the amount of support the person *actually experiences* from these same sources. Moreover, the actual sources of intimacy available will also be an important resource to reduce stress.

Recreational Repertoire

The more "creative operants" (Johnson, 1977) the person employs to actively use his or her time, the greater his/her adjustment will be. For example, learning to play the guitar (versus passively watching television) is a "creative operant."

COPING WITH DIVORCE: INITIAL PHASE

The abandoned cope as best they can with the adversities of separation and divorce—some more effectively than others. This section begins with a discussion about the time immediately following the abandonment.

Dysfunctional Responses

Ineffective or dysfunctional coping responses following abandonment may be divided into four categories utilizing two dimensions. The first dimension notes whether the behavior is primarily "destructive to self" or primarily "destructive to others" (principally the spouse but secondarily one's children, friends, or parents). The second dimension delineates whether these behaviors are "active" (aggressive) destructive or "passive" (non-aggressive) destructive.

Self-destructive Active. Behaviors which are actively destructive and also primarily destructive to one's self include suicide or self-maiming. In addition to overt self-destructions are actions which seek pleasure at the expense of one's well being: abuse of chemicals, over- and undereating. Finally, active self-condemnation is an act of self-destruction and often leads to long-term self-anger, guilt, or self-deprecation (Johnson, 1977; Weiss, 1975).

Self-destructive Passive. People may also engage in unconscious, passive actions which often result in harming themselves. This may include various forms of physical neglect, such as not attending to one's health (Goetting, 1980) or becoming so self-absorbed that accidents occur. McMurray (1970) has cited the high automobile accident rate among the recently divorced compared to controls, which suggests the self-destructive nature of this group. It is quite common, from our experience, to find that recently divorced persons withdraw from all forms of social contact, become listless and unable to work, or sleep excessively.

Other-destructive Active. Behaviors which are actively destructive and primarily focus on the spouse include various forms of physical and psychological abuse. The most radical forms include attempts at murder, maiming, or kidnapping the spouse. Name-calling, harassing telephone calls, and attempts to sabotage the ex-partner's relationship with children, friends, lovers, and employers are not uncommon. Angry spouses frequently raid bank accounts, abuse credit cards, or hire "bomber" attorneys to flagellate the other (Wallerstein & Kelly, 1980).

Somewhat less punitive but nonetheless destructive are those behaviors which inappropriately promote the continuation of attachment between ex-partners: spying, reading his or her mail, driving by his or her apartment, or engaging in other forms of "checking-out" behavior.

Sometimes the anger of the abandonee becomes displaced on persons other than the ex-spouse. Children may be abused out of a sense of frustration and helplessness. If there is a lover involved, frequently the abandonee directs his/her anger at the lover rather than the ex-spouse. Abandonees may also direct hostility at the ex-partner's friends, family, or even all members of the opposite sex.

Other-destructive Passive. Passive-destructive behaviors which focus primarily on the spouse include the various ploys which abandoned partners use to solicit sympathy from their ex-partners. Threatening suicide or feigning illness as a means of soliciting care-taking or pity are common behaviors. Appearing helpless or incompetent as a means of provoking the other person's guilt or sense of responsibility may also occur.

Neglecting significant others, including one's children, also occurs. A particularly perplexing, yet very common social problem related to divorce is the father who seldom, if ever, sees his children. We hypothesize that many men never learned to deal actively and creatively with emotions. As a result, the pain of reuniting and then separating from their children, so typical of post-divorce fathers, is unbearable and, for many, avoidance is the only recourse. To withdraw from the children supports their belief of "out of sight, out of mind."

Functional Responses

Although the coping behavior just discussed is virtually always unproductive, there are several transitional coping methods which would be dysfunctional if they persisted, but which may be functional if only temporary.

Repression and Denial. Just as denial is a typical and functional response to the news that one has a terminal illness (Horowitz, 1979; Kübler-Ross, 1969), this defense mechanism may mitigate the threat of "psychic annihilation" in a sudden divorce. Persons in this stage typically are numb, have a dazed expression, and articulate their feelings through words like, "I just can't believe this is happening to me." Although reality must eventually be faced, the temporary protective value of this defense is self-evident.

Blaming. Blaming the spouse and concomitant anger directed at the spouse are also useful transitional behaviors. Although there is some value in pouring out these negative feelings, the major value of this anger is to galvanize the abandoned mate's energy (Krantzler, 1974). We believe it may be temporarily functional for the abandonee to have the attitude, "I'll show that bastard that he can't ruin my life." Our clients frequently report that they are amazed at what they were able to accomplish during this anger phase of their response to sudden divorce.

Self-indulgence. A third transitional behavior is self-indulgence. This may take the form of engaging in excessive amounts of travel, buying sports cars, wearing fad clothing, spending money compulsively, joining groups, becoming involved in cults, excessive socializing, and being promiscuous. Kessler (1975) writes that a "second adolescence" is a typical transitional phase in divorce, and Fisher (1979) has documented the "horny" phase of sexual acting-out that frequently follows an initial lack of desire. Taken together, these forms of indulgence probably are an immature means of "self-care" that may temporarily enhance self-esteem until more mature methods can be found. They are also a means of structuring time, coping with loneliness, and contributing to a sense that one is at least "doing something."

While there is no empirical evidence which suggests when these transitional behaviors would cease, it is our clinical impression that repression and denial would probably be dysfunctional after a short time; excessive blaming and anger at the spouse should not be a predominant force after six months and extreme manifestations of self-indulgence should abate within a year.

COPING WITH DIVORCE: LONG-TERM RECOVERY

It is much easier to delineate criteria for a constructive adjustment to marital abandonment than it is to *achieve* such an adjustment. It will be virtually impossible for any person to achieve all of what the following describes, either completely or quickly. Since the divorce adjustment literature suggests that it takes somewhere between two to four years to "recover" from a divorce, the progress will be slow if not plodding. Also, the "graph" of divorce recovery typically is not straight, but rather jagged. For every several steps forward, there seem to be several backward. The best one can hope for is a general trend of progress toward recovery. The following, then, is an ideal rather than typical process of adjustment. Some of these dimensions are adopted from the work of Kressel and Deutsch (1977).

Avoiding Destructive Feelings

As previously mentioned, repression and denial may be appropriate at first, as well as anger and rage. Certainly the experience and expression of grief and sadness are appropriate and valuable. It is best, however, that the abandonee not resort to a pattern of long-term self-blame, guilt or anger. It is most constructive not to ruminate excessively about the past and what "might have been."

Fisher (1979) reports a true story about a recently divorced woman who came upon her ex-husband and his girlfriend lying on a blanket in a local park. She literally ran over them, back and forth, several times with her car. One client, even several years after his divorce, frequently committed acts of vandalism on his ex-wife's house and car. It is easy, yet destructive, to remain a "hostility junkie."

Acceptance of the Divorce

As hard as it may be for the abandonee, eventually he or she must come to accept that the relationship is over and there is no use continuing to invest in a relationship to which there is no return. It is helpful if the person realizes that, although divorce is incredibly painful, a worse fate is being married to someone who does not want to be married to him or her. A part of this dimension of acceptance is for the partner to achieve a balanced view of the marriage, to recognize the good things as well as the bad, and eventually accept his or her contribution to the dissolution of the marriage. Moreover, it will be beneficial for each partner to learn about the reasons for his/her choice of mate so that similar mistakes can be avoided in the future (Kressel & Deutsch, 1977).

Divorces are most constructive if the settlement is not contested, or at least neither partner feels embittered by the adversary legal process. Abandoned partners must learn to walk a fine line between taking care of themselves and being assertive about their own rights and using the legal process as a punitive measure (Irving, 1981).

Rapport with the Abandoner

Eventually the divorced must learn that nastiness only begets nastiness and that acting in aggressive and hostile ways ultimately hurts themselves and is especially detrimental to the children involved. Part of "becoming free" of the other person is the capacity not to engage in tit-for-tat retribution. The ultimate expression of this freedom is the capacity to forgive the other for his or her contribution to the demise of the marriage.

The amount of ongoing tension in the relationship with the ex-spouse will increase stress. As previously mentioned, Weiss (1975) has demonstrated that even after the erosion of love in the relationship there is a continuation of attachment, and this attachment works against the development of autonomy and independence necessary to function as a single adult. Several research studies (Hynes, 1979; Marroni, 1977) have confirmed empirically that the higher the lingering attachment to the former spouse, the higher the stress associated with the divorce. It seems reasonable, therefore, that interaction with one's ex-spouse that promotes lingering attachment would work against adjustment to sudden divorce. If, for example, the abandonee must be in frequent contact with his or her ex-partner due to employment, social networks, or the sharing of parental responsibilities, this will increase stress. If the abandonee must or chooses to drive past his former partner's house or apartment or engages in behaviors such as snooping, badgering, or pleading, stress will be increased. Naturally, frequent altercations and the bitterness associated with the legal dissolution of the marriage will escalate stress as well. The abandonee must, therefore, refrain from unnecessary contact with the former spouse and, when contact is necessary, try to work toward civil interactions.

Interpersonal Support

Alternate sources of social support, other than the ex-partner, are vitally important. There is consistent evidence in the literature that high levels of social support are related to lower distress and better adjustment for divorcees (Kitson & Raschke, 1981). By social support, we mean formal and informal contacts with individuals and groups that provide emotional or material resources (Kitson & Raschke, 1981).

In most studies, higher dating activity is related to lower trauma or distress and higher adjustment (Hetherington, Cox & Cox, 1976; Raschke, 1974). There is also at least impressionistic evidence that participation in counseling and divorce adjustment groups is helpful (Sprenkle & Storm, 1980).

Reworking the Parenting Role

It is important for the abandonee to compartmentalize negative feelings about the ex-partner and work cooperatively together as parents. It will benefit both the custodial and noncustodial parent, as well as the children, if both parents have ready access to the children. The most functional response for an abandonee is to facilitate such access. He or she should recognize that it is important that the children believe that *both* parents still love them, even if they no longer love each other. It is also essential that the children do not believe that loving either parent will jeopardize their place in the affections of the other. Moreover, children should not be used as weapons in an ongoing struggle with the ex-partner. It is wise to facilitate the children's expressions of painful emotions so that they may feel listened to and cared for. Finally, the parents should help the children dispel any beliefs that they have caused the divorce and should not nurture the children's fantasies that their parents will reconcile (Hetherington, Cox & Cox, 1977; Wallerstein & Kelly, 1980).

Personal Growth

The divorce will ultimately be most constructive when the abandonee is able to use it as an opportunity for personal growth—to develop feelings of competency and mastery as a single person. It is important for the abandonee to remember that "in divorce you always get custody of yourself." Part of this growth process will be finding sources of meaning in one's life other than the ex-partner, which will entail the establishment of a new identity and the setting of new goals. Obviously, it will also include the development of a whole new set of roles, whether these be learning to cook, becoming a professional person, or caring for children alone.

INTERVENTION: HELPING THE ABANDONEE RECOVER

As we have reviewed the literature, every possible therapeutic approach has been adapted to working with individuals experiencing the catastrophe of divorce; transactional analysis, rational-emotive, analytic, gestalt, behavioral and several other theoretical approaches have been attempted for this purpose. There is also no empirical evidence to prove that one approach is more successful than another (Kaslow, 1981) or that any specific therapy is appropriate for working with abandoned spouses. We do believe, however, that certain *general guidelines* should be followed by persons working with the suddenly divorced regardless of their theoretical orientation.

Supportive

Initially, intervention needs to be highly supportive. Relationship skills such as warmth, empathy, and unconditional positive regard (cf., Guerney, 1977) cannot be underestimated. The suddenly divorced feel deeply "wounded" and the short-term goal is not so much "healing" as it is "sustaining." As a result, therapy with the suddenly divorced is more like crisis intervention, where the clients need affirmation and to know someone cares.

Didactic

At the same time, it is important for therapy to be didactic. A didactic or teaching emphasis is necessary because people experiencing the typical symptomatology of sudden divorce frequently think that they are "crazy." It is important for the therapist to be able to teach the client about the divorce recovery process and what is likely to happen in the ensuing months. The professional must also be familiar with a specific body of knowledge on such practical matters as law, finances, and household management.

Confrontive

Furthermore, therapy must eventually be confrontive. Clients need to face the fact that they are at least partially responsible for where they are at this point and are totally responsible for where they go from here. In short, the therapist cannot afford to reinforce the "helpless victim" mentality. Therefore, an important goal is to help these persons gain a sense of power and control over their destiny. To the extent that they realize that they had something to do with where they are now, they also can more easily understand that they are in charge of their future. Naturally, however, this confrontation must be judiciously blended with support and affirmation, and such a balancing act requires consummate skill.

A General Strategy

In terms of the aforementioned discussion of adjustment to sudden divorce, a general strategy would include: 1) helping the client to revise self-destructive meanings attributed to the event; and 2) helping him or her to maximize resources so as to develop alternatives to the now defunct relationship. These two thrusts are interdependent. As the client learns to develop his or her resources, this makes it easier for the client to attribute less destructive meanings to the sudden divorce. Conversely, to the extent that the client diminishes making catastrophic interpretations, he or she will also be free to develop resources. Although a variety of theoretical approaches may be used to engender change in these ways, we believe these methods should impact the areas of the clients' feeling, thinking, and behavior.

Revising Self-destructive Meanings. Ways in which the meaning of the event affects the stress of abandonment were explicated earlier in this chapter. Although it would be naive to expect that a person would interpret the event positively, certain interpretations of the situation must be removed in order to fully recover. The most debilitating of these interpretations can be categorized into three basic types: unworthiness, meaninglessness, and helplessness.

1) *Unworthiness*. The reasoning here (generally unconscious) is as follows: "Since I have been rejected by my mate, I am inherently rejectable or worthless." There is, of course, a grain of truth in this interpretation. The person has been rejected and rejection is painful. The fallacy is the client's generalizing from a specific reaction of one person to a statement about his or her personal worth as a whole.

2) *Meaninglessness*. Here the reasoning may be, "My spouse means everything to me. Without him or her, life has no meaning." The rational component of this self-statement is that the spouse was an important (if not the most important) component of one's identity and carving out a new one will be difficult. The fallacy is the client's deleting other sources of identity, however dim. Regardless of how intertwined the client may have been with the ex-spouse, he or she did exist prior to meeting the partner and can continue to exist now and in the future.

3) *Helplessness*. The client frequently thinks, "My life is in turmoil, I'm overwhelmed by my emotions and I can't do the simplest things like get out of bed or write a check." Here again, there is sufficient truth in this plea. Nonetheless, generalizing from the temporary effects of a highly stressful situation to permanent behavior engenders a negativism which produces self-fulfilling prophecies.

Maximizing Resources. The ability to engage in constructive or helpful behavior depends upon tapping into resources that have either been underutilized or outside the clients' awareness, including friends, family, children, community, work, and most importantly, self. A general strategy is to help the client identify his or her resources and to strengthen those that seem most amenable to amplification. Obviously, this varies from client to client. There is evidence, for example, that the family can either be a resource at the time of separation or an additional burden, depending upon individual circumstances surrounding the divorce. As previously mentioned, there is considerable empirical evidence that a support group of friends and social participation abet divorce adjustment. Similarly, a job for which one is adequately compensated had been shown to be highly related to adjustment (Kitson & Raschke, 1981). Frequently, men and women differ in the extent to which these resources need to be cultivated. Typically, men need less help in developing their vocational resources and more help in the friendship and social areas, whereas the converse is often true for women (Johnson, 1977).

Developing the "self" as a resource is the most challenging and crucial task of the therapist. This generally entails:

1) *The development of certain basic life skills.* As noted earlier in this chapter and by Ahrons in Volume I, Chapter 7, one source of stress for the recently divorced is management of the household and other demands of living. Men, for example, frequently need to learn to cook and sew, whereas women may need help with fiscal management and basic maintenance and repairs.

2) *Time management skills.* Most abandonees need help in learning how to utilize time. In coming to terms with loneliness a program of "loneliness tolerance training" (Johnson, 1977) may be helpful where clients are introduced to progressively longer periods of time alone. Clients also need to learn how to use their time in ways that maximize their creativity.

3) *Accessing inner strengths.* Clients need help learning how to access personal sources of strength and competence that have been useful in the past. For example, Kirsten and Robertiello (1978) describe a method of helping the client to separate and distinguish his or her "Big You" and "Little You." The latter is the part of us that represents our emotional and belief system as a frightened small child. The abandoned often feels overwhelmed, incompetent, frightened, and demanding as a child would in a state of panic. Minimal attention is given to either consequences or delayed gratification. Conversely, Kirsten and Robertiello (1978) note that the "Big You" represents a part that is competent, confident, and capable of weighing consequences and delaying gratification. The therapeutic process is helping the client learn to better utilize his or her more competent self.

Salvaging the Constructive Elements

Fortunately, the long-term results of sudden divorce are often salutary.

Regardless of the intervention, most of those who are abandoned seem to fully recover from their experience. Many find they have actually benefited from the experience. Some of the constructive residue of the experience includes independence, growth, adventurousness, and acquiring new priorities.

Independence. Some people acquire, for example, a sense of autonomy through this experience. One middle-aged man in his forties said,

> At the time my wife left me I was a highly dependent person and my identity was very much wrapped up in my wife and children. I had few autonomous life skills, virtually no close friends who were not also close or closer to my wife. For me, just fixing Hamburger Helper was as significant as others might find preparing a gourmet meal. Writing my own monthly checks was more of an accomplishment than authoring the great American novel.

Growth. Many people find that sudden divorce is a significant catalyst for growth, change, and a general reassessment of life that might otherwise have been postponed indefinitely. Many therapists have learned that although people come to them for "change," a considerable portion of their energy remains invested in not changing. For most people, change is frightening, anxiety-arousing, and therefore resisted. Many of us postpone face-to-face confrontations with ourselves until our proverbial backs are up against the wall. Something like a brush with divorce or death will frequently precipitate life-changing revolutions concerning our needs, dreams, and acceptance of mortality.

Adventurousness. Perhaps another way of looking at what happens in sudden divorce is that it forces people to become more adventurous —to take risks that they would never do otherwise. As one woman client in her thirties put it:

> I've always been hesitant to make friends on my own because I assumed that nobody would really want to be my friend. But now, I had to make some friends. Besides, what did I have to lose? I had survived the worst possible rejection; one more could not add up to that much more pain; and I had nowhere to go but up

New Priorities. A final benefit of sudden divorce is that it frequently helps people to reevaluate their priorities. Divorce frequently pushes people to struggle with a question: "Just what does it mean to be a success?" or "What do I really need in life to make me happy?" As one 50-year-old man put it:

> I was one of those driven workaholics who kept building bigger barns to harvest all the money I was making. When my wife left me, I realized that what I had really reaped had all the substance of cotton candy.

CONCLUSIONS AND RECOMMENDATIONS

Only recently have scholars begun to recognize that divorce is not a unitary phenomenon, and this chapter is one of the first attempts to examine both theoretically and practically a specific type of divorce—abandonment. Since this demarcation of divorce types is in its infancy, it is not surprising that there are virtually no reliable normative data about even such basic information as the prevalence of abandonment, or the extent to which it is related to a number of other potentially significant demographic variables like age, sex, race, or socioeconomic status. Moreover, since type of divorce has not been controlled in divorce adjustment research, we do not know the extent to which the previously discovered associations hold for divorces of the unwanted-unexpected type.

Finally, outcome research on divorce therapy in general is meager and such research on abandonment therapy is non-existent. The first step will be to compare these interventions with no-treatment control groups. Clients may improve, for example, only because time has passed and not because of the curative nature of the intervention. Eventually the treatments need to be compared with each other and the links among treatments and types of clients assessed.

We hope the very gaps in our knowledge will spur the reader to investigate the unwanted-unexpected divorce more fully. We believe it is a fascinating phenomenon, in that it is both incredibly stressful and yet paradoxically affords a significant opportunity for growth. As one person expressed this two-edged sword so well:

> Even with my bills, my job, my exhausting routine, my two sons, I know I'm happier than before he left me. Several years ago I would have told you I was miserable. But now I know what I want out of life and who I am.

5

Death: Family Adjustment to Loss

JOHN F. CROSBY and
NANCY L. JOSE

Thomas Hollister died very suddenly almost one year ago. He had a massive coronary without any warning or prior history of heart disease. Since his death, the family has had difficulty in adjusting. Mrs. Hollister, Irene, continues to work as a teller at the bank. Before Thomas died at age 53, it was not crucial for her to work. Her paychecks covered extra things which she and Tom enjoyed. Since Tom had no mortgage insurance, Irene's check now must cover both the mortgage and living expenses. Tom's life insurance benefits are a help to Irene, but even so she is barely able to make ends meet.

The Hollisters have two children, a 27-year-old son, Hal, who is married with two small children, and a 21-year-old daughter, Chris, who lives with a girlfriend in Chicago. Recently, Irene has complained that her daughter is unsympathetic with her, showing little concern for her situation. Irene says that Hal is a bit more understanding of her plight but he is so busy with his job and his own family that he cannot really be of much help to her.

Irene complains that she has very little energy and that oftentimes she feels as though she cannot make it through the work day. She complains of depression and pressure, stating that "life just isn't the same anymore" and "I feel I can't cope with all the demands put on me." Irene says she has not considered taking her own life because "that would be wrong," but she has felt and expressed a persistent wish to die.

When Tom died, the entire family went through a time of chaos and disruption. For many months, no one touched any of Tom's clothes or possessions. Chris and Hal kept their feelings to themselves. They both had had clashes with their father and there had often been unpleasant exchanges between Tom and his children.

Shortly after Tom died, Irene had urged Chris to move back "home" to Peoria and share the house with her. Chris took off work from her job in Chicago for one month but then returned to Chicago. Hal continues to stop by and see his mother on weekends and sometimes leaves his two children in his mother's care.

Irene, even after one year, often feels depressed and is irritable with others, especially her children and friends. Yet she refuses to face what may be at the root of her changed behavior: the death of her husband. She has adopted "busy" behaviors to keep her mind off her problems. Chris and Hal do likewise, especially around Irene. Tom's death is a family topic which is taboo by unstated consensus.

Are the Hollisters typical of other families facing the unexpected loss of a loved one? Why are they still experiencing difficulties a year after Tom's death? Will they ever recover from the death? The answers to these and other questions hold the key to understanding the catastrophe of death in the family and will be discussed in this chapter. We will first consider the nature of death and dying which helps us understand it as a source of stress. Second, we will inventory the major sources of stress as well as characteristic ways families cope with them. Finally, we will speculate on the most prudent strategies for intervention, followed by a brief consideration of the policy implications. In addition, throughout the chapter we will refer to the Hollisters as a means of illustrating several theoretical ideas which may serve as an effective device for grasping the dynamics of family reactions to death.

DEATH AS STRESSOR

"Death be not proud," wrote John Donne, in HYMN TO CHRIST, "though some have called thee mighty and dreadful, for thou art not so. . . . " Since the beginnings of mankind, death has been the target of human thought and analysis. Efforts to scientifically determine the degree of stressfulness for various life events have been underway for over a decade (see Chapter 1). Every scale which assesses stressful life events ranks death of a family member quite high and unanimously agrees that the death of one's spouse is the most stressful (Dohrenwend & Dohrenwend, 1974). Clinicians have noted (cf., Hare-Mustin, 1979) that the death of a child may be, for many, the supreme crisis creating unparalleled stress for the parents. The loss of a parent, on the other hand, especially for young children and adolescents, may be the most profound event shaping the subsequent development of the child (Solomon & Hersch, 1979). Sibling loss, grandparent loss, aunts, uncles, stepparents, and the loss of long-standing family friends can be equally stress-producing, depending on the meaning attributed to or symbolized by the relationship.

Meaning Attributed to Death

The meaning the family ascribes to death depends on many factors, including both personal and sociocultural. Personal factors affecting meaning for friends, family, kin, and other survivors include the nature of the relationship between the living and the deceased; the role of the deceased as perceived by the living; the intensity of the relationship; the degree of dependence (both psychological and economic) upon the deceased; the significance of the relationship; and the memories associated with the deceased. Sociocultural factors affecting response to death are often less obvious due to the fact that family members are less aware of their impact. Examples of sociocultural factors include a societal attitude toward pain which teaches that pain is to be avoided at all cost; depersonalization of death ranging from the use of "funeral homes" to increasingly highly technical hospital facilities; and loss of the primary linkage role of the family and intimate network during the transition from life to death.

Loss Associated with Death

Inherent within death is the aspect of loss. Loss of any kind, any quality, any quantity and of any possible significance to the subject may have a profound effect on emotions, thoughts, and behaviors. Loss, in its most profound and severe manifestations, strikes at the core of the self by posing a threat to the essence of our being. Security becomes insecurity; safety becomes perceived threat; the adjustment becomes imperiled.

Loss is a unique life experience. Kalish (1981) suggests that the loss of experiencing, loss of people, loss of control and competence, loss of the capacity to complete projects and plans, the loss of things, and the loss of one's body are losses of major significance. The death of a family member often includes many or all of these losses, producing high levels of stress.

Sources of Stress

While death is usually the most catastrophic event for an individual or family, the degree of stress experienced is dependent on several interacting variables.

Many families experience extreme stress when the death of the family member is unexpected. They are totally unprepared for such a loss and the family system is thrown off balance. Conversely, when death has been prolonged over a period of months or even years (e.g., a hospitalized family member with a degenerative illness such as heart disease or cancer), the stress is continuous with no end in sight. Families are trapped in an ambiguous circumstance, not knowing when or even if death will occur, all of which leaves them emotionally depleted. Families experience the stress of death during this period—when their loved one is still alive—and when death finally comes, it is often far less traumatic due to the earlier preparation and acceptance of the loss. The grief work is still as stressful as it would be for families with an unexpected death; it just occurs at a different time in the process.

Second, if the family is experiencing other stressful crises, the death of a family member will increase the level of stress to an almost intolerable level. That is, personal and interpersonal resources may be depleted by the other stressors, leaving little in reserve to cope with the death. As McCubbin (1981) has pointed out, the pile-up of many stressors acting upon the family may lead to or compound the crisis, taxing the family's resources and coping ability to such a point that coping becomes increasingly dysfunctional.

A third variable contributing to the family's stress is the numerous "arrangements" that require attention following the death. Initially, for example, the family must deal with the funeral and burial. This includes contacts with morticians, cemeteries, and well-meaning sympathizers. Moreover, the family is inundated by a myriad of professionals involved in settling the estate (lawyers, employers, insurance company and government employees). All combined, these will greatly intensify the stressfulness of the death.

Additional stressful problems associated with death include: new role realignments and structures within the family; the need to establish new patterns of authority and decision-making; loss of economic (financial) security; establishing a new social support network; concern for children's and other family members' grief; finally, and perhaps most stressful, the loss of emotional support.

There are situational circumstances and personal resources available to families at the time of death and after which will serve as mitigating factors to help manage or reduce the stress. Such factors as previous experience with death, sufficient financial resources, positive outlook on life, religious faith, self-esteem, and interpersonal support networks both inside and outside the family system will all be useful in countering the stress associated with death.

STRESS REACTIONS TO DEATH

The Grieving Process

Although models and theories of human behavior for the most part attempt to identify major factors and their interrelationships, most importantly they provide an understanding of the various reactions people have to stress. The problem arises when generic, abstract models are imposed on others (e.g., "You *must* be feeling this way; you are at that stage!"). Thus, the application of theories to predict human reaction to death and dying must be prudent. Perhaps the most frequently-cited model applied to the process of grieving was developed by Kübler-Ross (1969). In it, she postulated five stages through which the dying person passes: denial, anger, bargaining, depression, and acceptance.*

The importance of research in the stages and phases of grief resolution for the dying person lies in what we can learn about the entire process of recovery for the family. Indeed, families experience similar phases/stages in the period prior to or following the death. The recovery-reorganization process is characteristically cyclical rather than linear. We move back

---

*Since Kübler-Ross, there have been other models. Some, such as the Frears and Schneider model (1981), move on a continuing line from simplicity to complexity. Pattison (1977) cautions that his three phases exist as a method to divide the process into dimensions having clinical utility to aid understanding. Schneidman (1973) sees a constant ebb and flow of affect between acceptance and denial. Smith (1975) describes her own dying as moving back and forth through several stages a number of times. Rodabough attempts to combine both Kübler-Ross and Pattison by using a model of repetitive alteration which allows for mood swings back and forth in a circular motion (Rodabough, 1980).

and forth, two steps forward and one step backward; we appear to be on top of things one day and then find ourselves overburdened the next day. The process varies according to individuals and families as well as the circumstances and situations surrounding the death event. Familial and individual resources of both a physical and psychological nature will also influence the passage through the stages and phases.

Application to the Hollisters

Looking at the Hollisters again, we note that the family conspires to seemingly deny that death has occurred. For example, Kübler-Ross stage one, denial, seems to be present for all the Hollisters. The denial is not that Tom Hollister has died; rather, it is a denial of the fact of Tom's death as a subject worthy of ongoing attention and discussion. In short, the mutual pretense insures that feelings will not be shared. Each person is prisoner of his or her own experience without benefit of open expression of grief, loss, and memory of happy times and associations. Irene also shows signs of anger, especially toward her children, and depression due to the many changes in her life. Neither Chris, Hal nor Irene have been able to resolve Tom's death and break through to an acceptance phase. Thus, instead of a gradual *recession* of stress, we find a continuous *increase* in stress—a symptom of unresolved grief.

AN ANALYSIS OF COPING WITH DEATH

It should be apparent by now that death introduces multiple changes which demand immediate attention. Individuals and families react to these demands in ways which either promote recovery (functional) or impede recovery (dysfunctional).

Dysfunctional Coping

Avoidance. One coping strategy that pertains to dying and death is referred to as the "Keep Busy" strategy. This strategy is often thought to be functional and/or therapeutic. In truth, it more often serves as a dysfunctional ploy which lengthens the denial process. By keeping busy we defend ourselves against the anxiety that arises when we "are doing nothing." Irene did this. Keeping busy enables us to put our mental-emotional energy into the task at hand, thus diverting thoughts and feelings away from death. As we struggle with our grief, we likely will have tasks to perform and worthwhile work to do. Keeping busy is, in itself, not wrong; the wrongness is in the fact that it turns into a dysfunctional strategy when it becomes the primary method of coping.

A second dysfunctional method is the "Take a Trip" or "Get Away" strategy. Grief resolution requires coming to terms with loss, loneliness, emptiness, personal effects, routines, rituals, and all manner of behaviors of the deceased. When a person in grief takes a trip (visits relatives, vacation, tours, etc.) soon after the death of a loved one, the grief work is *partially* postponed. The portion that is postponed is precisely that which begs to be dealt with first. One only needs to fantasize coming back home after such a trip (i.e., walking into the empty house, seeing the empty dining room chair, the empty bedroom, the driverless car, etc.), in order to appreciate that the first level of grief work needs to be dealt with in the context of the deceased person's position, role, and immediate family environment prior to death.

Obliteration. Just as an ostrich chooses to solve its problem by sticking its head in the sand, obliteration is an attempt to erase or wipe away the former existence of the deceased. Obliteration on the part of any one member of the system, if not challenged, is likely to close the system down, at least temporarily. Obliteration goes beyond denial and avoidance. Obliteration involves the attempt of total erasure of the deceased person's prior existence. This may involve disposal of all personal effects, belongings, collections, hobbies, pictures, and other possessions. Obliteration is akin to "wiping away" all memory traces and clues. It is to live "as if" the loved one never existed (Satir, 1972).

Idolization. The polar opposite of obliteration, idolization, makes the deceased greater in death than he/she was in life. The deceased is endowed with a quality of perfection that is supra-human. It is to restore life by holding fast to the belief that the deceased is really present. Personal effects are left intact. Possessions, momentos, pictures, and hobbies are endowed with an importance they previously lacked. No survivor can ever hope to measure up, and shame, self-doubt, guilt, and inferiority are prescribed feelings for those who must live in the wake of such splendor.

Dysfunctional coping, then, is generally avoiding, denying, or in some way escaping from the reality of the death and subsequent demands to react and change. These actions prevent resolution of the grieving process and ultimate accommodation and adjustment to the catastrophe, unencumbered by the past to meet future demands. But what are the ways in which families manage that ultimately lead to effective coping?

Functional Coping

Constructive grief work depends on the ability of the network to be permissive of feelings. Additionally, the network needs to be positively accepting and supportive. This implies the ability to engage in "leveling" types of communication and that energies should be directed at the actual loss as experienced collectively and individually. In order to accomplish this freedom of mutual acceptance, there needs to be an absence of scapegoating and blaming, placating and excessive caretaking, and computer-like rationale which substitutes reason and logic for feelings and emotion. Commitment to the process of communication creates an atmosphere or context wherein the individuals may feel secure in their grief. This security means that they are free to self-disclose or to be "into themselves." They are free to feel whatever they feel but they are also free to challenge their own beliefs and the beliefs of others, knowing that feelings are often the result of internalized beliefs which are mythological, irrational, illogical, or erroneous.

Once feelings are permitted and openly accepted within the system, there is an unlimited range of possible courses of grief reduction and resolution. If feelings are shared (even if not in identical ways), there is an open stage for talk, recall, memory association, fantasy, rehearsal of future scripts, and reliving of past episodes. At this point, beliefs and values may need to be questioned openly, i.e., challenged and confronted. Further, the open confrontation of beliefs may help us see the sometimes irrational assumptions we make regarding our personal role and responsibility in events that, in actuality, are far beyond our control. People who are in mourning and grief sometimes have a gigantic overestimation of their own power: They reason that if they had done something differently, the death would never have happened. Thus, the stage is set for prolonged grieving due to the fact the person takes upon him/herself responsibility for things far beyond his/her control. This accounts for much of the "guilt" that becomes mixed up with "grief." Grief work, reduction and resolution, can hardly be carried out when the overriding agenda is the survivor's guilt.

Special Circumstances of Children's Coping

Let us now consider children and their reaction to death. It is of first importance that the adults within the intimate environment do not become so preoccupied with their own grief that they fail to consider the emotional dilemma of the child.

> Adults who respect children's right to grieve teach them that loss is natural to life, people and objects do not have permanence, grief feelings are normal, grief offers opportunities to help establish or re-establish values and goals (Tanner, 1976, p. 49).

Functional coping entails sharing with children on a level commensurate with their cognitive and emotional levels of development (Glicken, 1978).

> Adults frequently deny children opportunities for learning about loss. They rationalize that they are sparing the feelings of the child by not sharing facts and their own emotions. Thus, children are more likely to find loss confusing and may act out instead of expressing their own feelings (Frears & Schneider, 1981, p. 343).

Responses to children which are characterized by fairy tale explanations are, in the long run, dysfunctional. *Excessive* reliance on simplified theological or religious explanations, "God wanted Daddy to live with Him," may be counterproductive since, as the child grows and begins to question, the image of God may take on a negative connotation, and God can then become a target of the child's anger or an object of his/her fear.

The handling of death with children of all ages including early adolescence is a subject of vast significance. Suffice it to say here that the grief resolution process is a familial concern of the first order and that most of the basic principles outlined above apply to children and adolescents as well as adults. Specifically, children need:

1) space and time to absorb the fact of loss;
2) help in labeling and identifying the finality of death;
3) models who are themselves able to grieve and express the range of emotional response;
4) to be listened to attentively and with respect; and
5) to express themselves by giving their own individualized account of what happened.

Their loss needs to be recognized, even if it cannot be totally explained. Perhaps, more than anything else, the adult members of the family network need to be aware that children are *persons* with all the capacity to grieve, suffer, mourn, yet without full cognitive ability to comprehend and understand. Childhood and adolescent reaction to loss, therefore, dare not be underestimated. The grief resolution process of children may have significant impact on the future functioning of the family system (Glicken, 1978).

Summary

The focal point of death grief for the family is, of course, the loss of the deceased family member: the tragedy of the end of a worthwhile human being. The second focal point is the loss and disruption of the survivors. A content-focused grief is limited to these two aspects of loss. In contrast, the process-focused grief turns inward, encouraging free expression of feelings ("I really hated him at times"); challenge and confirmation of assumptions and beliefs ("He was more worried about his reputation than us—but he loved us in his own way"); recall of past events ("Remember when he fell asleep in church?"); reflections on the future ("Christmas will be lonely"); and a reorganization and/or mobilization of family resources ("We need to call each other more frequently—go camping again").

An open, functional family system such as we have described is growth-producing, integrative (melding past with present and future realistically), and positive, because its members are able to work through the content of the grief ("What do we do now?") in such a manner that it is less likely to become a permanent part of family living. A closed family system, on the other hand, is often unable to achieve growth, integration, and resolution and thus, unable to incorporate the grieving process into its identity and activities. This may lead, for example, to setting a place at the dinner table for the missing member or speaking to and about the deceased as if that person were still present.

Table 1 provides a good summary of the contrasting elements of functional versus dysfunctional coping of individuals and families following the death of a family member.

INTERVENTION IMPLICATIONS

Briefly, we have reviewed the sources of stress and characteristic ways individuals and families cope with these stressors. An effective coping method, as well as an important community resource for families, is

Table 1
Contrasting Elements of Dysfunctional and Functional Coping

Dysfunctional	Functional
Closed	Open
Individual Focus	System Focus
Content Focus	Process Focus
Illusion-oriented	Reality-oriented
Role Rigidity	Role Flexibility
Resources Non-utilized	Resources Utilized
System Reorganization	System Reorganization
—Resistant	—Flexible
—Static	—Dynamic
Vulnerability Defended	Vulnerability Accepted
Beliefs Unchallenged	Beliefs Confronted
Feelings Need Justification	Feelings Accepted without
High Control of Grief	Defending
Reaction	Low Control of Grief Reaction
—Suppression	—Acknowledgment
—Denial	—Sharing
Reorganization and/or	Reorganization and/or Mobilization of Re-
Mobilization of Resources	sources is Open, Flexible, and Adaptable
is Rigid	

utilization of a professional adept at supplementing the coping process. Our direct experience with the dying has gradually diminished in recent years (Steele, 1977). As a result, families and the intimate network have had decreasing opportunity to serve as primary linkages during the transition from life to death. In short, the death professionals have unwittingly served as buffers, protecting us and shielding us from the pain of loss, suffering, and bereavement. This, in turn, has the effect of reducing or preventing the family from experiencing the meaning of the death in more existential terms (Frankl, 1963).

Among the professionals involved in "healing" or helping the family in times of death, perhaps the clergy have had the most experience. In addition to officiating at funerals, the clergy provide emotional support and guidance to families at all stages of the grieving process. In addition, there is a growing movement within the medical profession to provide family-centered services for dying patients. Social workers, psychologists, psychiatrists, family life educators, and therapists have varying experiences and expertise in assisting families and family members dealing with death.

The field of family therapy has developed at an astonishing pace over the past several decades. Increasingly, the emphasis is on discovering the unwritten rules under which families function, develop, and maintain coalitions and strategies. Moreover, family therapy centers on the system and how individuals function within and independent from the family (Madanes, 1981) and the use of various intervention techniques, such as paradoxical suggestions to "treat" the family (Selvini Palazzoli, Boscolo, Cecchin & Prata, 1978).

Regardless of the type of intervention, facilitating the grief resolution process is the goal, and this most often entails establishing independence and self-sufficiency. The process of reorganization in reaching this goal requires many and varied efforts and elements. Following is a list of tasks appropriate for any interventionist intent on facilitating the grieving process. It is by no means exhaustive, only suggestive, serving as a starting point in tailoring a plan for the particular circumstances of the client.

1) *Role clarification:* At death, there is a high likelihood that roles will become confused, accompanied by unclear assignment of responsibilities to the surviving family members.

2) At death, the *patterns of authority and decision-making* are often blurred, especially in cases of death of a parent of children and/or adolescents.

3) The tone of intervention should be positive with an emphasis on the *strengths of the surviving family members rather than on their weaknesses.*

4) After strength assessment may come *need assessment.* A prioritizing of immediate and long-range needs gives structure (and hence, security and confidence) to the grieving and stressed family.

5) There needs to be a definite emphasis on *planning and implementation* of new and/or changed behavior patterns. This amounts to a strategy for taking steps to meet the needs already prioritized.

6) *Generational and hierarchical boundaries* need to be clarified and sometimes reestablished.

7) Following McCubbin's (1981) emphasis on independence and self-sufficiency, a crucial emphasis must be placed on the *prevention of over-dependency.* In grief work, there is a distinct difference between fostering a sympathizing self-pity and a caring-sharing, empathic relationship. The former reinforces dependency; the latter reinforces independence and autonomy.

8) Issues dealing with too much familial *isolation and enmeshment* (loss of personal boundary) need to be worked through. This

      is best accomplished by encouraging cohesiveness as a family
with freedom for individual flexibility.

9) *Financial restructuring* may be a first-level priority, especially in
cases where the deceased was a breadwinner-provider.

10) *Mobilization of community, state, and federal resources* may be pivotal, especially in situations where families have little or no prior
experience with societal support structures.

Reconsideration of the Hollisters

Looking back at the Hollisters, let us focus on possible points of intervention. As noted earlier, Irene is not out of her denial and depression. In addition to facilitating the expression of grief, the helping
professional will hopefully challenge Irene's desire for emotional dependency, especially upon Chris. The expectations of Irene for Chris to
be more sympathetic and understanding arise from Irene's dependency
upon Tom. This dependency was financial as well as emotional and, as
such, is a fairly common occurrence. However, it begs to be dealt with
by all three adults. For example, here are several questions which illustrate the uncertainty of this family: Are Hal and Chris avoiding their
own grief at the loss of their father due to guilt and bad feelings they
encountered in their relationship with him? Has Irene made a saint of
Tom, thus causing Chris and Hal to remain silent? Have Chris and Hal
discussed with one another and with their mother the entire long-range
financial implications for Irene? Should Irene be challenged by her children to become more self-sufficient and less dependent?

      The above questions reveal the need for strength assessment, need
assessment, role clarification, planning and implementation, consideration of generational boundaries and responsibilities, financial restructuring, and perhaps mobilization of community resources.

      The meaning of Tom's death for Irene explains much of her present
stress. Irene was psychologically invested in Tom to a far greater extent
than she had ever realized. The loss of Tom was catastrophic for Irene,
almost to the point of functional immobilization. The intervenor will
readily identify the need for Irene to become increasingly independent
and self-sufficient. In order to accomplish this, a great deal of effort may
need to be expended in helping Irene, Hal, and Chris share their feelings
and thoughts with each other.

      It is of crucial importance not to minimize or overlook the anger stage
in grief resolution. Has anyone been allowed to express anger over Tom's
death? Doubtless Irene is angry at Tom for not taking better care of

himself (he was overweight and an incessant smoker). Yet Irene cannot own her anger feelings because of guilt. She does not know why she feels guilt. The actual cause of Irene's guilt is because she holds the belief that "it is wrong to be angry at anyone who is dead because they can't defend themselves." Consequently, her anger is repressed and she is unable to move further in recovery.

Chris and Hal have their own anger/guilt problems due to unfinished business with their father.* Somehow, the professional must get the survivors to confront and resist the belief that "it is a sign of weakness to share our deepest feelings and thoughts." Until this harmful belief can be challenged and discredited, there can be no openness, sharing, or leveling (Satir, 1972). Recovery remains at an impasse and the stress level increases.

Obviously, the Hollisters represent only one type of bereavement-death situation. The range is limitless inasmuch as there is sudden, unanticipated death due to accidents and other catastrophic events, and there is anticipated death due to age, declining physical condition, chronic illness, and other "normative" developmental sequences.

---

*The use of the empty chair may be quite helpful in facilitating the verbal expression of these feelings. Williamson (1978) even plans a trip to the cemetery when it is necessary for a son or daughter to separate from a deceased parent.

CHAPTER

6

Unemployment: Family Strategies for Adaptation

PATRICIA VOYDANOFF

Ralph Brown was numb, barely able to comprehend that after 10 years he was suddenly indefinitely laid off from his job. Sure, he had heard rumors of impending layoffs, but he had reasoned that certainly 10 years of seniority would prevent him from being affected. Soon he would have to face his family with the word. What would happen to all of their plans—the addition he was going to build on the house, skis for his daughter, camp for his son, the new freezer for his wife? How could he explain that he had no job, no plans for getting one, and no knowledge as to whether or when he would be called back to his old job? What would they think? What would they say? Of course, they knew times were tough. Several friends and neighbors had already been laid off. But that was different. What would happen to him, his family? What if his wife were laid off too?

Sudden, unpredictable unemployment has devastating effects on individuals and families. It introduces a set of stressors into an individual's life situation and family system with no opportunity for preparation, either psychological or financial. This lack of preparation intensifies an already stressful situation for individuals and families—unemployment of any kind.

Research on unemployment since the 1930s reveals effects on the mental and physical health of individuals and on family relationships and stability. Many studies show strong relationships over several decades between unemployment rates and indicators of mental and physical health, including state mental hospital admissions, suicide, homicide, total mortality, and cardiovascular-renal disease mortality (Brenner, 1973, 1976, 1977). More qualitative research indicates less severe psychological effects, e.g., lowered self-esteem, anxiety, and psycho-physiological distress (Cohn, 1978; Krause & Stryker, 1980; Powell & Driscoll, 1973; Schlozman & Verba, 1978).

In addition, unemployment affects other family members and the functioning of the family as a system. In his analysis of work experience and family life, Furstenberg (1974) states that "economic uncertainty brought on by unemployment and marginal employment is a principal reason why family relations deteriorate" (p. 355). Unemployment is related to family instability and family functioning in the areas of marital power, family violence, spending behavior, division of labor, and parental authority and discipline (Voydanoff, 1978).

What are the sources of stress for the suddenly unemployed and his or her* family? What resources are available to families to deal with these stressors? What are the effective as well as ineffective methods families use to cope with sudden unemployment? These and other questions will be considered in this chapter.

SOURCES OF STRESS FOR INDIVIDUALS AND FAMILIES**

Unemployment, sudden or otherwise, is a complex event occurring in varying contexts with differential impacts according to sex, race, age, and occupational skill level. Unemployment rates vary over time and by industry and geographic region. Unemployment in these various con-

---

*Although existing research only examines the unemployment experiences of men, job loss for women, especially those whose income is critical to the family and whose identity is closely associated with a work role, can also be expected to produce considerable stress. The precise differences between men and women must await future research results and will not be discussed here.

**The analysis of sources of stress and mediating factors incorporates the work of Voydanoff (in press).

texts is accompanied by several potential hardships. The number and type of hardships associated with an individual's unemployment experience influence the likelihood and extent of individual and family stress.

Financial Hardship

Financial hardship frequently results from the unemployment of a family earner. The extent of hardship has been defined in two ways: 1) an income level insufficient to meet family needs; and 2) economic deprivation, i.e., the loss of at least 30% of the income earned before unemployment (Elder, 1974; Moen, 1980). These hardships may occur independently of each other; both are related to patterns of family functioning (Elder, 1974).

The magnitude of individual and family financial hardships depends upon eligibility for Unemployment Insurance and other benefits, the length of unemployment, and prior income level. Company and union policies also influence the extent of financial hardship associated with layoffs and plant closings. Short-term financial hardship is reduced by policies such as the continuation of fringe benefits, especially health insurance; severance pay based on length of service; and the vesting of pensions.

Financial hardship resulting from the unemployment of a major family earner is associated with a shift in the family work effort (i.e., the pattern of labor force participation and earnings among family members) (Ferman & Gardner, 1979). Spouses may become employed outside the home or increase their level of labor force participation from part-time to full-time. Children, especially adolescents, may take part-time jobs to reduce the level of financial hardship in the family (Elder, 1974).

Financial hardship is extended to the community when a company laying off workers or closing a facility is the major employer in the community. The lack of alternative sources of employment results in widespread long-term unemployment. High unemployment in a company employing a substantial percentage within the community can have a ripple effect, creating financial hardship in other sectors (e.g., among those providing goods and services that unemployed workers can no longer afford to buy).

Loss of the Earner Role

Hardships associated with unemployment extend beyond the financial to the social and psychological. The loss of work involves more than the loss of income. This is rather obvious in our case example of Ralph Brown. It also means the loss of a major role, a role that is considered desirable, socially valued, and even essential for men with rigid, traditional values, or for either men or women whose identity is part of their profession (e.g., police officer, fire fighter). Work is a major source of social integration; it structures the way people spend their time, and it provides a sense of accomplishment and purpose. The sudden loss of this role can result in a period of shock, lowered self-esteem, and anxiety and depression. Work also determines the amount of time spent with the family and the structure and pattern of family activities. When a family member becomes unemployed and spends substantially more time at home, family routines are disrupted and tensions increase (LeMasters, 1975). The psychological effects on the unemployed lead to strain and concern among other family members (Root, 1977). Children of the unemployed also are at higher risk of illness (Margolis & Farran, 1981).

In addition, plant closings, which are often sudden, have another effect on integration not occurring in other types of unemployment. Victims of plant closings report a feeling of separation and loss comparable to the death of a relative (Slote, 1969). A plant closing usually consists of several stages: economic difficulties and uncertainty; announcement of closing; anticipation; staged terminations; and final closing. Workers report several emotions during this process including anger, denial, acceptance, and anxiety. The knowledge that the plant is not continuing after the worker has left creates a sense of grief and loss among workers with high seniority and attachment.

MEDIATING FACTORS

Before considering how families cope with unemployment and its associated stress, it is important to examine factors that, under certain conditions, can reduce the level of family stress associated with sudden unemployment. The likelihood that unemployment-related hardships will produce high levels of family stress depends on two major mediating factors: the family's definition of the event and family resources.

Family Definition of the Event

Suddenness. Sudden, unpredictable unemployment is more likely to result in stress than expected or routine unemployment (e.g., layoffs for automobile changeovers or unemployment among construction workers in bad weather). When unemployment is perceived as normal or manageable (e.g., when it has occurred before, when it has a specified duration, or when there is a period of anticipation and preparation), it is less stressful for individuals and families (Angell, 1936; Bakke, 1940; Cavan, 1959; Powell & Driscoll, 1973). Although the length of time that an event is anticipated is related to a family's definition of the event as noncrisis-producing (Burr, 1973; Hansen & Johnson, 1979), the period of anticipation can be stressful. In their study of a plant closing, Cobb and Kasl (1977) found the anticipation period to be the most detrimental to the mental and physical health of the workers. However, this period may have reduced the stress that otherwise would have occurred *after* unemployment by providing a time for psychological and financial preparation.

Responsibility. A second aspect of a family's definition of the event is the extent to which the unemployed person is considered to be responsible for unemployment, including the worker's sense of blame from the family. During the Depression of the 1930s, many workers and family members blamed the unemployed person (Bakke, 1940; Komarovsky, 1940). This tendency now exists mainly among the long-term unemployed (Briar, 1978; Calavita, 1977; Cobb & Kasl, 1977; Greenwald, 1978). Self and family blame for unemployment are related to family stress and limit adjustment to unemployment (Burr, 1973; Furstenberg, 1974; Hill, 1958; Rainwater, 1974).

Sense of Failure. In addition, even if a worker is not blamed for being unemployed, he or she may be seen as failing in the role as family provider. This may be especially troubling for men, since the role of economic provider is perceived to be the primary family responsibility of men by both husbands and wives (Bernard, 1981; Cazenave, 1979; Lein, 1979; Nye, 1974). The loss of the provider role was a key element in those families where the husband lost his authority in relation to his wife and adolescent children during the Depression (Komarovsky, 1940). The sense of failure may be intensified when wives and adolescents take jobs or when family members hold rigidly traditional sex role norms (Anderson, 1980; Angell, 1936; Cavan, 1959; Voydanoff, 1963). With the emergence of egalitarianism within the family, however, such sex-specific findings may not be as pervasive today (cf., Perrucci & Targ, 1974).

Family Resources

In addition to a family's definition of unemployment, several family resources mediate between unemployment and its hardships and individuals' and family reactions. These include financial resources, family system characteristics, and social supports.

Financial Resources. Unemployed earners with financial resources to draw upon, e.g., savings, home ownership, and lack of debts, are protected from financial hardship for a period of time and have higher morale (Voydanoff, 1963). The level of family financial resources is dependent upon family size and composition and the family's life cycle stage. These factors determine the number of earners available to the family as well as the number and ages of dependents. For example, families with young children must support dependents with limited earning resources, especially among single-parent families (Moen, 1979). Families with adolescent children are more likely to have a mother and/or teenagers working to supplement family income (Elder, 1974). Women heading families are especially vulnerable to stress because they are less likely to have financial resources, other available earners in the family, or marketable job skills and experience.

Family System Characteristics. Several characteristics of the family system as it was operating prior to unemployment influence the level of stress occurring during unemployment, especially adaptability, cohesion, and authority patterns. The extent of change in authority patterns during unemployment is related to the type of authority existing before unemployment (Anderson, 1980; Komarovsky, 1940). During the Depression, unemployed husbands were most likely to lose authority based on economic need or fear and least likely to lose authority based on love and respect (Komarovsky, 1940). Research during the Depression also found that integrated and adaptable families remained so during unemployment, while previously disorganized families became more disorganized (Angell, 1936; Cavan & Ranck, 1938). These data support the circumplex model of family systems which hypothesizes that families with moderate levels of adaptability and cohesion are best able to respond satisfactorily to stressors (McCubbin et al., 1980).

Social Support. A third significant resource for the families of the unemployed is instrumental and expressive support from friends, relatives, and neighbors. Limited research indicates that help from friends and neighbors contributes to family stability and that social support, especially from other family members, mediates the effects of unemployment on individual mental and physical health (Cobb & Kasl, 1977; Gore, 1977, 1978; Kasl & Cobb, 1979).

These mediating factors influence the extent of stress resulting from the unemployment of a major earner. Unemployment is less stress-producing when preparation occurs, when the unemployed husband is not blamed for the unemployment, and when he is not perceived as a failure in his provider role. Family stress is also reduced by the existence of financial resources, adaptive family system characteristics, and social supports.

COPING WITH SUDDEN UNEMPLOYMENT

The concept of mediating factors suggests that families differ in the number and combinations of characteristics available to resist or limit family stress following unemployment. However, families are also able to manipulate these characteristics in a more active fashion to prevent or handle family stress. Coping is an active process in which families take direct action to use other resources to deal with unemployment and its associated hardships. McCubbin and Patterson (1981a) conceptualize coping as follows:

> Although family resources and perceptions have been studied independently and offer investigators a gauge of family capabilities used to meet demands, these same observations suggest that we could improve upon our understanding of family adaptation to crises by looking at these two variables simultaneously along with what families do to cope with the situation. Coping appears to be a multifaceted process wherein resources, perception, and behavioral responses interact as families try to achieve a balance in family functioning (p. 10).

In this context coping is what families *do* with their resources and perceptions to meet the demands of unemployment as a stressor. Coping may reduce the vulnerability of the family to the stressor, may strengthen or maintain family system characteristics, may reduce or eliminate stressor events and their hardships, and may alter the environment by changing social circumstances (McCubbin et al., 1980).

Coping with unemployment is a process that occurs over time. The process begins before unemployment if there is a period of anticipation and continues after reemployment as individuals and families adjust to new, sometimes less desirable, jobs. During a period of unemployment, coping strategies must accommodate to changes in the extent of hardships, the level of resources and support, and family definitions. Several formulations of the adjustment process are similar in basic structure (Bakke, 1940; Eisenberg & Lazarsfeld, 1938; Powell & Driscoll, 1973; Zawadzki & Lazarsfeld, 1935). Bakke's formulation serves as a good example. He outlined the following stages of family adjustment to unemployment: momentum stability; unstable equilibrium; disorganization; experimental readjustment; and permanent readjustment. Each stage is characterized by a complex pattern of family functioning and coping in the areas of financial management, family work effort, family division of labor, authority and discipline, and use of social support.

Effective Coping Methods

Family Work Effort. During a worker's unemployment, other family members frequently increase their participation in the labor force to provide financial resources to the family. They either take jobs outside the home or increase their work effort from part-time to full-time. Children, especially adolescents, take on part-time employment to help out. Although individually wives and children usually earn less than husbands, families may approach their former income level by everyone seeking some work and contributing a large percentage to the household (Ferman & Gardner, 1979). This realigning of the family work effort provides financial resources and reduces anxiety about the future.

Financial Management. Effective financial management is an important aspect of family relationships at all times; its significance grows during unemployment as resources shrink and family tensions increase. Handling financial resources is often stressful for families and is a major source of family disagreements. Working together as a family to manage limited resources effectively is an important coping mechanism both for practical purposes and as a means of maintaining family cohesion. A consistent strategy for budgeting and bill-paying is crucial for the efficient management of limited resources, especially when it is uncertain when unemployment will end.

The types of cuts in expenditures vary with the duration of unemployment. Early research shows that during the first weeks cuts are limited to recreation, luxuries, and social contact expenses. Later, some essential items are replaced with less expensive alternatives, clothing is not replaced, and recreation is severely limited (Bakke, 1940). The use of credit attenuates the severity of cuts for several months. More recently, studies show that families make cuts in housing, food, clothing, transportation, and recreation (Briar, 1978; Nicholson & Corson, 1976;

Rosenfield, 1977; Sheppard, Ferman & Faber, 1959). Housing costs are reduced by moving to less costly quarters or sharing quarters with friends or relatives. Many goods and services are obtained more inexpensively through the irregular economy, e.g., purchasing or trading items and services with friends and neighbors. Garage sales and moonlighting plumbers and carpenters are examples of this type of activity. The unemployed with a variety of skills often earn some income by providing services to others on a cash or barter basis (e.g., housekeeping, carpentry, painting).

Quality of Family Relationships. Attempts by family members to maintain and strengthen the adaptability and cohesiveness of the family unit are essential coping strategies among the families of the unemployed. It is important for the family to be flexible enough to reorganize the roles performed in the family and remain a cohesive family unit. Maintaining cohesion through communication, empathy, and joint activities is a second important element. These coping mechanisms are important ways of sustaining family relationships during unemployment.

The Use of Social Supports. Isolation among the unemployed is detrimental to individual and family well-being. It is crucial for unemployed workers and their families to maintain contacts with friends, relatives, neighbors, and former co-workers who have been helpful as emotional supports in the past. In addition, supports are useful in more concrete ways, such as giving job leads and job-seeking advice, providing transportation to job interviews, and caring for children.

Definitional Coping. Definitional coping can decrease stress by altering the perceptions of family members toward unemployment, (e.g., by reducing blame, supporting flexible family role definitions), and perceiving unemployment as an opportunity. It is helpful for the unemployed man and other family members to recognize that most unemployment is structural and not the fault of the unemployed person. A recent study of a plant closing reveals that the level of self-blame is relatively low immediately after the closing; however, it is substantially higher six months later. Thus it is necessary for the long-term unemployed to maintain their perspective on the social context of unemployment.

Regarding traditional views of sex roles, it is also important for family members to have a flexible view of the contributions of husbands and fathers to the family. Unemployed men with traditional sex role ideologies have lower morale (Voydanoff, 1963). Families perceiving husbands and fathers as more than economic providers and supporting alternative value contributions to the family during unemployment (e.g., housework and childrearing) can develop a more effective and less stressful pattern of family functioning during unemployment. This is especially important if other family members are employed outside the home.

Some families facilitate coping by perceiving unemployment as a challenge, a growth experience. This is particularly likely among dissatisfied workers who use unemployment as an opportunity to get into a more desirable occupation or job situation (Little, 1976; Root & Mayland, 1978).

Certain combinations of definitional coping and family resources can create a situation in which unemployment is relatively unstressful. For example, in a recent study a majority of wives thought that unemployment following a plant closing had been "generally good for their family" (Root, 1977). This perception was much more likely, however, among wives from families with the following characteristics: substantial family resources, including wife employment, high income, and family cohesion; the definition of unemployment as an opportunity; and the perceived ability to make plans.

Ineffective Methods of Coping

Recent work on family stress indicates that coping strategies themselves can become sources of further stress (McCubbin et al., 1980). Coping mechanisms effectively meet some needs while at the same time creating new problems. For example, shifting the family work effort from the unemployed member to other family members is effective in coping with reduced financial resources. However, it can lead to stress in family relationships if either the unemployed or other family members feel resentment, or if it appears that the unemployed has failed as a provider. Tensions can result from wife employment when men are unwilling to assume household chores (Powell & Driscoll, 1973). The same phenomenon may apply to unemployed wives reluctant to assume or resume the homemaker role her employment once freed her from. These shifts have implications for the entire fabric of family relationships, in some cases undermining the cohesion of the family unit and the quality of husband-wife and parent-child relationships.

The use of social supports and cutting expenditures for recreation may also have mixed results. Social supports effectively mediate between unemployment and mental and physical health and the quality of family relationships. However, the expected loss of support from those in their family, community, and workplace contributes to a reluctance to move to another area with better job prospects. Reducing expenditures for recreation helps families manage limited financial resources; however, it also limits the use of social supports and increases isolation and boredom (Rapoport, 1981). In situations such as this, trade-offs exist between the costs and benefits associated with various coping strategies.

Another form of ineffective coping includes generally dysfunctional methods of dealing with stress (e.g., alcohol and drug abuse, withdrawal from interaction with others, and lashing out in violence against family members).

IMPLICATIONS

Policy Interventions

What can be done about the Ralph Brown families of tomorrow? The analysis of mediating factors and coping strategies suggests several types of intervention to reduce the level of family stress and to assist recovery from crisis. The most direct approach would eliminate unemployment and economic uncertainty through increased economic stability. Uncertainty regarding the onset and expected length of unemployment influences a family's ability to deal with unemployment. In this context it is important for families to have a period of preparation before unemployment occurs. Controversy surrounds proposed plant closing legislation requiring notification before closing. Time requirements for notification vary from a month to a year or more. In his study of a plant closing, Cobb concluded that two years was too long a period. He recommended two or three months as optimal for preparation without drawing out the process longer than necessary and creating additional stress (Cobb & Kasl, 1977; see also Slote, 1969). This period may need to be extended, however, when management and workers attempt to negotiate alternatives to closing, e.g., employees purchasing the plant.

Unemployment Insurance and other benefits, (e.g., Supplemental Unemployment Benefits) have reduced the financial hardships associated with unemployment. However, many unemployed family members do not qualify for UI and SUB and most workers still lose health insurance and pensions. These hardships can be alleviated by severance pay and the maintenance of pensions and medical and life insurance. Reduced work time and job sharing can spread out limited employment opportunities and reduce unemployment. When layoffs are necessary, a flexible schedule can facilitate individual planning and reduce community impact (Teague, 1981).

Recession-related unemployment is often accompanied by cutbacks in the programs and services most needed by the unemployed, e.g., mental health programs. These programs lose government and private support as part of the same economic processes that create unemployment. Policy initiatives that cannot reduce unemployment should at least be able to limit the cuts in programs needed to cope with unemployment.

Implications for Professionals

Several approaches by professionals can be helpful in increasing the coping abilities of families during unemployment. First, many unemployed workers have not been in the job market for several years and need assistance and support in looking for a job. Companies laying off workers or closing plants can serve as a focal point for efforts in this area, e.g., providing job placement services, job-seeking skills and advice, and information about community resources. Family service programs and individual and family counseling can be important in sustaining or improving individual mental health and family functioning and cohesion, as well as encouraging the development and use of social supports. Often, community services appropriate for the unemployed are available; information about these services needs to be available in a compact package of resource and referral material. A critical need for many unemployed is financial counseling and financial management skills. The availability and awareness of credit counseling centers and programs to build skills in family money management is a crucial first step in coping with unemployment.

These services need to be provided within a context that emphasizes that structural unemployment is not the fault of unemployed family members. This perspective is most important for the long-term unemployed and for those who are among the last rehired after a recession or plant closing. An understanding of labor market dynamics is important for professionals and the unemployed in clarifying that age, local unemployment rate, and demands for specific job skills are significant, yet impersonal, factors in the timing of reemployment.

To increase understanding of unemployment, coping strategies, and family-oriented policies and programs to deal with unemployment, further research is needed. Much of the current research base was developed during the Depression of the 1930s. It is important to update this research to account for the vast social and economic changes since that time. For example, the increases in female labor force participation have not been accompanied by research on the individual and family effects of unemployment among women. This is a major deficit which must be redressed immediately.

CONCLUSION

As illustrated by the case study at the beginning of this chapter, sudden unemployment affects families in different ways because of variations in the circumstances associated with unemployment and with family structure and functioning. Family stress theory clarifies these sources of variation. The presence of hardships influences the potential for family stress. In addition, families vary in the nature and extent of resources available to deal with unemployment. Lastly, the coping strategies families are able to mobilize and use effectively influence the ways in which families are affected by unemployment.

These coping strategies include realigning the family work effort by having other family members take on employment; learning techniques for managing limited financial resources; maintaining strong and healthy family relationships; and developing and using social supports to alleviate stress and provide concrete help in family problem solving. However, the use of coping strategies is complicated by the fact that some coping strategies are effective in meeting certain needs, while at the same time creating difficulties in other areas. For example, employment by the unemployed spouse helps financially while changing the balance of and supplementing family roles. This dilemma points out the complexities involved in dealing with external stressors such as unemployment. The family is truly a system interacting with other systems. It is not possible to introduce a sudden stressor like unemployment into these complex interrelationships without expecting multiple repercussions.

Our knowledge in this area is quite unsophisticated. We have data on the effectiveness of individual coping strategies; however, we know very little about the interactions among strategies and their combined effects on family relationships. Examples presented here are just the beginning of knowledge about these complex interrelationships.

7

Rape: Individual and Family Reactions

SANDRA K. BURGE

David Como was glad to hear the familiar click in the lock of the apartment door. He and baby Laura were growing impatient for the arrival of their wife and mother, Marilyn. She rarely stayed very long past 5 P.M. at her job as administrative assistant, never this long. A surprise awaited her: a cake to celebrate her recent promotion to assistant branch manager. Laura wanted to blow out the candles as soon as possible.

The door swung open and David and Laura's smiles turn to looks of terror. Marilyn collapsed in the doorway. Her hair and clothes were disheveled, a shoe was missing, her stockings tattered. Laura started to cry. David stood frozen in terror and disbelief for seconds, then raced to his wife's side. "Darling, what's wrong, what happened?" Marilyn bristled uncharacteristically at David's touch and began to sob, "I was raped! I was raped! I can't believe this is happening to me!" David became incensed. His grip tightened. His questions shot at her like a machine gun: "When? Where? Who did it? I'll kill the son-of-a-bitch." With this Marilyn became hysterical: "No, David, please don't leave me, please, please. Don't go, please!"

David did not go. They called the police who arrived within minutes followed closely by a Rape Advocate worker from the local Rape Crisis Program. She will accompany Marilyn to the hospital and through the maze of paperwork, interviews, and examinations. She will help Marilyn discuss her feelings and her willingness to testify in court if the rapist were apprehended. David, together with his and Marilyn's parents, will endure the ordeal along with Marilyn. They will feel a mixture of rage, shame, pity, fear, and vengefulness. They are victims of rape, too, because it happened to Marilyn.

Since the resurgence of the women's movement in the late 1960s and the early 1970s, rape and other atrocities against women have been identified, publicized, and politicized. Because the crime of rape is a traditional act of physical violation against women,* it has received substantial attention as a feminist issue. Prior to the late 1960s, women who were victims of rape were not recognized as individuals who needed special treatment. On the contrary, they were more often subject to scorn and blame. At the same time that sympathy for the plight of rape victims increased, social scientists began to investigate the dynamics of the psychological and interactional aftermath of rape. After a mere decade of research on rape, much has been discovered about rapists' motivations and rape victims' reactions to their experiences. This new information repudiates traditional myths about rape which, unfortunately, are still held by most people in our culture.

Societal conceptions about what constitutes rape are complex, situational, and usually inaccurate. More attention is focused on the sexual aspects of the crime than the violence. Rape is expected to occur at night in sinister-looking places, and to be inflicted on scantily-clad, promiscuous women who lure sex-starved madmen into treacherous abandon. However, the facts about rape (Norsigian, 1979) repudiate the myths:

FACT 1: Rape occurs during the day, as well as under the cover of darkness.

FACT 2: Rape occurs in "safe" locations as well as in sinister ones. One-half of all rapes occur in the victim's home.

FACT 3: Rape victims are usually neither sexy nor promiscuous. Rapists more often choose women who appear to be vulnerable. Women as old as 93 and as young as 6 months

---

*Although it is recognized that men, too, can become victims of rape, the overwhelming majority of rape victims are in fact women. Thus, when referring to victims of rape throughout this chapter, the female gender will be used.

have been raped. However, most rape victims are 15-22 years old, approximately the same age as their assailants.

FACT 4: At least two-thirds of all rapists have regular sexual outlets (such as wives or girlfriends) and are not "starved" for sex. In fact, sexual desire appears to be merely a secondary motive for rape. Rapists rape primarily because of a need to express anger or to dominate another human being (Groth, Burgess & Holmstrom, 1977).

FACT 5: Rapists are generally not what we would consider "madmen." They do not appear to differ from the average male. About half of all rapists are known (and often trusted) by their victims.

FACT 6: Sixty percent or more of all rapes are premeditated—not abandonment to primitive desires.

Because rape is believed to be motivated out of strong sexual desires, victims are regularly accused of being seductresses and, consequently, devalued and blamed for the assault which they have experienced. The tremendous underreporting of rape can be attributed largely to this widespread disapproval of rape victims. Although 65,000 rapes per year are reported to legal agencies, it is estimated that two to 10 times that number actually occur (Schram, 1978). Rumors of harsh treatment by hospital personnel and police, dramatic courtroom scenes, and societal reproach cause most rape victims to shy away from public declarations of the assault.

As complicated as the issue of rape may seem, the definition is actually very simple and straightforward: *rape is sex without consent*. The dictionary (Webster's, 1981) defines rape as:

Sexual intercourse with a woman by a man without her consent and chiefly by force or deception.

This definition embraces a wide variety of situations, ranging from a struggle with an over-aggressive date to a brutal, bloody encounter with a stranger in a dark alley. Differences in rape circumstances may trigger varying degrees of distress among victims. Regardless of the details of the incident, rape represents a crisis in the victim's life, primarily because *rape is a crime of violence*. A woman submits to rape neither out of excitement nor willingness, but because she fears injury or death.

These threats to her safety, in addition to actual physical harm, precipitate intense emotional responses for the victim as well as her family (Burgess & Holstrom, 1979a; White & Rollins, 1981). The victim's stress involves behaviors which may seem bizarre and out of character to those who know her best. A sudden change in behaviors in one family member causes abrupt changes in the balance of interpersonal relations and becomes a source of enormous stress, as family members adjust their roles and behaviors to deal with the effects of the traumatic incident. Thus, the rape generates a crisis for the family as well as for the victim.

Following rape, most victims find they are subject to the "second rape" of societal disapproval. The stigma attached to the impact of the violent act of rape is compounded by victimization by rape, which constitutes a second barrier to recovery. Like the general public, the family of the rape victim may feel that she was at fault. Consequently, family members may withdraw affection for, and approval of, the terrorized woman. Breakdown of her network of support serves to undermine her feelings of security and self-worth, thus adding an enormous strain to her attempt to recover from the trauma.

The violent impact of the crisis in combination with the shame and degradation brought about by the stigma of the experience sharply affect the behavior and personality of the rape victim. This behavior change in one individual will disrupt the routines and coping mechanisms necessary for family stability. In addition, the attitudes of other family members toward the rape may, in turn, change their feelings and behaviors, obstructing the social support which the victim so sorely needs. The crisis of rape does not occur to an individual within a void, but strongly influences the behaviors and interactions of those within the victim's social network. In order to understand the family's reaction to the transformation which occurs in the rape victim, it will be beneficial to first explore the dynamics of the individual's response to the assault.

REACTIONS TO RAPE

Victim Reactions

The first emotional reaction to a crisis (Weiss & Payson, 1967), such as rape (Burgess & Holmstrom, 1979a; Sutherland & Scherl, 1970), is a period of shock and disbelief. This stage of chaos and disorganization may last from a few hours to several days. Following this stage, the victim begins to feel a need to "get back to normal." The process of recovery and reintegration of this experience may consist of one or two stages of reorganization and relapse and may take from a few months to several years. During all stages of a rape victim's recovery, a variety of specific emotions are manifested which constitute the symptoms of the emotional disorder that Burgess and Holmstrom (1979a) have named the "rape trauma syndrome." As one would expect, the severity of the stress response varies widely among rape victims. However, nearly all do experience at least some of the symptoms in the following description.

Surprisingly, feelings of humiliation, degradation, guilt, and shame are only secondary emotions experienced by the rape victim (Burgess & Holmstrom, 1979a; Katz & Mazur, 1979). Although the rape victim rarely feels that she held any responsibility in inviting the attack, she may anticipate public scorn as well as nonacceptance by significant others (Burgess & Holmstrom, 1979a; Weis & Borges, 1973). The immediate and primary emotional reaction experienced by the rape victim is *fear* (Burgess & Holmstrom, 1979a; Katz & Mazur, 1979; Kilpatrick, Veronen & Resick, 1979). She has encountered an overwhelmingly frightening ordeal in which she fears for her life and pays for her release with the sexual act. Feelings of terror continue long after the assault is completed. The victim may fear a return visit by her assailant, particularly if the rape occurred in her home.

The loss of control experienced during the rape may cause feelings of excessive vulnerability and mistrust of situations which were previously considered safe (Brodsky, 1976; Katz & Mazur, 1979). Horrifying nightmares may disrupt her sleep (Burgess & Holmstrom, 1979a; Brodsky, 1976; Katz & Mazur, 1979). Phobic reactions to circumstances which are reminiscent of the rape often disrupt her daily routines (Burgess & Holmstrom, 1979a; Katz & Mazur, 1979; Wilson, 1978). Sex, which for most women is a source of pleasure, becomes an agonizing reminder to the victim of her degrading experience (Burgess & Holmstrom, 1979a; Holmstrom & Burgess, 1979; Masters & Johnson, 1976; Woodling, Evans & Bradbury, 1977). Sexual aversion, mistrust of men and strangers, and general irritability provoke interpersonal conflicts (Burgess & Holmstrom, 1979a; Katz & Mazur, 1979; Notman & Nadelson, 1976; Woodling et al., 1977) at a time when the rape victim needs enormous amounts of emotional support (Burgess & Holmstrom, 1979a; Werner, 1972; Woodling et al., 1977).

The rape victim's experience incurs a mixed bag of feelings toward her loved ones. Although she may feel totally helpless and dependent on her family to pull her through her trauma, she may also experience periods where she is completely indifferent to them. At these times she may prefer to detach or estrange herself from everyone. She may restrict her affection toward those people who are really very important to her. As mentioned earlier, dynamics of her reaction to the crisis lead to other nonsocial behaviors—mistrust, avoidance, moodiness, and sexual aversion. Social support is believed to be an effective buffer against stress (Dean & Lin, 1977); it can protect people in crisis from a wide variety of pathological states (Cobb, 1976). However, following a rape, a victim, as badly as she may need that emotional support, is not likely to exhibit behaviors which would encourage healthy, positive interactions.

Maladaptive Family Reactions

Just as rape represents a crisis in the life of the victim, it may also assault the delicate equilibrium of the couple and/or family relationships (Silverman, 1978). Although the family's responses may be influenced by the stigma of rape as well as the physical harm to the victim, generally the family's crisis arises from the victim's distress. That is, the more agitated a victim becomes (or the greater the personality change), the more disruptive the rape will be for the family (White & Rollins, 1981). The impact of the rape on the family causes them to move through stages of shock and recovery in a manner similar to the victim's own experience. As a result, family members may exhibit specific emotional responses and symptoms, such as anger, revenge, helplessness, and guilt, that are typical catastrophe reactions. In addition, the stigmatic sexual nature of the crime incites other debilitating emotions within the family which may be particularly destructive to the victim's recovery. It is unfortunate when the misconceptions which dominate the general public's attitudes toward rape also cloud the perceptions of the rape victim's loved ones—the people she turns to for support. However, it is a common tendency for family members to react more to the sexual than to the violent aspects of the assault (Silverman, 1978). This bias may be reflected in any of the family's responses to the rape, but is particularly prevalent in reactions of revulsion and victim-directed blame.

Anger and Revenge. Historically, women have been viewed as the property of men, first as their father's property and later as possessions of their husbands (Brownmiller, 1975). Current laws against rape still reflect this concept of "ownership".* Additionally, societal stereotypes about

---

*For example, rape of a woman by her husband is legally undefined in most states. Additionally, vaginal rape usually incurs greater punishment than sodomy (anal or oral rape), although sodomy during rape is usually more painful and traumatic for the victim. However, vaginal rape treads on a husband's right to exclusive procreation and a father's right to a chaste daughter (Brownmiller, 1975).

male roles and responsibilities perpetuate men's feelings of right to ownership of women. When a woman is raped, often her mate or father will feel *personally* wronged and attacked by the defilement of "his woman" (Silverman, 1978; White & Rollins, 1981). He may display a wronged property-holder's rage which, instead of expressing his "deeply-held personal philosophy," protects him from his own "unconscious sense of vulnerability" (Silverman, 1978, p. 168). Male family members may experience thoughts of revenge—extracting violent retribution from the rapist on behalf of the woman. These thoughts may function to protect the man against his own sense of utter helplessness. However, the victim, whose resources are already depleted, has to bear an extra burden of calming, placating, and reassuring the man who would be her avenging protector (Silverman, 1978).

Helplessness. Frustration may build within the family members at not being able or knowing how to "undo" the effects that the rape has had on the victim and themselves. Loss of control over the events in their lives causes a sense of helplessness and vulnerability which leaves the family grasping at random coping strategies in an effort to do *something* which would relieve their frustration. Plotting revenge is one such strategy. In their concern to aid the victim and contain their own feelings of helplessness, family members may attempt to rally the support of the victim's friends, clergy, co-workers, teachers, supervisors, and others (Silverman, 1978). Such attempts may be considered invasive by the victim or may serve to humiliate her further by causing her traumatic experience to become public knowledge.

Guilt. Often parents or mates of rape victims experience considerable guilt and a sense of responsibility for the rape (Silverman, 1978). Interpersonal difficulties may lead individuals to place themselves at greater risk of personal harm. For example, a family fight may send an adolescent female out of the house in a rage. If she is subsequently raped, while away from home and emotionally distraught, her parents may experience a frenzy of self-blame, feeling responsible for their daughter's vulnerable state. Issues of self-concept or role expectations may also play a part in the manifestation of guilt. Following a rape, parents and husbands of victims may feel that they have failed in their duties as protectors. Just as rape victims experience "if-only" feelings ("if only I had stayed home," or "if only that window had been locked"), family members may feel that lack of precautions or a flaw in their behavior precipitated the rape episode.

Sexual Revulsion. Feelings of revulsion on the husband's or mate's part may have a significant impact on the couple's sexual interactions following a rape. The woman's husband may be repulsed by her discreditable experience for a variety of reasons. Some men feel that their wives have been dirtied or contaminated by the rapist—this idea is perhaps motivated by a fear of catching a venereal disease or by anger at having to share their woman with another man. Some of the feelings of distaste arise from their beliefs that the women, in some way, desired the encounter. Sexual dysfunctions are common among rape victims and their mates. Not only can the rape incident cool the victim's appetite for sex and emotional involvement, but also the mate may find resuming sexual activity very distressing when preoccupied with thoughts about the victimization of his mate.

Blame. Anger may be directed at the victim, manifested in blaming or doubting behaviors and statements such as: "Why weren't you more careful?" "Did you enjoy it?" "She's allowed herself to become damaged merchandise!" and "Is she telling the truth?" Mates of rape victims may sincerely believe that the assault was prompted by the behavior, appearance, or wishes of the woman. After all, traditional conjectures concerning rape situations dictate that "nice" (i.e., respectable, decent) women do not get raped, and consequently, any woman who is raped must have invited it. Again, emphasis here is placed on the sexual aspects of the crime. The violence which the victim experienced is overlooked, and she is given little credit for escaping the situation with her life. Obviously these critical responses from her loved ones reinforce the victim's sense of humiliation and devaluation (Silverman, 1978), as well as provoke interpersonal conflicts within the family unit.

Secret-keeping. Although the act of secret-keeping imposes an extra burden upon an already overwhelmed rape victim, she may wish to refrain from telling the entire family about the rape episode in order to protect herself from such negative feedback as described above. In most cases, unless a victim's family lives in another city, reporting the crime to the police ensures that the family will be informed. Many victims of rape, anticipating the withdrawal of affection from their present support network, will bypass the legal reporting system and tell no one of the event or select a few persons to tell whom they feel will be supportive and sympathetic. Occasionally, one or more of these confidants may be family members who have agreed to keep the rape concealed from the rest of the family, or from one particular member—"Please don't tell

Dad; he already believes I'm a troublemaker!" Regardless of how many family members are aware of the incident, the marked personality changes in the victim, as well as the attitude adjustments which may occur in the confidants within the family, are bound to affect the interactions which occur between family members and thus disrupt the usual patterns of day-to-day existence.

COPING WITH STRESS

Dysfunctional Coping Methods

As a response to the crisis of rape and to the sudden onset of a host of undesirable emotions, troubled family members will tend to mobilize strategies aimed at soothing the victim and protecting her from further harm. However, even with the best of intentions, an issue as sensitive as rape is very difficult to manage. Coping mechanisms which the family may try to employ, such as patronization, distraction, or protective silence, can negate the victim's attempts at recovery, as well as inconvenience and frustrate other family members, resulting in increased interpersonal tension. The major flaw with coping tactics such as these is that they serve more to reduce the family's feelings of helplessness and vulnerability than to aid the victim's readjustment processes.

Patronization. The family may attempt to overcompensate for their perceived lack of protectiveness prior to the rape by guarding the victim's every action and by controlling her environment. Parents of a teenage rape victim may enforce new curfews; single women may be urged to move back home with their parents; husbands may desire to accompany the victim anywhere that she needs to go. The danger in such actions as overprotectiveness is that they communicate the idea to the victim that important people in her life see her as a vulnerable child in need of caretaking (Silverman, 1978). This only serves to reinforce her feelings of dependence and helplessness, and prevents her from using adaptive coping strategies which would enhance her self-esteem and sense of autonomy.

Distraction. In an attempt to "keep her mind off things," or to "cheer her up," the family may employ a tactic known as distraction. The victim may find herself suddenly occupied with shopping sprees, vacation trips, and/or group activities. The idea is to keep the victim too busy to think, and thus, hopefully, undo the effects of the rape. An underlying hypothesis in connection with this coping style is that "time heals all wounds," and if the allotted healing time passes quickly and painlessly, the trauma will evaporate with a minimum amount of stress. Basically, the distress which the victim is feeling is played down in the family's attempt to distract her from it. This deprives the woman of the opportunity to mourn her lost autonomy and self-respect and denies her the acknowledgment of her right to be upset.

Protective Silence. Too often, the stigma associated with the act of rape is overwhelming to the family. Because of the perceived shamefulness of the incident, family members may presume that the victim is too embarrassed or humiliated to talk about it or that discussion of the trauma keeps painful, disruptive memories alive in a destructive way. They attempt to protect her with their silence, being careful not to violate her need for privacy and confidentiality. However, from the victim's point of view, this protective silence may be interpreted as shame or disgust. She may fear rejection if she mentions the rape or her consequent emotional reactions to it. This cycle of avoidance is unfortunate because of the need of all family members for mutual support and to work through the feelings precipitated by the rape.

Resources for Coping with Stress

In light of the destructive emotions and reactions which may characterize a family distraught by the occurrence of rape, the question naturally follows: How may a family best cope with the sexual assault of one of its members? Silverman (1978) states:

> the very difficult reality is that there is no single "magical" or "right thing" that can be said or done to make "everything better" (p. 172).

Lack of a specific answer to the family's collective problem may be extremely frustrating for all persons in contact with the rape victim. Concrete strategies or traits which would cause a family to be crisis-proof are difficult to pinpoint. Having maintained a healthy family environment prior to any threat of misfortune is of primary importance as a crisis-meeting resource. Attributes such as good communication skills and role flexibility exist in some families which tend to help them adapt to major disturbances quite effectively. In the event that the family cannot reach a satisfying solution to their conflicts on their own, there are outside resources in most communities to which they can turn for help, such as family therapy, religious counseling, rape crisis intervention, and mental health counseling centers.

Quality of Relationships. Quality family relationships prior to a rape can be an important resource for a continuance of family stability and mutual support. However, the rape experience will add stress to vulnerable areas in any relationship (Silverman, 1978). Although a family may be supportive and attempt to rally together to aid the victim and each other, problems which lie unresolved at the time of the rape will certainly be amplified by the additional stress brought about by the new obstacle. For example, couples who experience sexual problems prior to a rape may find their sexual relationship is in serious jeopardy following the assault. Those with healthy sexual interaction prior to a rape will experience relatively little trouble in resuming their romantic activity (Burgess & Holstrom, 1979b; White & Rollins, 1981). Within a trusting and supportive network, family members can count on one another for continuing aid and nurturance, even as they function under the shadow of a calamity. Strengths, as well as weaknesses, may be emphasized in the context of a crisis situation (White & Rollins, 1981). A woman who feels humiliated by her experience and who fears rejection by her family if she discloses the details of the crime may be surprised and relieved to discover that her husband and her children are sympathetic and non-accusing. The rape episode may stimulate a reevaluation and awareness of the quality of the relationships, as the family collectively responds to the crisis and strives toward a mutual goal of recovery and reintegration.

Communication. One of the most critical resources of the family for dealing with the crisis of rape is a pattern of open communication within the family system (White & Rollins, 1981). Burgess and Holmstrom (1979b) found that when the family discussed the rape, phobic responses of the victim were likely to be resolved and the victim was more likely to resume sexual relations. Silverman (1978) felt that ventilation of feelings in a nonjudgmental environment would help family members realize their underlying negative attitudes toward the situation. Recognition of those emotions would then allow for greater control of the potentially confused communication between victim and family. According to White and Rollins (1981), the welfare of the family is best served if anger is recognized by all members and externalized. If the blame and anger for the rape can be directed to a source outside of the family unit, rather than toward one another, support and compassion can be nurtured among family members. A delicate balance must be maintained for *all* family members between the need to ventilate negative feelings within a presumed supportive environment and the willingness to offer support to other troubled family members. The family should allow, but not force, open expression of feelings, acknowledging the idea that rape is indeed emotionally distressing for all members, yet recognizing that the changes and feelings will not be permanently debilitating.

Flexibility. A major effect of a catastrophe such as rape is to create a need to change alignment of the roles of family members (Hill & Hansen, 1962). The victim's distress may prevent her from performing certain tasks or from interacting with others as she did before the traumatic incident. As a response to her role transformation, the family structure may change in terms of power, responsibility, interfamily coalitions, or economics (Stanton & Figley, 1978). Consider, for example, the case of a working mother who, following a rape, became too distressed to be efficient at her job. Her decision to take a leave of absence substantially affected the economics of her family. The financial power and responsibility fell into the hands of her husband. Due to the victim's extreme feelings of helplessness, the husband additionally found that he was making all of the major family decisions without her help or input. The "mother role," or that of primary nurturer, was shouldered by her eldest child, because the victim was perceived both as needing more nurturing and as being unable, because of her distress, to fulfill her accustomed nurturing role. Just as the victim's disability need not be permanent, so the structure transformations within her family will be temporary. Later, this woman may return to work and the role assignments which the family once knew will shift back into the routine that existed prior to the traumatic incident.

Clearly, the ease with which the family structure can responsibly undertake the realignment of roles during the recovery phase of the trauma will affect the amount of conflict experienced in their daily interactions. Families with rigid expectations of each other will experience intense disruptions as they try—and fail—to accomplish their customary tasks in the face of the breakdown of other members' (particularly the rape victim's) abilities to function as before. Flexibility of roles, then, is seen as an important resource in weathering the long-term distortion and subsequent readjustment of the family structure following the crisis of rape.

External Support Services. Another important resource for families troubled by rape is the availability of family-oriented support services (White & Rollins, 1981). As a result of increased interest in the needs of rape victims in the 1970s, rape crisis centers were developed to offer immediate intervention to rape victims and their families following a rape, as well as to direct them to other services which would address medical, legal, and long-term emotional concerns. Most rape-victim-oriented programs have staff who are prepared to accompany the victim (as well as her family) to the hospital and the police station immediately following a rape in order to provide emotional support and general information regarding medical and legal procedures which are utilized in rape cases. In later stages of the legal and recovery processes, a rape crisis center may provide such services as counseling, referrals to other helping agencies, escorts to legal trials or interviews, and/or securing medical or legal advice. Although rape crisis centers exist, for the most part, only in the larger American cities, most communities maintain mental health agencies and family service agencies which can administer to the psychological and interactional problems of troubled individuals and families. Families of rape victims may seek out these community services as a supplemental stress-buffering resource if they are amply distressed and motivated to do so. The accessibility and use of such services are important influences on the ability of a family to deal with the disruptive effects of rape (White & Rollins, 1981).

IMPLICATIONS

The primary slant of rape literature to date is to guide therapists into creating a safe and supportive environment for the rape victim. A boundary is clearly delineated which separates the care and counseling of the rape victim from the therapy of her family. There appear to be two distinct therapeutic tasks required in this situation. One is to help the victim to "get back to normal" as quickly and comfortably as possible. The other job is the preparation of the family for supporting the victim, making the first job easier while minimizing the traumatic impact on the other family members. This task of mobilizing the family to aid the victim involves several strategies which are described by Silverman (1978):

1) *Encourage open expression of feelings from family members.* An interventionist may provide an atmosphere where it is safe for family mem-

bers to express those feelings which may be injurious to the victim or to other family members. Those who believe that the rape event involved seduction are likely to feel anger, resentment, disgust, or blame directed toward the victim and/or another family member. The therapist can help these family members to unearth their underlying emotions which will then allow them to control the feelings and attitudes that they communicate to each other (Silverman, 1978). Individual sessions lend both confidentiality and privacy to the family members and protection to the absent victim.

2) *Provide education about rape and rape myths.* Because of the sexual nature of the crime, victims are often denied support or sympathy for their plight. The therapist may find that clients who are affected by the crisis of rape will cling to the belief that the victim, in some way, invited the assault. It is important that the therapist redirect family attitudes toward the violent nature of the attack—that victims are selected because of their vulnerability, not because of sexual enticement—in order that those family members be more supportive and accepting of the victim. In addition, it would be extremely useful to educate them regarding the psychological reactions which they may expect from the victim, so that when (and if) these symptoms do occur, the family's concerns may be minimized and they may respond to her in a more calm and reassuring manner (Silverman, 1978).

3) *Encourage receptivity to the victim's concerns and feelings.* Following the realization and acceptance of their own feelings, in addition to education regarding the facts of rape, an important concept for therapists to transmit to the family is that of "containment" of the victim's feelings. Silverman (1978) states:

> This means explaining how to provide an accepting and safe "holding environment" into which the woman can release her troubling thoughts and feelings without fear of condemnation or critical response born of a shared sense of helplessness (p. 172).

Her need to ventilate her emotions and to mourn her lost sense of control and self-worth should not be hindered by the family's refusal to talk about or listen to concerns resulting from the rape. Being emotionally available to, caring of, and concerned for the victim offers her an invaluable aid to recovery from the trauma.

4) *Allow and encourage the victim to reestablish her autonomy.* Therapists may direct family members' behaviors toward acceptance and support of the victim, but without overprotectiveness and smothering behaviors.

When family members forcefully attempt to "undo" the trauma which the rape victim is experiencing, she is again denied control over her destiny. Family members will aid the victim most when they assist her in remobilizing her own best coping abilities as an autonomous adult rather than a sheltered child (Silverman, 1978). Granting her independence in a supportive environment will aid her in regaining control over her own life.

Although professional therapy may be a valuable resource for those coping with a crisis such as rape, these programs reach only a minority of families who are affected by this traumatic experience. Indeed, several variables operate which may prevent a family from approaching professional interventionists—lack of motivation, ignorance of their existence or the nature of their services, insufficient funds, distance or inaccessibility (especially for rural families), stigma attached to help-seeking, or stigma attached to the incident of rape. How, then, can a community help those who do not seek outside intervention in times of intense stress? Perhaps preventative approaches can be very useful. By improving a family's interaction skills, their own best internal resources may be available during a crisis. There are programs of a nonclinical nature which may help couples or families secure specific strategies which may function as future barriers against trauma. A variety of relationship enhancement workshops are offered in many communities by family life educators, churches, and cooperative extension agencies. These programs primarily focus on improving communication and listening skills in an effort to establish methods of openly sharing feelings, improving interactions, and dealing with family issues in a calm and rational manner. For those who may be potential crisis victims, these workshops can help to establish resources of quality relationships and improved communication which may be invaluable in times of extreme stress.

Education may serve to de-stigmatize the victimization by rape. Just as a therapist seeks to redirect a family's attention away from the sexual nature of rape and toward the violent aspects in order to enhance compassion for the victim, so educators can help to mold universal attitudes which will be more accepting and less stigmatic for potential victims. Rape crisis centers and other groups concerned about violence against women are working to enlighten the general public about rape-related issues. Their speakers' bureaus address sororities, church groups, women's clubs and organizations, high school and college classes, and other community organizations. They additionally attempt to reach a larger audience in their community by publishing series of educational articles in local news publications. Topics discussed may include prevention, self-defense, incidence of rape, emotional response to rape, and what to do if one is raped; but invariably, all presentations include education regarding rape myths in an attempt to correct misconceptions about rape and thus to elicit more sympathy for rape victims. By trying to reach a large segment of their community population with rape presentations, these individuals hope to educate those people who may someday have to personally deal with the issue of rape.

CONCLUSION

The incident of rape brings about remarkable stress, both because of the violent impact which shatters established patterns of coping with daily life, and because of the sexual stigma associated with the act which serves to further threaten the victim's self-image and self-respect. In order to achieve recovery from the rape trauma, it is of extreme importance that the rape victim be surrounded by persons who are noncondemning, sympathetic, and caring. However, those who would make up the victim's safe and comforting environment are at the same time suffering from a crisis precipitated by that very assault. The victim's personality swings which result from the violent impact cause the established family structure to waver as members realign their personal roles and expectations of the others. Consequently, the whole family is in turmoil and must rally their collective strengths in order to survive that disruption.

In general, characteristics of families who best weather stressful experiences include quality relationships prior to the crisis, open and effective communication, and role flexibility. However, societal scorn for victims of sexual assault may serve to undermine the family's attitude toward the victim and thus destroy what would be her supportive and remedial environment. Two preventative strategies can be promoted by community service agencies to prepare families for a possible rape catastrophe. First, the family's internal resources must be strengthened. Communication and problem-solving skills may be improved through community-sponsored relationship enhancement programs. To reach a broader audience, perhaps the media can be utilized to encourage enriched family relationships. Second, universal attitudes toward rape victims must be reshaped so that rape is considered a violent crime and its victims are dealt with as survivors of a life-threatening event. Widespread educational programs may help to accomplish this task of eliciting sympathy and understanding for rape victims. In the event that family members cannot overcome their interpersonal difficulties, it is important that quality helping agencies exist in their community as resources to allay the traumatic stress reactions caused by rape.

Although much has been learned about rape victims in the past 10 years, most of the research has been of an exploratory nature with very little attention directed toward the families of the victims. Social and emotional support is vital to the recovery from rape trauma and other stresses, yet it is unknown what style and structure of support systems best benefit the rape victim. The degree of disruption in the victim is believed to affect the stability of her family structure, but little is known about which variables primarily affect the victim's emotional state. Is it the severity of the assault? Her coping strategies? Her personality traits? Existence of support? Certainly there is much to be learned concerning the individual victims of rape as well as those who live and work with her. Although it is certainly not expected that the crime of rape will be eliminated from our society, increased knowledge about rape should help to reduce the severe stress reactions which are experienced by families of rape victims.

8

Disaster: Family Disruption in the Wake of Natural Disaster

SHIRLEY M. SMITH

It was all gone. In less than 40 seconds a killer tornado had completely destroyed a home the Flores family had built and lived in for 18 years. But they were unharmed; they had sufficient insurance (they thought), and the neighbors, friends and family would pitch in. That was for later. Now they had to think about salvaging a lifetime's belongings. Everywhere they looked were personal belongings—photographs, clothing, a matchbook from a local restaurant, pieces of furniture. It was the first house Ramon and Mary had owned and the only one their children, Bennie and Sue, ever knew. Eighteen years of memories were strewn everywhere for neighbors and insensitive sightseers to see. They would gather the most important items together in plastic garbage bags and store them in a neighbor's garage. And only then would they seek refuge at the National Guard Armory set up by the Red Cross for survivors who were displaced by the freak May storm.

The four huddled together with their ration of food, clothing, and bedding. Slowly they met and talked with other survivors—first with those they knew, then with total strangers. But very shortly they would be friends for life: fellow survivors.

Natural disasters have caused human agony since earliest recorded history. They strike indiscriminately, inflicting death, suffering, physical devastation, social disruption, and economic loss. Over the centuries, societies have learned to cope with these disasters by making adjustments that often become part of the culture. In spite of these adaptations, however, a major natural disaster generates extraordinary stresses on individual family members, the family itself, and the community in which the family lives.

Historically, families have always been primary units of response to large-scale disasters. Families act as natural stress buffers and support groups for family members. They can also contribute to community recovery and general mental health after disaster. Their role during periods of threat, impact, and post-impact recovery is of central importance to professionals concerned with handling disaster-related stresses.

Leading scientists (e.g., Burton, Kates & White, 1978) warn that the human and economic costs of disaster are increasing even in this time of extraordinary efforts to control the natural environment. Each year, on the average, 30 major natural disasters occur somewhere on earth, killing 250,000 people. These catastrophes drain the global economy by at least $40 billion a year: $25 billion is in damage loss and $15 billion goes to prevention and mitigation activities. Approximately 90% of the world's natural disasters originate in four hazard types: floods (40%), tropical cyclones, called hurricanes in the Western hemisphere (20%), earthquakes (15%), and drought (15%). About 95% of disaster-related deaths occur among the populations of developing countries. Wealthy countries suffer greater economic losses, but developing nations have more casualties and sustain a much higher proportion of loss to income (Burton et al., 1978; Kates et al., 1973).

In the United States, an estimated average of $5 billion and 600 lives are lost each year to natural disasters (Lander, Alexander & Downing, 1979). Following a super-force disaster, reconstruction can take several years of sustained effort, cost many millions of dollars, and directly affect thousands of households (Dworkin, 1974). Data bases for establishing total losses nationwide for all types of disasters are highly inadequate and may grossly underestimate total costs, both damage losses and costs of mitigation and recovery (Drabek, 1981).

While the average number of natural disasters has remained fairly constant worldwide, death rates and economic losses have climbed sharply. This is due to the rapid growth of civilization into hazardous areas and the high dollar value of technological societies. For example, those areas of the United States most vulnerable to catastrophic disasters are coastlines—earthquakes on the West Coast and hurricanes on the Gulf and East Coasts. Over half the population of the United States lives on these coastlines and the percentage is increasing at a faster pace than in inland areas (Schnabel, 1972). The value of human resources and property in these areas is astronomical.

With more people vulnerable to natural disasters than ever before, families as well are more likely to be involved in a disaster during their lifetime.* Particularly in the United States urban environment, we rely on more services and are therefore less self-sufficient in many ways than our ancestors. Our technological, social, and economic systems are so interdependent that major disasters cause massive disruptions in lifeline services and family support systems. Most families do not prepare for a low-probability hazardous event ahead of time. Thus, most households are more vulnerable to physical and psychological damage than if they had taken steps to prepare ahead of impact (Janis, 1969; Mileti, Drabek & Haas, 1975).

As noted throughout this volume, traumatic stress is a common by-product of severe catastrophes. A considerable amount of scientific literature confirms that disasters can be especially traumatic (Chamberlain, 1980; Erikson, 1976; Leopold & Dillon, 1963). Two factors appear to account for the differences between disaster-related traumatic stress and other types of catastrophes affecting the family. First, the stresses of a major disaster are most often shared directly or indirectly by the community. The family is not alone in its suffering. Disaster experiences can be evaluated relative to the losses of others. Second, family members often jointly experience the terror-filled moments of impact and extended period of cleanup, in contrast with victims of rape or distant war, who share the catastrophic experiences with their untouched families. Roles within the family may be very different when members are responding to a shared catastrophic event. Disorganization of the family system can be swift and dramatic during a disaster.

---

* For example, flooding disasters are among the most common catastrophes in the United States. Flood losses presently average $2.2 billion annually and are projected to increase to $4.3 billion in the next 20 years. An average of 200 flood-related deaths occur each year and another 80,000 people must evacuate their homes (Maywalt, 1981). West Coast earthquakes are another common hazard. Scientists warn that a super-force earthquake can be expected to occur on the West Coast within the lifetime of most readers of this volume (Kates et al., 1973).

If the family members are aware of their inherent abilities to prepare for disasters and to give mutual support after a disaster, and if relief programs are designed to supplement the family's traditional support roles, the family as a whole should be able to adapt to the demands of disaster and recovery with a minimum of stress.

A THEORETICAL FRAMEWORK FOR VIEWING DISASTERS

Given this introduction to disasters and their potential for producing stressful changes in normal life patterns, it is important to provide some theoretical perspectives on disasters and their impact on individuals, communities, and families to guide the analysis that follows.

Disasters—The Stress Agent

Disasters are defined as calamitous events, especially those occurring suddenly and causing great damage to property and hardships for human beings. While some disastrous events can affect only an individual family, most larger disasters impact some portion of the community. Thus, the widespread social disruption that accompanies disaster may be an important factor for the family. It reduces the family's access to outside resources and throws the family back on its own resources.

Natural disasters refer to those extreme events, caused by natural forces like wind, water, fire, volcano, or earthquake, that are life-threatening and/or destructive for human beings. The direct impact is felt upon the physical structures, land, and inhabitants of the areas affected (Rossi et al., 1978). Manmade disasters are caused by man-produced agents like chemicals and nuclear products or by negligent or hazardous business practices.* This chapter will focus on natural disasters, though manmade disasters may cause similar stresses (cf., Cornell, 1976).

Natural disasters vary in cause (an earthquake, a hurricane, a flood), length of warning period, duration and intensity of impact, number of people affected, amount of property damage, number of deaths and injuries, and problems encountered in the recovery period. In addition

---

*Man-caused disasters that introduce novel hazards are an increasing threat. Illustrations of these types of incidents are Three Mile Island, various hazardous materials accidents, or fast-spreading fires fueled by synthetic materials. Some of these incidents may take on the nature of a social disaster, even though no lives are lost or property damaged in the usual sense.

to the physical impact, they also have a psychological impact (the emotional reactions and subjective evaluations of the traumatic event) and a sociological impact (the social disruption created). All these variables contribute to the type and severity of problems the families caught in disaster will face (Farberow, 1978).

Disasters will create maximum social and psychological disruption when they are sudden, occur at night, impact an unprepared family or community, create many uncertainties, or have a prolonged duration (Bolin & Trainer, 1978; Fritz, 1957; Mileti et al., 1975). Disasters that develop slowly and/or have a long aftermath drain the resources of family and community alike, making it more likely that important kin and friendship networks will be disrupted and property damaged. Brief-duration disasters may create long-term injury and destruction, but relief and recovery are unhampered by further impacts (Perry & Lindell, 1978). Recurrent hazards, such as seasonal hurricanes or floods, make it necessary that communities develop institutionalized ways of coping with chronic uncertainty and recurring impacts. A type of disaster subculture, capable of efficient response, evolves and assists the family and community in coping (Anderson, 1965).

In assessing the impact of disaster, we must consider both the individual and social perspective (Rossi et al., 1978). The long-term effects of a "typical" disaster (i.e., one occurring in the low- to mid-spectrum of severity) on a larger region may be negligible while effects on the level of individuals, families, or businesses may be catastrophic. The critical factor is the impact ratio—magnitude of losses involved against the resources of the impacted unit. The higher the impact ratio, the larger the need for outside help. Several widely-quoted studies (Buffalo Creek—Erikson, 1976; Friesema et al., 1979; Managua earthquake—Haas, Kates & Bowden, 1977) have focused on high impact ratio disasters and thus paint portraits of extreme misery. However, this perspective alone is too narrow, for the great majority of disasters are not as overwhelmingly catastrophic for entire communities as these examples (Rossi et al., 1978; Tierney & Baisden, 1979).

In fact, disasters may have some "therapeutic" features. It is not uncommon for victims to express positive feelings from participating in the community recovery process. A sense of adequacy, mastery, increased community solidarity, and general optimism often comes from collectively responding to the challenges of a crisis (Fritz, 1961; Tierney & Baisden, 1979). However, when the disaster overwhelms the resources of community or family, people are robbed of this positive element.

A disaster progresses through several stages. Disaster literature commonly describes these stages as warning, threat, impact, inventory, rescue, remedy, and recovery (cf., Dynes, 1970; Farberow, 1978).* However, another description of phases has evolved, based more on the emotional states of victims (Farberow, 1978). These phases help us better understand family reactions and coping during and after impact:

Heroic Phase. This period occurs during impact and immediately after. Emotions are strong and direct. People respond to the need for heroic action to save lives and property. Altruism is prominent and people expend major energy helping others survive and recover. Family groups, neighbors, and emergency teams are important actors.

Honeymoon Phase. This period usually lasts from one week to six months after impact. The victims share in the common catastrophic experience and losses. Encouraged by official promises of assistance and the anticipation that considerable help will soon be available to solve their problems, victims start the massive cleanup. The activities of community service groups become more important during this phase.

Disillusionment Phase. This stage lasts from two months to as long as two years. Strong feelings of disappointment, anger, resentment, and bitterness surface if delays or failures occur and the promised aid does not materialize. Victims gradually lose their sense of community sharing as they begin to focus on rebuilding their own lives and solving personal problems. Simultaneously, outside agencies pull out of active disaster relief roles.

Reconstruction Phase. In the several years following a major disaster, victim families finally realize they will be solving their problems largely by themselves and therefore assume responsibility for the task. The emergence of restoration activities reaffirms the victims' beliefs in their community and in their own capabilities. When these signs of healthy regrowth and positive coping are missing, serious and intense emotional problems may appear.

---

*This chapter examines human responses to disasters which have occurred, as well as feelings and problems generated by threats of impending disaster. In contrast, a few researchers have recently begun to study responses to disaster mitigation efforts (cf., Kunreuther, 1978, on purchase of flood insurance; Mileti, Hutton & Sorensen, 1981, on family response to earthquake prediction; Palm, 1981, on family reactions to the new California earthquake disclosure law requiring that families be told they have purchased a home in a seismically active area).

The Individual in Disaster

To better understand family reactions to disaster, we must first know a few things about the individual's feelings in disaster. Why is a disaster such an upsetting event to the individual? Figley (1979) has constructed a conceptual framework that helps us anticipate individual reactions in disasters. He identifies four perceptions common to survivors of major disasters which make their experiences catastrophic. First, people perceive disasters as *highly dangerous*.* They fear for their lives and the lives of loved ones. They fear recurrences of situations which would put them in such danger again.

Second, disasters cause a *sense of helplessness*. People feel powerless to stop the wind, flood water, or earth movement. They are unable to control their fate and the unfolding destruction. Moreover, during impact, they may feel that their courses of action are severely limited or escape routes blocked. Their shelter may seem inadequate to withstand the full force of impact. They may be trapped under debris. In the aftermath, they may literally be unable to do much for a while to restore their lives to normal.

Third, disasters cause community-wide *perceptions of destruction and disruption*. People can no longer deny the reality of impact on their lives. Few living in the impact area escape completely. Most are either direct or "hidden" victims, many of whom have not suffered direct damage but whose lives, homes, and jobs are seriously affected (Janis, 1971; Moos, 1976; Schanche, 1976). Victims perceive immediate and alarming disruptions in living; they realize that their family and perhaps whole community have suffered a disabling blow. They see death and physical devastation all around them. They interact with family members and neighbors who are emotionally distraught. In large-scale disasters, such as the Managua earthquake or Buffalo Creek flash flood in 1972, they live among reminders of the traumatic moments for long periods of time (cf., Erikson, 1976; Haas et al., 1977).

Fourth, disasters result in a *sense of loss*. Victims report being overwhelmed by the loss of many of the things they care most about in the world. Losses of home, neighborhood, loved ones, or belongings that

---

*Drabek cautions the reader to differentiate between extreme events and the far larger number of disasters which are not so defined. He points out that most American losses, economically speaking, are due to flooding and only a few of these are flash floods. Typical riverine floods do not generate a public perception of being highly dangerous or life-threatening (Drabek, personal correspondence, 1981).

took a lifetime to accumulate leave deep psychological scars. One important psychological loss is the illusion of personal invulnerability to tragedies that strike others (Janis, 1971); another is a feeling of control over the environment (Chamberlain, 1980; Lifton & Olson, 1976; Titchener & Kapp, 1976). Economic estimates do not convey the true loss. For example, a photo album may not have been expensive, but to the parent who cannot replace it, the cost is defined as very great (Kilijanek & Drabek, 1979).

Disasters force man to survive in a radically changed environment. Suddenly, it becomes difficult to provide the basic human needs for water, food, shelter, and safety (Maslow, 1954). Because it takes such effort just to sustain life, victims have little time for the social interactions and personal pursuits of pre-impact days.

The more death and devastation an individual witnesses, the more indelible will be the mental imprints. Indeed, these images will last a lifetime for some (Chamberlain, 1980; Figley, 1979; Janis, 1971). Once a person survives a catastrophe, he or she then feels especially vulnerable to future brushes with death, injury, and psychic trauma. Future crises may overwhelm him or her more easily. This kind of dread may become a collective family experience that stimulates further anxiety in each individual (Lifton & Olson, 1976).

Disasters produce a variety of emotional or psychosomatic aftereffects such as nervousness, excitability, hypersensitivity, sleep disturbances, inability to concentrate, nightmares, or headaches (Fritz, 1957; Gleser, Green & Winget, 1981). These disturbances vary in intensity and may disappear quickly or remain to cause long-term distress. Disasters also produce intense feelings: fear, helplessness, anger, bitterness, frustration, or survivor guilt, which may in turn lead to lowered self-esteem (Chamberlain, 1980). The ego may have difficulty integrating and controlling these feelings. Titchener and Kapp (1976) argue that, after overwhelming disaster, a personality reorganization or character change may interfere with full recovery. This takes the form of rigidity, aimed at prevention of recurrences of the traumatic event, and can actually preserve symptom patterns and forced changes in life-style. Psychological damage incurred in life-threatening trauma, if unrecognized and untreated, tends to grow worse with time (Leopold & Dillon, 1963).

Figley (1979) predicts that the intensity of the stress caused by the disaster event is a function of both the stress-coping ability of the individual (based on his knowledge of coping, previous disaster experiences, and temperament) and the degree to which he was in either an active role (could act to save himself and others) or passive role (at the mercy of others or fate) during the emergency.* Chamberlain (1980) points out that pre-disaster personality characteristics may do no more than determine how long an individual can withstand prolonged extreme stress.

One cannot underestimate the effects of an individual's prior experiences with disaster. These experiences could be positive in the sense of better equipping individuals to withstand future disasters, or negative, if the individual was unable to cope with past problems and stresses. Bell, Kara, and Batterson (1978) suggest that those accumulated experiences may help many older persons develop a resilient character, one more suited to the adjustments required after large disasters.

There is growing evidence that psychological readiness for a stressful event provides a kind of emotional inoculation. When individuals do the "work of worrying" prior to the event, they increase their tolerance for stress. By mentally walking through realistic scenarios of the event, they begin to develop coping mechanisms and effective defenses (cf., Janis, 1971, pp. 100-105, 196-197). This method has been successfully used with pre-surgical patients, prepared childbirth classes, and in cardiopulmonary resuscitation training.

The Community in Disaster

In general, disasters usually have mixed effects on a community. They can be viewed as both creating and increasing community problems, as well as affecting psychological and physical well-being. They may also generate a sense of community esprit de corps which may have salutary effects for some.

The community is affected at many levels. Physical destruction may be visible everywhere, but significant changes in normal patterns of community life are not always as apparent. However, individuals and families struggling to return to normal after a catastrophe find this social disarray painfully real. In addition to normal life problems, the community suffers when jobs and incomes are disrupted, when schools and shopping facilities are closed, when social and recreational activities are curtailed, and when community support systems are not functioning. Thus, social disorganization compounds the physical devastation (Dynes, 1970).

---

*Drabek and Key (1972) have interpreted data from a long-term follow-up of disaster victims in the 1966 Topeka tornado as indicating that the greater the degree to which individuals participated in the post-disaster therapeutic community, the less the negative psychological impacts.

A disaster can never be conceptualized as if it were a simple uniform stimulus (Erickson et al., 1976). Communities will suffer greater or lesser loss according to the magnitude of the event, the nature of the community, the degree of community preparedness, and the extent of warning of impending disaster (Friesema et al., 1979). Perry and Lindell (1978) list several factors characteristic of social systems that mediate the psychological impact of disasters:

1) the level of community preparedness;
2) the presence of a disaster subculture;
3) the development of a therapeutic community;*
4) the destruction of kin and friendship networks;
5) the extent of property damage; and
6) the presence of institutional rehabilitation.

The social shock to a community is proportional to the percentage of the population directly affected through ties to the human victims.

Only within limits can a society or community equitably "prepare" for disaster (Mileti, 1980). Given the rare occurrence of truly extreme events, total community preparedness or prevention raises plausible questions about the benefits versus costs of these adjustments. Mitigation measures always include value conflicts, both for the community and the family. Community adjustments cannot mitigate all risk. At best, they can reduce the risk imposed by environmental extremes to lower levels. Thus, families in a community must live within the levels of protection deemed adequate by community decision-makers.

In a classic analysis of families in disaster, Hill and Hansen (1962) describe communities as being either *individuated* (usually urban, industrialized, predominance of nuclear families, more activity between neighbors and friends) or *kinship* (rural or mountain villages, predominance of extended family networks, less activity outside the family). The individuated community better adapts to changes and, as a byproduct, arms its citizens for disaster and short-term recovery. Intense interaction with non-family groups soon after disaster offers support and adds to the family's own resources, but this ad hoc support system dissipates rather quickly. In contrast, a kin-oriented community will be less well

---

*Barton (1970) has created the most elaborate theoretical model to date wherein numerous variables are integrated so as to create a predictive estimate of the rise of the therapeutic community which may alter the social system and psychological impact on individuals.

prepared, less flexible, and less quickly adjusted to immediate aftermath, but will provide better long-term support through kin group interaction.*

Very often, a "therapeutic community" of survivors emerges immediately after disaster impact (Dynes, 1970; Mileti et al., 1975; Perry & Pugh, 1978). A spontaneous band of victims comes together and plunges into the work of search and rescue, care of the injured, and provision of basic needs. A kind of euphoria uplifts people. Social status and organizational rules fall away. It is a time of intense concentration and activities toward common goals. The family's coping resources are extended during this short cooperative time period. However, the most severe disasters fail to generate this therapeutic community. For example, the Buffalo Creek flood, which wiped out all the small hamlets along a narrow canyon in West Virginia, was so severe that communality was destroyed and people never did unite into this common bond (Erikson, 1976).

The Family in Disaster

The major dimensions affecting family behavior in disaster are the stress agent and its characteristics, the community milieu in which the disaster takes place, the family's organization resources, and the family definitions of the event (Hill & Hansen, 1962). The urgent problems created by the disaster itself are compounded by the problems inherent in the post-disaster environment. Some families are better equipped than others to cope within this changed world (Haas & Drabek, 1970). To a significant degree, the well-being of the post-disaster family is determined by the wider responses of community, state, and nation. In other words, external resources which aid the family are important. No stress agent is uniformly the same for all families but varies in striking power by the hardships that accompany it.**

---

*In an insightful commentary, Kates and his coauthors (1973) compare three types of societies threatened or struck by large-scale disaster: the folk society, the industrial society, and the transitional society which has elements of both. Transitional societies, which still have pervasive kinship systems, are particularly vulnerable to natural disasters.

**Hill (1958) observes that families are increasingly vulnerable to disasters as they are shorn of kin, friends, and neighbors. Once a self-contained economic and social unit buttressed by kinship support, the family is now more dependent on other agencies in society for fulfilling its purpose and responding to its emergencies. As early as 1958, Hill warned that modern American families, centered around a husband, wife, and their one or two children, are highly mobile, precariously small, and poorly structured units to withstand life's stresses. This observation would be even more true today with less than 15% of American families living in the "traditional" configuration of a working father, a stay-at-home mother, and one or more children (Taubin & Mudd, 1981).

Inadequate family functioning before disaster predisposes a family to adjustment problems after disaster (Haas et al., 1977; Hill & Hansen, 1962). A crisis may become a disaster as a result of the family's perceptions of the event, the kinds of problems created, the resources available, and the family's experience in coping with previous crises. All these perceptions are filtered through the family's value system and result in a view of the situation as crisis-provoking rather than challenging. Multiproblem families will be especially vulnerable to the stresses of disaster.

We suggest that the normal family functions of protection and leadership of members produce more appropriate behaviors in disaster-related situations. Hill and Hansen (1962) make this observation: the more clearly defined the responsibilities, the more effectively a person meets a disaster. Fritz and Marks (1954) demonstrated that, compared to persons without dependent children, men in homes with dependents both prepared better and acted more rationally in all stages of disaster.

In any type of community, the extended family may offer more intense and lasting therapy to suffering victims than other elements of the community. Strong kin relationships before disaster are highly supportive and add to post-disaster recovery resources for victim families. Conversely, the destruction of these kin relationships can produce negative psychological consequences (Perry, 1979). In fact, the importance of kin ties, especially in the recovery process, holds true across sex, age, ethnicity, education, income, and religious categories (Bolin, 1976). The more geographically or socially distant the kin, the less effective they are in meeting the needs of victim families. Also, kin become less and less helpful in a widespread disaster with intense impact because they are likely to be victims also (Hill & Hansen, 1962; Mileti et al., 1975).

The number and strength of linkages to the support systems in the outside world also increase a family's resources and help determine the family's capacity to recover (Bolin & Trainer, 1978; Drabek & Key, 1976). Linkages to support networks outside the family are important in that they become the social routes through which much economic and emotional support is channeled in the aftermath of disaster. Chamberlain (1980) suggests that stable, strong relationships with significant others prior to disaster provide resources for psychological reorganization in the aftermath.

Family welfare is of central concern to people caught in disasters. Family members show an immediate and powerful concern for the safety of their loved ones (Hill & Hansen, 1962; Kates et al., 1973; Killian, 1952). Most individuals will be less effective in relief efforts until they are assured their loved ones are safe. In receiving warnings about possible impact, the family is the primary group in which an individual is *most* likely to take adaptive actions, the peer group the *least* likely. Warnings may require evacuation. Studies show that, where possible, families choose to evacuate as units; families need to remain together after disaster; and intact families rarely show panic-type behavior in catastrophic situations (Drabek & Stephenson, 1971; Mileti et al., 1975).

The family's protective and security functions are heightened during disasters and provide important contributions to the survival and psychological well-being of victims. Thus, the family more than ever requires the intimate environment and privacy of a home to confront the traumas and disruptive experiences precipitated by such an extreme event (Bolin, 1976). When the physical home is destroyed or severely damaged, the family's deep feelings of loss often reflect the meaning and security attached to the home and its contents, rather than its actual dollar worth. Older families have a greater sense of loss and deprivation because they are losing things symbolizing a lifetime of work which they probably will never regain (Bolin & Trainer, 1978).

SOURCES OF STRESS

The disaster impact itself is a powerful and immediate primary stressor. Many other variables within the disaster situation become sources of secondary stress: pre-impact predictions, warnings, and evacuations; death, injury, property damage, and community destruction; personal disaster experiences; and pre- or post-disaster adjustments. Sources of stress that seem to impact only the individual eventually affect his or her family.

Stressors Impacting the Individual

The individual in disaster suffers through a variety of stress-generating experiences. The terrifying threats to his or her physical and psychological survival as well as to his or her home and loved ones immediately produce deep distress. Traumatic memories of the event can bring on more reactions: survivor guilt; feelings of incompetence that he or she did not "perform" adequately during the disaster; frustration and anger if the disaster was preventable; feelings of isolation; or psychosomatic problems (Chamberlain, 1980; Farberow, 1978). The victim often finds it difficult to relate to others. Interpersonal relationships are impaired at a time when he or she desperately needs support and nurturing. The individual feels a loss of control, not only over the environment, but in matters that affect the family. Normal family roles and functions may be taken over by others within the family or by outsiders.

Individuals usually do not have a "blueprint" that helps them know for sure what to do in a disaster; thus the vivid destruction and repatterning of home and their world leave them feeling disoriented. Uncertainties abound as questions about survival, additional impacts, financial losses, how to provide basic necessities, where to settle, or unemployment demand attention. In addition, changes in loss of community support mechanisms or legal problems further stress the victims (Friesema et al., 1979).

In our American culture which is largely without ritual formulae for working out sorrow, the individual finds it difficult to express his or her grief and other feelings about the disaster (Wilson, 1962). The unvented emotions accumulating within the victim further stress his or her relationships and can contribute to divorce, loss of ambition, and other family problems.

Stressors Impacting the Family

Threats and Warnings. Threats of disaster and resulting warnings of possible impact are sources of stress for the target population. Research on reactions to disaster warning shows that the individual almost immediately thinks of his or her family. If children are separated from parents at the time of urgent warnings or impact, most will suffer separation anxiety. Once the family has been reunited, circumstances which force further separation will cause renewed anxiety (Hill & Hansen, 1962). Predictions of very severe and/or long onslaught events create maximum anxiety (Drabek et al., 1973; Haas & Mileti, 1977; Turner et al., 1979). Warnings giving alarming but confusing hazard information can raise anxiety levels to such an unmanageable point that the family either denies the threat completely or becomes immobilized. False alarms make the public less receptive or more skeptical the next time.

Evacuations. Evacuations in any phase of disaster cause stress. If the evacuation is expected, has been clearly defined, eliminates uncertainties as much as possible, evacuates the family as a unit, provides safeguards for the home left behind, and offers an acceptable destination and shelter, the family will more likely experience tolerable levels of stress and be willing to cooperate. Violation of any of these parameters will cause families to be anxious, ambivalent, or downright resistive (Drabek & Stephenson, 1971; Perry, 1979).

Roles and Relationships. Disasters require that certain important roles such as protective leader, comfort giver, and provider of basic necessities be adequately performed to help the family successfully adjust to the crisis. The supreme stressor upon the family is probably the death of a primary family member, followed by a long-term severe injury or other incapacity (Mileti et al., 1975). The resulting grief and drastic reallocation of critical roles within the family create coping and adjustment problems.

Due to its small size, the nuclear family has a limited number of roles, thus inadequate role performance has greater negative impact (Wilson, 1962). Important family roles that conflict with urgent emergency roles in other groups may cause ambivalence and stress. Individuals or families forced to remain in passive roles during any stage of disaster will suffer more stress since active roles can be highly effective in regulating emotional states in crisis situations (Gal & Lazarus, 1975). Family members requiring special consideration during disaster (for example, infants, young children, and bedridden, handicapped, elderly, or foreign-speaking members) make family coping that much more difficult. Evacuation and long-term housing in temporary quarters are especially stressful when considering the needs of any of these groups.

The stresses induced by parent-child interactions during disaster are considerable. Parents have difficulty dealing with their own fears and are thus less effective in providing support for their anxious children (Farberow, 1978; San Fernando Valley Child Guidance Clinic, 1972). Parental fears that are unrecognized or denied heighten a child's fears and interfere with the satisfactory performance of parental roles.*

Destruction of Home and Near Environment. Since "home" often includes the neighborhood and near-community, seeing neighbors upset and the community devastated makes it seem as if the whole world is destroyed. Families experience stress if they continue to live in surroundings that daily remind them of the disaster. Moving away to another area, either

---

*For example, following the 1971 San Fernando earthquake, parents expressed considerable uncertainty and hesitancy in setting limits or dealing with their children's maladaptive behaviors (Blaufarb & Levine, 1972). This reluctance to restore appropriate limits actually delayed recovery within the families.

temporarily or permanently, will also produce stress, but for different reasons. Moving often implies significant changes in patterns, perceptions, and friends. Most families will put up with intense hardships rather than leave the location meaning "home" to them (Mileti et al., 1975).

The mental and physical fatigue after the terrors of impact is compounded by the destruction left behind. The long hours families spend on major cleanup are tiring and even dangerous, leaving little time for rest and leisure activities. Repairs can be costly and delays frustrating. While repair bills mount, economic aid from the government to help pay for the damage may be slowed by bureaucratic red tape.

Economic Losses. Economic problems* after disaster can severely challenge a family. Property damage, uncertainties about employment and income, or post-impact inflation create budget and psychological stresses. Families are especially hard-hit if they have inadequate insurance to help cushion the financial shock. Their standard of living may be appreciably lower than before the disaster. If they suffer long-term deprivation of regular housing and services while families in undamaged sections of the community do not, they may feel like "have-nots," with resentment towards the "have's." Whatever the socioeconomic status, the family faces abnormal and limited problem-solving options after disaster.

Recovery Resources. Families that rely heavily on urban services, that are not involved in kin interaction, or that have never been self-sufficient for any reason, will find adjustments during the recovery period especially stressful. American families are conditioned to expect immediate help from the government when emergencies strike, but with super-force disasters, this help may be hours or days away. The need for family self-sufficiency under calamitous conditions often runs counter to customary habits, expectations, and capabilities and thus produces stress. As highly mobile Americans who have moved far from established support systems and who often do not know about hazards common to their new homes, many families will be more vulnerable to disasters.

---

*Families have three financial resources: their earning power, their home and possessions, and their accumulated wealth. With loss of either home and possessions or their wealth, they would need to start over to restore these resources. The loss of earning power (for example, through the loss of a small business or through an injury that makes it impossible to work) is a far more serious problem.

As described in the previous section, the warmth, support, and extended resources of a therapeutic community drop off rather quickly after impact, to be replaced by more impersonal bureaucratic relief efforts (Mileti et al., 1975). Survivors grow frustrated and angry if they must wait in long lines, deal with multiple agencies, or fill out complicated forms.* These bureaucratic procedures are especially confusing, intimidating, and distressing for elderly citizens, minority families, or others unused to accessing this type of government assistance (Bell et al., 1978).

In large and/or spectacular disasters, a generally uncoordinated outpouring of goods, services, and miscellaneous people converges on the impact area (Perry & Pugh, 1978). These people want to see, help, research the situation, or get the news story out. But this massive load of well-meaning stimuli may overwhelm victim families and community workers at a time when they already have enormous coping problems.

Changes in Routine. Abrupt changes in normal, daily-life patterns can also be very upsetting. The family suffers stress when many necessary services are unavailable, when transportation, work, school, and shopping patterns are disrupted, and when less time is available for social interaction or leisure activities. The longer this period of upheaval and the greater the changes, the more severe will be the resulting stresses.

FAMILY COPING IN DISASTERS

The greater part of disaster theory and research has focused on complex organizations, the community, and individuals during threat and immediate post-impact phases. Only cursory attention has been given the family as a unit and its problems during the long-term aftermath (Bolin, 1976; Mileti et al., 1975). Yet, compared to other social groups, the family is a highly adaptive and protective unit during all stages of disaster. The family's established patterns of authority, communication and support usually facilitate functional adaptive behavior (Hill & Hansen, 1962).

With natural disasters, active manipulation of the stressor is usually impossible. Therefore, families must cope with the consequences. Coping refers to family members managing the requirements of the external

---

*One-Stop Assistance Centers have improved the uncoordinated multiple agency situation greatly.

situation while also attending to their own feelings about that traumatic situation (Moos, 1976).*

This section describes common family responses during threat, impact, and aftermath. Some methods families use to cope are dysfunctional and contribute to survival and recovery problems; others are functional and will clearly help the family make the best possible adjustments.

Dysfunctional Coping

In general, families that cope with disasters least effectively are those that have low family adequacy in normal times, those families that are recurringly overwhelmed by crisis situations. These "crisis-prone" families have little in the way of resources to meet the disaster and they tend to define accompanying hardships as crisis-producing (Hill, 1958). Individuals and families who have not envisioned the problems attending a large-scale disaster or emergency *before* the event are at a disadvantage during and after impact. This avoidance may cause them to ignore or deny the threat and contributes to general confusion in the aftermath.

Families that are rigid and unresourceful in reallocating roles and spreading post-disaster responsibilities among family members will fare poorly. Also, when a family is intolerant of the reactions and needs of individual members, recovery for the individual and the family will be delayed. It is dysfunctional for the family to allow serious and/or long-term disturbance in family members to go untreated, just as it is to discourage expressions of grief. Those families that insist on denying or underestimating their problems will have no basis for positive actions to cope with the situation. Parents who do not resume a normal lead-

---

*Moos (1976) divides the overall coping process into two phases: an acute phase, in which energy is directed at minimizing the impact of the stress, and a reorganization phase, in which the new reality is faced and accepted. In disaster-caused crises, we add a third phase which requires coping: anticipation of impact, triggered by predictions and warnings of threat. Typical reactions range from denials or downplaying the importance to some form of preparation. During the acute phase (impact and immediate aftermath), attention is directed at practical matters while feelings are largely denied. The victim is thus able to ration out his limited physical and emotional energy while adjusting to the changes in his life. If successful, the reorganization period (longer-term aftermath and recovery) leads to a gradual return of normal functioning and a new equilibrium. Changed circumstances and new feelings are integrated into the victim's life and self-image. The acute phase corresponds to the heroic phase described on page 125, and the reorganization phase to the honeymoon, disillusionment, and reconstruction phases on page 125.

ership role as soon as possible after impact leave their children to cope in a disturbingly unstructured world. The child who is allowed to continue abnormal behavior patterns, such as school avoidance or sleeping with a parent at night, will have more recovery problems.

The loss of home and destruction of neighborhood cause unique coping problems. With a loss of this magnitude, families of low adequacy may find good reasons for their apathy and feelings of helplessness. They consider the financial and disaster relief situation so hopeless that they resign themselves to a temporary living situation. Since most of these arrangements are makeshift and inadequate, the longer families stay in temporary housing, the more stresses they accumulate (Haas et al., 1977).

Those families that do not use outside aid recover more slowly and have a lower post-disaster standard of living (Bolin, 1976). In contrast, families that depend solely on the government to solve their problems are also coping dysfunctionally. It slows recovery to take no personal or family responsibility for disaster-related problems like unemployment or to feel anger and resentment against the employer.

Finally, it is reasonable to expect that families that have inadequate plans for meeting crises, that do not learn from their experiences, that deny problems, that are inflexible in response to crisis, that do not make positive progress toward recovery, and that do not have a network of help and support are likely to experience more severe stresses each time a crisis or disaster happens.

Functional Coping

Families best able to cope with disaster-caused stresses are those that successfully adjust to other normal life crises. Wilson (1962) states it well when he observes "competence begets competence." These families define hardships as opportunities. They are survivors, which implies a positive assault on the problems, not victims, which here implies passive or ineffective reactions. The following paragraphs describe functional coping methods used by families during various phases of disaster.

Preparation for Disaster. One of the most effective ways to cope with disaster-related stresses is through preparedness. Families that behave most competently in disasters have determined ahead of time how best to physically cope with impact and aftermath (e.g., go to the basement,

seek cover under heavy furniture, evacuate under certain conditions).*
Planning within the family context reduces uncertainties, gives the family more appropriate procedures for coping, prepares psychological defenses, helps reduce anxiety to manageable levels, and provides for basic needs (Drabek & Stephenson, 1971; Lafferty, Paine & Smith, 1979). In short, the family setting provides an appropriate environment for carrying out the "work of worrying." This type of emotional inoculation helps a family feel more in control and less helpless. Because many aspects of preparedness are generic,** preparations for one kind of disaster will better prepare the family for other emergencies and disasters.

Anticipating Impact: Warnings and Threat. In general, adequate warnings can do much to save lives and facilitate coping, though property may not be spared. If the warning provides a graphic portrayal of expected impact accompanied by clear instructions on what to do, families develop an "optimal anxiety level" that both mobilizes their defenses and makes it more likely that they will take protective action.

Official warnings often include urgent recommendations to evacuate. Families make better evacuation decisions if they receive the warnings as an intact family unit, perceive their risk to be high, have specific emergency evacuation plans, and have past experiences with disaster (Perry, Greene & Lindell, 1980). If given a choice, they will usually take refuge in the homes of relatives or friends rather than a public shelter (Drabek, 1969). This kin sheltering over a short period is usually positive in that it allows the natural family support network to operate.

Impact and Immediate Aftermath. Response to sudden impact is largely individual, reflexive, and aimed at personal survival (Mileti et al., 1975). But once the intense trauma of impact is over, victims soon become concerned for loved ones, neighbors, and community. The family is the major focal point and main source of help to victims during this period (Erickson, 1976; Kates et al., 1973; Quarantelli, 1960). Some researchers

---

*In addition to large-scale disaster, parents could teach basic first aid and survival skills which could apply in everyday family situations such as winter storms or summer camping vacations.

**Certain aspects of emergency response are generic to most disasters: the need to save human life; the need to provide water, first aid, food, shelter, or clothing in the aftermath; the possible need to evacuate or get messages to family members; the need to provide comfort support for victims; the need to survive economically; and the need to survive the aftermath in reasonable psychological shape.

have found that, with sudden, widely devastating impacts, victims will be collectively and temporarily stunned for a brief period (Janis, 1971; Perry & Pugh, 1978). But in contrast to stereotyped images of victim reactions as panic, mass disorganization, or irrational behavior at this stage, most people act in controlled and adaptive ways in disaster (Mileti et al., 1975).

Families spend the first hours in purposeful actions to rescue loved ones and other victims and repair as much damage as possible. These activities are functional in that they help ease the initial shock. Voluntary search and rescue efforts, care of the injured, attempts to gather the family, damage assessments, restoration of vital services, and helping others are common activities after disaster that contribute to recovery.

The family can play an important part in helping the individual adjust to new realities. Families that face the reality of death or severe injury to their members and encourage each other to work out their grief will move toward healing more quickly. They must reallocate the roles and responsibilities of the dead one among remaining members. With a severely injured member, families are careful to attend to his or her needs but not to create a dependency or to isolate him/her from family life.

Victims desperately need to talk out their traumatic experiences, repeatedly if necessary (Figley, 1979; Perry & Perry, 1959). They need a place to grieve, to be angry, to be bitter, to go through the stages of adjustment. Some members may be experiencing brief emotional or psychosomatic disturbances soon after impact (Fritz, 1957; Gleser et al., 1981). The family that expects these reactions, encourages their expression without condemnation, and is accepting of the sufferer will speed individual healing. While the family can be an ideal stress-buffering environment, it does not always perform this function well. Those families that have trouble providing this kind of milieu or defusing serious disturbance in a family member should seek professional help.

It is beneficial when family leaders move quickly to help all members reassume their usual roles or assist them in taking on new roles. Parents who firmly but sensitively reinstate normal patterns will function as guiding, steadying influences in the family. Rapid restoration of as many of the usual parent-child, child-sibling, and child-peer behavioral patterns as possible provide children with the security and certainty of the familiar (Blaufarb & Levine, 1972; San Fernando Valley Child Guidance Clinic, 1972). Families find it difficult to give young children the extra comforting they need and still carry out other urgent duties, but parents should make an extra effort to spend more time with their children and involve them in restoration activities wherever possible.

Recovery and Restoration. After the acute emergency period ends, the anticipation of a favorable recovery is critical to families struggling to cope. Without that hopeful outlook, demoralization and decline are likely to occur (Farberow, 1978). Therefore, family activities which give tangible evidence of progress toward "successful recovery," as defined by the family, will be most beneficial.

The reestablishment of a home base is an important initial step toward recovery. Thus, families that take advantage of their natural urges to rebuild a shattered home, coupled with wise use of disaster relief resources, will more quickly restore a satisfactory environment in which to deal with their other problems. Families will be more satisfied if they can keep some ties with their familiar neighborhood and friends. Families housed in temporary living quarters will fare better if they make the best of the situation, are flexible, and rediscover talents for living with less.

Since activity is a good means of diverting our attention from our distress, post-disaster chores can actually be therapeutic if handled correctly (Gal & Lazarus, 1975). The immense job of cleanup is not so burdensome when shared among family members and even neighbors. Teamwork allows individuals to prioritize jobs and monitor one another, heading off such problems as exhaustion before they become too severe. However, families must be careful to recognize the special needs of this period to maintain social contacts and to engage in some recreational and leisure activities, and strive to devote time to these pursuits.

Families that sustain substantial economic losses might try to cope through making a realistic assessment of their losses, insurance coverage, and relief programs available. They would then prioritize needs and outline steps toward financial recovery. Ideally, the most functional way to cope would be to include an emergency/disaster component in the family's overall financial management plan long before the crisis materializes. But sometimes even this foresight is not enough to cover losses in major disasters.*

---

*Disaster-related economic problems are so difficult and the solutions so unique to each situation that recommendations on functional coping methods are highly general and probably not too useful.

Families adjust better to necessary dependency on outside assistance by being flexible and tolerant. However, family members need not feel helpless to influence the handling of their problems. Ideally, they would be assertive rather than passive and would find someone to assist them who understands the aid systems. They would have a clear idea of their priorities when working with relief personnel. As a preparedness measure against future crises, they would keep kin support networks activated by occasional contacts.

In summary, we predict that families will cope more adequately with disaster and its aftermath if:

1) they have prepared themselves to survive emergencies and disasters, both physically and psychologically;
2) they have previous successful experiences in meeting crises;
3) they have more depth in coping resources;
4) they work as teams to solve problems;
5) they are flexible and tolerant of changes;
6) they accept and support family members during other kinds of crises; and
7) they have an active network of kin and/or friends' support.

These families will function as units to solve their problems and will be a resource to the community recovering from disaster, rather than a burden. Indeed, the resiliency and adaptiveness of American families are highlighted throughout the research literature—problems are conquered, life goes on.

THE PROFESSIONALS: HELPING FAMILIES COPE WITH DISASTER

Although families are primary and natural stress-buffering units, they seldom can solve all the complex problems caused by disasters impacting a complex society. Thus, disaster relief professionals deal directly with individuals and families to provide the additional human services necessary after major disasters. The partnership among federal, state, and local emergency services personnel, help organizations like the Red Cross and Salvation Army, emergency medical professionals, and mental health workers has developed into an impressive emergency management program in the United States.* Within this program, planning has centered on community preparedness and individual and community reactions in the aftermath. Nuclear war has been a primary focus of preparedness efforts. Recently, emphasis has been broadened to include natural disasters as well as family reactions and needs.

This chapter has highlighted some of the important needs of families as victims of catastrophe. Professionals can help families meet these needs and cope in more functional ways. Tierney and Baisden (1979) suggest that most difficulties experienced by victim populations involve problems in everyday living. These problems require solutions in order to preclude more serious, long-term effects. Thus, disaster-response professionals will be dealing mostly with everyday-life problems and transient symptoms of various forms of emotional disturbance.

Emergency Services Professionals

These people come from several government agencies and coordinate the entire emergency planning and response operation, from the community up to the national levels. Their extensive planning operations are designed to provide rapid response to overall community problems and thus deal with individual families only as a set of generic needs. However, if they became more knowledgeable about families in disasters, they could base more of their planning on known family responses. Their public service messages would be an ideal place to urge *family* preparedness for possible disasters, with instructions on how to become prepared. In their disaster relief activities, they should take special note of the need to deal with families as units and plan to assist in keeping them together wherever possible. If they know the family demographics of their area, they should be able to map out strategies that better anticipate realistic family reactions and problems. These professionals work closely with community decision-makers and thus can urge a higher priority for disaster preparedness activities, including education.

---

*After a major disaster, a host of helpers from federal and state agencies will seek to coordinate family assistance through establishing One-Stop Assistance Centers. This aid augments the massive efforts made by numerous voluntary agencies like the Red Cross, Salvation Army, and religious groups. Thus, the post-disaster scene is a hotbed of activity.

Disaster Relief Professionals

Organizations like the Red Cross, Salvation Army, and other volunteer groups have a long history of aid to families of disaster. They are well-known and respected and have experience in providing for the most urgent needs. Thus, they are in a position to influence other disaster planning agencies to consider the crisis-coping capabilities of the family unit and the home environment when developing programs. These organizations often informally perform some of the functions that mental health agencies normally handle. Thus, the recommendations below also apply to these help organizations.

Mental Health Professionals

After disaster, early intervention by trained workers can prevent or significantly lessen the severity of later family problems (San Fernando Valley Child Guidance Clinic, 1972). Intervention programs planned around the family's natural support networks will provide more effective recovery services. Given the context of family-wide trauma caused by disaster, the whole family may often be the most appropriate unit for therapy rather than only the troubled individual. Simple crisis intervention programs built around a few persuasive ideas have a better chance of adoption by both community and family (Drabek & Stephenson, 1971). Professionals are in a position to gather specific information for the community on how families are doing, what they actually need, and the requirements of special populations like the elderly or minority families, so that the community can provide appropriate types of aid.

Many of the mental health problems in disasters are not classic psychoses but rather stress precipitated by innumerable "hassles" victims experience in the aftermath. Mental health professionals can usually view individuals and families after disaster as normal people temporarily disrupted by a severe stress; thus, they can give concrete types of help for normal problems of living (Farberow, 1978). They can provide services to families through empathetic listening, nonjudgmental acceptance, showing interest and concern, helping focus and define problems, and helping establish priorities for recovery. They can also show the family how to provide this kind of therapeutic environment for their own members. Professionals have found their services are more effective when taken out into the community following disaster, rather than expecting families needing assistance to come to offices or clinics (Farberow, 1978).

One of the chief aims of mental health professionals should be to help families develop their own resources for recovery. If outside caregivers try to do everything, they offer victims so much help that there is little room for self-sufficiency, thus encouraging dependency.

CONCLUSIONS

Natural disasters change the physical and social landscapes of our lives. They produce changed people within changed families within changed communities. A single disastrous event can leave behind great diversity in the kinds and amounts of stress it creates in families. These stresses should not be viewed in isolation but rather as one point on a continuum of stresses the individual and family face every day.

The family's traditional ways of dealing with stress, its repertoire of coping resources, can be directed to meeting the challenges of disaster. As a stress-buffering environment, the family forms the first line of defense against the post-traumatic stresses precipitated by disaster. Thus, family capabilities to respond to disaster should be reflected in community disaster planning.

The most effective adjustment the family can make to lower the toll of disaster is to *prevent* as much physical and mental damage as possible.* Prevention includes family planning for possible emergencies, knowledge of the best ways to survive, some form of psychological preparation, and overt actions to prepare.

In the aftermath of massive disaster, the family should unify as quickly as possible and try to stay together; offer encouragement and emotional support to one another; reach out for help from relatives, friends, neighbors, or relief agencies; and reestablish normal roles and patterns as soon as possible. Long-term psychological trauma affecting the individual and/or family can be expected when the catastrophe is overwhelming or when recovery progress is significantly delayed. When disaster-related stresses accumulate and have no healthy outlet, emotional problems become likely.

Professional disaster planners and caregivers should broaden their perspective to include the whole family as a unit of concern. They are most successful when they help families develop their own resources

---

*Prevention could go even further if family members became more aware of the dangers confronting their communities and became interested in politically supporting mitigation efforts.

for recovery. The participation of families is pivotal to the morale and success of any community disaster prevention or relief program.

The many issues surrounding family behavior in extreme situations have only begun to be explored. Important questions needing further investigation are:

1) In what ways does the family support system foster better adjustments before and after disaster?
2) How can family disaster preparedness be fostered in spite of the natural reluctance of people to deal with the unpleasantness it suggests and to allocate the resources it requires?
3) What are the characteristics of people and families who do take adaptive actions compared to those who do not?
4) In addition to well-studied responses to warnings and evacuations, what are the family's common responses in other phases of disasters?
5) Why are disaster-related fears among children more intense in some families than in others? How could they be reduced? What long-term consequences might they have?
6) Do urban environments have higher proportions of nuclear families without relatives in the same area than rural environments? How dependent are urban families on urban-type services? Do factors like separation from extended kin and dependency on services make them more vulnerable to disasters?
7) In addition to insurance coverage and a financial reserve, are there other viable solutions to the family's economic dilemmas caused by disasters?
8) Where and how could survival-relevant skills and information be introduced into ongoing school programs, from elementary to university levels?
9) In what ways are the lessons from other successful prevention education programs for the public, like CPR training or prepared childbirth, applicable to disaster prevention programs?
10) Is the family capable of being a basic unit around which overall disaster planning can be tied?
11) How does government policy affect family coping and recovery after disasters?

The family can be a critically important resource for a community struggling to reestablish itself after a disaster. In light of this, more family-focused research and better family-oriented intervention programs will enhance the family's capability to survive disaster with a minimum of stress. Families that are coping successfully with disaster's problems will speed progress toward recovery for the whole community.

CHAPTER

9

War: Bringing the Battle Home

VICKI E. HOGANCAMP and

CHARLES R. FIGLEY

> When Tony left to go overseas, he was so full of enthusiasm and
> patriotism. He was proud to do his duty and serve his country.
> After he had been gone a few months, however, I began to sense
> a change in his letters. I couldn't quite put my finger on it, but
> there was something different. My suspicions were confirmed the
> day he came home. I looked into his eyes and knew this wasn't
> the same Tony who had left. The war had changed him.

The above quote is from a mother of a returned war veteran. The war
could have been any one of America's wars. Throughout America's
history—indeed, since earliest recorded time—soldiers have marched
off to war, leaving behind families and loved ones concerned for their
welfare during and following the campaigns. America is a nation of
veterans and their families. Of all the traumatic events that have affected
our citizens, none has impacted more of our population than war.

Although there is no precise accounting of the number of families and
dependents of American soldiers affected by war, available estimates
suggest the figure is considerable. According to a recent report by the

Administrator of Veterans Affairs (1980), approximately three-quarters of the living veterans in civilian life are married. Their 24.2 million spouses, 23.3 million dependent children (under 18 years of age) and 10.3 million other family members, combined with the 30.1 million veterans themselves, total up to more than 90 million. If we add the 3.4 million survivors of deceased veterans to this figure, the total number of families is *well* over 90 million or approximately 42% of the entire United States population.

The purpose of this chapter is to provide a counterpoint to the following chapter which focuses primarily on a special group of "warriors"—prisoners of war and hostages—and their families. Both chapters attempt not only to highlight the emotional upheaval for the victims, but also to discuss the special stressors and unique circumstances of the families. The memories of battle live on for those fortunate enough to have survived. The memories also live on in the families they rejoin. We shall examine the results of bringing the battle home.

STRESSORS FOR THE COMBATANT

In discussing the impact of war on both the combatant and his* family, it is perhaps appropriate to begin by identifying the elements of war which make it stressful.

Figley (1979) has identified four major components which constitute a traumatic event and has applied them to war. First, war is perceived as being *highly dangerous* by the combatant. The soldier fears for his life and for the lives of his comrades. For the combatant in the field, the fear of death is often present 24 hours a day, every day, for the length of his tour of duty. Second, the combatant experiences *a sense of loss.* Lives are lost, both friends' and enemies'. Youth and innocence are left behind. Illusions of the "glory" of war quickly vanish and the soldier's perception of immortality is destroyed. Third, war causes a sense of *helplessness.* The combatant is powerless to stop the fighting, devastation, and killing. Moreover, he has little control over the situation or even his own fate from moment to moment. Finally, the combatant is confronted with *destruction and disruption.* Everywhere he looks the physical signs of devastation are apparent: bombed-out buildings, burned jungles,

---

*The authors recognize that a small percentage (less than 2.4%) of women, too, have served in the military. However, the overwhelming majority of veterans in the United States (98%) are men. Therefore, for the purpose of this discussion the male gender will be used throughout.

wasted acreage. Moreover, with the technological advancements in warfare during the past 50 to 60 years, the physical devastation of war is even more blatant, serving as a constant, ugly reminder of war's aftermath.

It is not surprising, therefore, that social scientists and clinicians have observed, as early as the Civil War, psychopathological reactions among a small, but significant, number of combatants (Figley, 1978). The symptoms remain virtually the same, although the terminology has changed from war to war. "Prior to the First World War, psychological casualties resulting from war were seen simply as weak, lacking military discipline, or both" (Figley, 1978, p. xv). Then, with the onset of World War I soldiers were diagnosed as "shell-shocked," as a result of artillery fire which left them disoriented. Following World War I, the symptoms associated with combat stress were labeled "war neuroses" or "traumatic neuroses." During and after World War II all psychiatric casualties were subsumed under "exhaustion," later refined to "combat exhaustion" or "combat fatigue" during the Korean conflict (Figley, 1978). During America's most recent war in Vietnam, "acute combat reaction" was adopted as a generic term to refer to "all psychopathology associated with combat" (Kormos, 1978, p. 4). To some degree, all of these terms were used to describe typical symptoms associated with combat-related stress: irritability, disturbed sleep, disorientation, confusion, panic, apathy, etc.

However, despite commonalities of war that all combatants share—death, injury, destruction, emotional trauma—it is important to note that all wars are *not* alike. America has fought in a variety of different types of wars, in all corners of the world, for different political causes, using diverse military strategies, with varying societal responses and support. From the War of Independence to the Civil War, where brothers fought brothers, to the two World Wars that were to end all wars, to Korea and Vietnam, our "undeclared" wars, combatants have had to experience their own unique war and live through their own personal "hell."

STRESSORS FOR THE FAMILY

For the family of the combatant, the horror of war is no less real or intense. While the soldier is struggling to survive, the family at home is confronted with a myriad of adjustments as a result of the war-induced separation.

Separation Experiences

Miller (1978) describes the circumstances of the family during this period of waiting. He suggests that the family is a set of units with relationships among them. When a family member is lost—either temporarily or permanently, due to violent or nonviolent circumstances—the family is profoundly affected. In her work with families of prisoners of war, Boss (1980b) describes this as family boundary ambiguity (see Volume I, Chapter 2, for additional details).

Family members experience a wide range of emotions regarding the absent serviceman. Of primary significance is the possibility that their loved one is dead, injured, missing in action, or even captured by the enemy. This uncertainty leads to a reluctant, but inevitable, anticipation of loss (McCubbin, Dahl & Hunter, 1976). Their anxiety may be further heightened by the fact that at any given time they may not be aware of his exact location or be familiar with the type of environment in which he is stationed and fighting. Moreover, despite newsreels in the theater or nightly broadcasts on television, it is still extremely difficult for the family to fully comprehend what combat is actually like and what their absent member is experiencing. As a result of all these factors, the family's reactions to the separation may resemble a rollercoaster pattern ranging from optimisim to despair (McCubbin et al., 1976; Figley, 1980a,b).

Families may also undergo changes in their community networks, forced upon them by the military system. Some families may reestablish residence with relatives during the separation, while others are temporarily placed in military communities with other "waiting" families (McCubbin et al., 1976).

Additionally, the removal of the father/husband requires shifts in roles within the family system to compensate for his absence. Wives, perhaps for the first time, must learn to make decisions solo, take charge of the family, and fulfill the responsibilities of both parents. Children may be burdened with additional tasks because of the father's absence which require them to forego typical childhood activities and enjoyments and adopt a more mature and independent status. The family as a whole attempts to "close ranks" by separating out the servicemember's role and operate efficiently without him.

Added to these stresses are the typical pressures of normal family life, which often become exacerbated by the absent father/husband. For example, the normal period of adolescence can become further complicated as the male teenager rebels against the discipline and authority of the mother. For adolescent girls, during this normal period of increased interest in sexuality, father absence often manifests itself in an inability to relate to men and male peers (McCubbin et al., 1976).

Finally, the family is concerned that *if* the soldier returns, what will he be like? Will he have changed? What will he look like? Will he act the same? Will he still care for them? Moreover, the family members will probably experience doubts about their actions during the servicemember's absence: Will he be happy with the changes we have made? Will he be angry that we did this? Will he judge the way I have taken care of the children?

Homecoming and Reintegration

Whereas the experiences for the combatant and his family *during* the war produce intense stress, dealing with the process of integration upon return is equally, if not more, stressful. The veteran and his family may encounter numerous obstacles to successful readjustment and eventual adaptation. Based on more than 75 years of research on combat veterans and the process of their reintegration into society, several major sources of stress have been identified: psychological residue of war; changes at home during the soldier's absence; changes in the family structure; pressures on the veteran to return to "normal"; employment difficulties; and medical problems.

Psychological Residue of Combat. As noted earlier, many combatants experience emotional problems *in* combat. However, there are also those whose reactions to the war are *delayed* until months or years following combat experience (cf., Figley, 1978). These men may experience one or more of a list of symptoms which similarly affect victims of other life-threatening events, such as rape and natural disasters. (Figley, 1979).

As noted in Chapter 1, the latest edition of the *Diagnostic and Statistical Manual of Mental Disorders* (DSM-III, 1980), unlike the previous edition (DSM-II), includes a category which encompasses those individuals affected by catastrophic events. This category is referred to as "Post-traumatic Stress Disorder (PTSD)." The inclusion of this disorder in the DSM-III is based on considerable research conducted with war veterans and other survivors of traumatic events, and a consensus opinion among mental health professionals regarding the psychological "fallout" of an overwhelmingly stressful experience such as war combat, rape, and natural disasters.

Symptoms of PTSD include reexperiencing the traumatic event or events (e.g., life-threatening and horrifying battle scenes) through flash-backs, nightmares, and dreams. Victims also often lose interest in activities they once enjoyed; for example, hobbies, sports, and work. In these instances, the veteran may feel detached from people, experience difficulty in establishing and maintaining interpersonal and social relationships, or often feel little if any emotion at all. Various related symptoms, such as hyperalertness, impaired memory, feelings of guilt, shame or depression, irritability, or anxiety, are also common. Any one or a combination of symptoms of PTSD may have significant implications for the veteran in his attempt to readjust to family life, and he may experience a "considerable amount of difficulty fulfilling his responsibilities as husband and father" (Figley & Sprenkle, 1978, p. 56).

Changes in Society/Homeland

The home to which he returns is by no means the home he left or the home which he recalled and longed for during his absence (Schuetz, 1944-45, p. 375).

The veteran's adjustment to civilian life may be further complicated by changes which have occurred in society during his absence: for example, changes in the government (new administration, new government policies and programs), changes in societal norms and values (e.g., liberalized male-female relations, family life, sexuality, education), and economic changes (higher unemployment, lower standards of living). "The soldier observes few of these changes, and suffers their full impact all at once when he becomes a veteran and returns to civilian society" (Waller, 1945, p. 176). Indeed, during his absence shifts may have occurred in society's attitude toward the war resulting in rejection of the very cause for which he risked his life. This was, perhaps, most evident for Vietnam veterans who returned home to find unprecedented opposition to the war and antagonism directed at them for fighting in it (Figley & Leventman, 1980).

Changes in the Family. As noted earlier, the family during the period of separation realigns to compensate for the father/husband's absence. When the veteran returns and is reintroduced to this new family structure at the time of reunion, there may be some initial tension as new roles and responsibilities are negotiated. For instance, the husband may discover his wife has become more independent, assertive, and accustomed to "heading up the household." Reshifting role assignments to incorporate the husband back into the system again may cause stress between the veteran and his wife (cf., McCubbin et al., 1974). Hill(1949), for example, notes that when the father returns, the mother will compete for functions that she has learned to perform during his absence.

In addition, the veteran may be introduced to infants he has never seen or who have grown and matured into virtual strangers during his absence.

> Father rejection, perhaps more aptly termed "father strangeness" so far as the child is concerned, is often very apparent to the men. The child born since his father's induction or who has matured considerably since that time has a social world in which he apparently needs no father (Cuber, 1945, p. 29).

Given the transformations within the family, the veteran will need to allow himself sufficient time to become reacquainted with each family member and not be disappointed or feel rejected if reassimilation is not immediately forthcoming.

Pressure to Return to Normal. It is not uncommon for the veteran to sense a lack of understanding or appreciation for what he went through in the war. As one veteran complained: "Friends and family treat me like I have only returned from a summer vacation and now it is time to get back to work!" Free from his military role, the veteran was expected to resume, in a very short time, the roles and accompanying responsibilities of being a loving, supportive family member and citizen. Many veterans were not ready. Another veteran stated: "There was this incredible sense of pressure. I got to find a place to live; I got to get this stuff moved . . . we gotta do this, we gotta do that . . . but wait a minute! I'm still somewhere between Vietnam and here" (Canzoneri & Simon, 1981).

Usually the family is well-meaning, assuming that the veteran wants to put the war behind him, to function normally again, and to make up for lost time. Conversely, the family who has been on hold during the veteran's absence is now anxious to make plans for the future. Unfortunately, this lack of time to debrief, review, and decompress from his war experiences and adapt to being a civilian again may place additional stress on the veteran. Cuber (1945), in his study of World War II veterans, discovered a frequent desire on the part of veterans to escape from the obligations of the conventional family man, at least initially.

> I feel as if I must have a little time to play around some more. I

want to spend at least a summer as a single man without any of the obligations or responsibilities of a married man . . . then I think I will be ready to settle down (p. 28).

Disadvantage in the Labor Market

When war comes, we take these young men trained for peace and send them off to fight . . . we compel them to sacrifice their personal good and their personal lives to the collective good . . . then with a pat on the back and some hypocritical words of praise, we return them to competitive society, where, for a time at least, they compete at a considerable disadvantage (Waller, 1944, p. 106-107).

When the veteran returns, he is once again expected to fulfill the role of financial provider for the family. However, due to the interruption of his years away at war, he finds himself competing at a disadvantage with those who remained at home during his absence. For example, military service during World War II kept the serviceman out of the labor market for an average of 36 months (President's Commission on Veteran's Pensions, 1956). He was just beginning his career, when he was called into duty. For Korean and Vietnam combatants, although their tours were generally shorter than those in World War II, they were younger in age and thus were just beginning to seek employment prior to entering the war (President's Commission on Mental Health, 1979).

Furthermore, wars rarely teach skills which prepare the combatant for civilian life. As one World War II veteran said, "It's strange, we don't want to continue our soldiering and yet we want to do the things we have learned how to do" (Cuber, 1945, p. 28). Expertise in hand-to-hand combat, interrogation techniques, digging foxholes, machine gunnery, and setting up land mines are rarely marketable in the civilian labor force. In other words, survival skills appropriate for combat situations are no longer acceptable or useful to the veteran in civilian life.

This lack of marketable skills had resulted in protracted periods of job hunting for some veterans and even extended unemployment for others. Gibbs (1920) observed over 60 years ago

What knowledge had they of use in civil life? None. They scanned advertisements, answered likely invitations, were turned down by elderly men who said, "I've had two hundred applications. And none of you young gentlemen from the army are fit to be my office boy" (p. 549).

In contrast to the years following previous wars, the U.S. economy in the post-Vietnam war years was in a record slump. The prolonged and often unsuccessful search for employment intensified the stress for those veterans. Indeed, Vietnam veterans have recorded one of the highest unemployment rates of any group of veterans: 15% overall, with 30% for Black veterans (Figley & Southerly, 1980). Included in these statistics are those veterans with less-than-honorable or dishonorable discharges (commonly referred to as "bad papers") who found it virtually impossible to find meaningful work. All indications suggest that the 1980s may be even worse for this cohort of war veterans as a result of cuts in social programs, the shrinking job market, and soaring unemployment.

The families, too, were burdened by the problems facing the veteran in his struggles to enter and stay in the labor market. Wives often became sole supporter for the family, sometimes resulting in feelings of resentment. Children occasionally accepted part-time work to help supplement the family income. Other families had to apply for some form of social relief to tide them over. Voydanoff (Chapter 6) notes that the unemployed husband/father who now spends more time at home often disrupts normal family routine, and tensions increase within the family system.

Disabilities. Significant among the group of veterans who returned home with health problems were the disabled—some 2.7 million from the last three wars (Phillips, 1980). Due to scientific advancements in the medical professions, the number of soldiers surviving combat wounds has dramatically increased since World War II. Eighty-one percent of wounded men in Vietnam survived, in comparison to 74% in Korea and 71% in World War II (Lieberman, 1971). These men often returned home feeling bitter and angry about the war and the sacrifice of their health and limbs—a bitterness often shared by the family. Many of these men and their families became dependent on the Veterans Administration benefits for living expenses. But, as Lieberman (1971) notes, the amount of payments for the disabled are inadequate and minimal, for example, in comparison to settlements received for domestic automobile accidents.

Depending upon the severity of the veteran's disability, role reversals within the family were not uncommon (Johnson, 1980). Perhaps for the first time, the veteran found himself dependent on his family to perform the simplest tasks for him. Also, because of his inability to work, his wife had to take over as financial provider for the family. This shift in the family's power structure often generated feelings of low self-esteem and caused the veteran to question his masculinity and authority to head the family. Conversely, the family, in attempting to help the veteran, often overdid its caretaking and reinforced the veteran's dependency and helplessness (Figley & Sprenkle, 1978).

Long-term Health Hazards. Other medical problems create special difficulties for veterans—namely those which do not surface until months or even years following the war. As a result and in an attempt to secure government assistance for these problems, the burden of proof as to the war-relatedness of the illnesses falls on the veteran and his family (Bitzer, 1980).

Prisoners of war, for example, appear to have the strongest case regarding certain maladies that afflict them long after imprisonment. Only until very recently, however, were efforts made to respond to the special medical and emotional problems of POWs. A recent government report (Veterans Administration, 1980) documented some of the effects of war imprisonment—disabilities resulting from diseases such as beriberi, optic atropy, malaria, parasitic infection—which have persisted throughout the veteran's life and account for signficantly higher mortality and morbidity rates.

Less research activity is being devoted to what may be an even larger problem—chemical poisoning. Various reports of long-term damage due to exposure to chemical warfare have emerged over the years, beginning with World War I and II veterans and more recently with the "atomic" veterans who served in special units located within five miles of test detonation sites of the atom bomb back in the 1940s and 1950s (Rosenberg, 1980; Saffer & Kelly, 1982).

The situation with Vietnam veterans and Agent Orange poisoning is particularly noteworthy. Agent Orange is the best known of several chemical defoliants sprayed throughout Southeast Asia (especially South Vietnam) between 1962 and 1971 to eliminate dense jungle cover and thus allow American and allied troops to spot the enemy. It was later discovered, however, that Agent Orange was contaminated with a by-product known as TCDD (tetra chlorodibenzo-para-dioxin) or *dioxin*, which is one of the most toxic and potent synthetic chemicals known. The symptoms associated with 2,4,5-T exposure include: skin conditions; gastrointestinal problems; vision and/or hearing impairments, respiratory difficulties; various cancers; numbness or tingling in extremities; psychological changes, such as irritability and depression; fatigue; and birth defects in offspring (Whiteside, 1979).

Although the Veterans Administration has received over 10,000 claims for damages, and the number is increasing daily, the government has denied responsibility and compensation, pending a national epidemiological study of the long-term health factors involved in 2,4,5-T poisoning (Watriss, 1981). As a result, the veteran's family has had to accept both the financial and psychological consequences of the poisoning, as well as the burden of proof for health problems. Many of these men have been unable to work because of their health problems and many families have accrued medical bills in the thousands of dollars (Linedecker, 1982).

Unfortunately no definitive research has attempted to detect a direct cause and effect relationship between war and medical and psychological problems among POWs and combatants.

Substance Abuse. Another significant problem for returning veterans is substance abuse. The various substances abused by veterans throughout the history of civilization have changed, but the use among veterans has always been problematic. Drug abuse was particularly prevalent among Vietnam veterans due to the special and pathetic nature of their war. In a recent study conducted by Nace, O'Brien, Mintz, Ream & Meyers (1978), "39% of the sample were drinking heavily enough to be experiencing alcohol-related problems; 21% of the sample used heroin in the period since discharge; and 38% had used a narcotic" (p. 78). Of these men sampled, depression, criminal behavior, and unemployment were also noted as problems.

Although the Veterans Administration, in response to political pressure to deal with veterans' drug problems, set up Drug Dependence Treatment Programs, most of the veterans with problems have not sought treatment. In the case of Vietnam veterans, this is partially due to the VA's original policy to deny medical benefits to veterans with discharges under other-than-honorable conditions, who were the majority of veterans needing treatment (Stanton, 1980b). Of additional interest here is a 1973 report conducted for the U.S. Senate Committee on Veterans' Affairs, which notes that one of the areas requiring improvement by the Veterans Administration's mental health program is specialized alcoholism programs for *aging* veterans (Schottland, 1973).

DYSFUNCTIONAL COPING

The myriad of problems faced by the returning veteran and his family are of major social significance. A vast majority of the men who serve in overwhelmingly stressful situations in war and return to civilian life *do* cope effectively. They are somehow able to find the strength to endure. Yet for a significant percentage of veterans and families adjustments are slow and often unsuccessful. It is important therefore to consider some of the ineffective methods veterans and families have used in attempting to cope with the problems noted earlier before considering those successful strategies.

Denial and Silence

In an effort to protect themselves and the veteran from unpleasant reminders of the war, family members may attempt to deny the veteran's involvement in the war with hopes that he will quickly adjust and any problems will disappear. Therefore, they may adopt a stance of silence. In doing so, however, they often send "messages to the veteran suggesting that he should not talk about the stressful situation (because it makes the family anxious) and, above all, he should not share his emotions" (Figley & Sprenkle, 1978, p. 57).

The veteran himself often encouraged the family's silence. He, too, was hesitant to be reminded of his war experiences and somewhat afraid that his family would not understand—or possibly condemn his actions during the war—if he opened up to them. As one recent veteran said:

> Who would understand. You can't talk about Vietnam with different people . . . there's so many moral judgments and different values about what happened to people over there. "Oh, you're a baby killer, you're a mutilator." Even if they don't say it, it's the expression on their face. I guess I wish everybody understood what it's like to take another human life and not know if it's right or wrong and to live with it (Canzoneri & Simon, 1981).

Conversely, the family's silence was a form of self-protection. Although children often wanted to hear bloodcurdling tales of war (glamourized through books, television, or the movies), rarely could they comprehend the realities of war. For adults, hearing in graphic detail about the horrors of combat could often be overwhelming. As one wife of a veteran related:

> I didn't want to hear any more. It would totally destroy my image of what he was. He was a real sensitive person that did that. And what do you think that felt like for him, to finally open up to somebody and have them shut themselves off (Todd, 1981).

Bitterness

The need to blame someone or something for the disruption in their lives is strong for some families. For example, the veteran often feels angry at the government which sends him to war and then easily forgets about him upon his return home.

> The veteran is often bitter, because he is the one singled out to fight and die and experience horrors, because he gives so much and others so little, because civilians see the glamour of war and he sees the dirt and the dead men, because of his comrades who have been killed or wounded and perhaps allowed to starve when the fighting is over—because he has been used as a means (Waller, 1945, p. 177).

As one Vietnam veteran related, all he got when he returned was a Red Cross key chain telling him: Welcome Home. Your Country's Proud of You (Goldman, 1981).

Sadly, this anger and resentment towards the politicians and government often becomes displaced on the family because it cannot be directed toward those who deserve it. It is not uncommon for such displays of hostility to be directed at the wife and children because of their easy accessibility. As one veteran commented,

> I guess I do fly off the handle a little easier now and it seems to be at her, and I'm not really meaning it for her. It's kind of a frustration type of thing (Todd, 1981.)

Waller (1945) notes that "this bitterness is closely related to the veteran's tendency toward explosive aggression" (p. 177). Other wives have been the recipients of more violent outbursts:

> He was angry at me a lot . . . and he snapped. He grabbed me by the throat and threw me into the wall screaming at me (Todd, 1981).

The children who either witness or are recipients of such violence may become fearful of their fathers and remain so in the future:

> He's seen Barry go crazy, seen Barry do a lot of wierd stuff and it's affected him . . . he's scared. I feel he may always have the fear of his father that he does (Todd, 1981).

FUNCTIONAL COPING

Although there is no single way to deal effectively with stress or any quick cure to the problems associated with serving in war, there are some constructive coping methods the family can employ to promote healthier family functioning.

Understanding Stress Reactions

Understanding the elements of combat and their interrelationships which are traumatic for the veteran, and having an overall knowledge of typical stress reactions, can go a long way in easing the transition period. If the veteran feels his experiences are at least minimally understood, that the family appreciates what he has been through, it will relieve some of the tension during readjustment. Moreover, the family that is familiar with the symptoms associated with PTSD and prepares for the possibility of emotional fallout will not be shocked or afraid if and when the veteran displays such behaviors. Indeed, family members can be more effective and involved during the healing process.

Communication

An open communication network among family members will provide both the veteran and the family with a healthy, nonjudgmental environment in which to discuss thoughts and feelings about the war experience. If the family can adopt an attitude of acceptance and tolerance for the veteran's suffering and ventilation, misunderstandings and "bottling up" of emotions and frustrations will be prevented. Moreover, it is important for the veteran to be aware that his family has been under considerable stress during his absence. An equal appreciation on his part for the family's suffering will ease their burden as well.

Flexibility

The family's willingness to be flexible, allowing the veteran time to readjust to being home and to the changes that have occurred within the family, community, and nation will reduce the tension. As Burge (Chapter 7) notes,

Clearly the ease with which the family structure can responsibly undertake the realignment of roles during the recovery phase of the trauma will affect the amount of conflict experienced in their daily interactions (p. 16).

Family members need time to become reacquainted with the returning veteran, and vice versa, and to educate the veteran as to what events have taken place during his absence. In addition, the family needs to recognize and accept that the veteran may not be willing or able to pick up where he left off or be interested in doing the things he used to do with or for them prior to the war.

Support Services

One of the most significant resources for the veteran and his family in their attempts to cope may come from support outside the family system. It is therefore important that families be aware and knowledgeable about public and private agencies which offer veterans assistance with employment, educational opportunities, medical services and benefits, loans for businesses and housing, and psychological counseling. An excellent example of a support service available to veterans and their families is the Veterans Administration's "Operation Outreach" program. This program has set up storefront centers in various cities across the country to provide assistance to all Vietnam-era veterans and their families.

> . . . The programs are operated mostly by Vietnam veterans. They are seeing anyone and everyone—wives, sisters, disabled, dishonorable guys with bad papers. The theme is really that we are all fellow survivors, we are in it together, we have been touched one way or another by the Vietnam experience, and we have a responsibility to each other (Figley & Salison, 1980, p. 139).

Figley's thesis of "contact with fellow survivors" notes that "those who share the injuries are major sources of reassurance, strength, encouragement, guidance and counsel" (p. 139).

Similarly, Waller (1944) notes that

> the tendency of veterans to stick together for a time is not altogether unhealthy . . . to establish relations with the rest of society may be for them to cling to their own group, to cleave to their own kind, for a while . . . the society of veterans will thus furnish a sort of causeway leading to normal readjustment . . . (pp. 180-181).

This concept perhaps best explains the numerous veteran organizations active in our society (e.g., the American Legion, Veterans of Foreign Wars, Disabled American Veterans, Vietnam Veterans of America). Throughout the years these organizations have become better incorporated into society. They have expanded beyond limited services to veterans to provide assistance to families and the general community. These organizations and various other self-help groups established throughout the country can provide aid to families in times of crisis and influence government policies to benefit veterans and their families.

IMPLICATIONS FOR PROFESSIONALS

Although family members can act as a stress reducer or buffer for problems originating outside the family system, they cannot always solve everything. When it becomes apparent that the family alone is not sufficient, professional help may be beneficial to assist the veteran and his family in working through the stressors associated with the war.

Currently, most of the approaches to the psychosocial management of war-related problems focus almost exclusively on the individual veteran. This is not surprising, since the accepted form of treatment for most victims of catastrophe centers around the individual, blatantly ignoring the family connection (cf., Figley & Salison, 1980). Individually-oriented therapy may be initially necessary, as the veteran seeks to resolve specific war-related issues. These issues may need to be dealt with prior to resolving interpersonal and family problems. For example, Tony (from our case illustration) may choose either individual counseling or a group approach, such as a fellow veterans' "rap" group to share and come to terms with his emotional reactions to the war (with the guidance of a professional) (Lifton, 1978).

These kinds of individually-oriented services are quite appropriate for some veterans, indeed most veterans, but eventually it is important to incorporate the veteran's network of social support. This is most often his family, especially his wife, and at times parents and children should be included. For, as the chapter has pointed out, not only has Tony changed, but his family has changed as well. Including the family in treatment is based on both research (cf., Figley, 1978; Wilson, 1980) and the impressions of clinicians (Williams, 1981; Wilson, 1980), and is related to the importance of helping the veteran effectively integrate himself back into his social support group. Another obvious reason for including family members in treatment is that they too have been affected by the veteran's experiences either directly (i.e., the family in waiting during the war) or indirectly, through the experiences and behaviors of the veteran (e.g., veteran's violent behavior directed at one or more family members).

Seeing all family members together, as a unit, early in therapy will enable the therapist to better determine: 1) how the combat-related stress and the family problem(s) in which it is embedded are affecting each individual family member; 2) how the behavior of the family members may be reinforcing or exacerbating the difficulties; and 3) whether the family members have any understanding of post-traumatic stress disorder or the veteran's military experiences and how they might best respond to his suffering (Figley & Sprenkle, 1978).

There are several basic issues the therapist needs to consider relevant to treating veterans and their families.

1) The veteran may be hesitant to discuss his combat experiences for fear of rejection. Thus, he may be very sensitive to any behavior seen as judgmental or condemning. It is therefore important for both the therapist and the family to show understanding, compassion, appreciation, and empathy for his unique experiences. As a means of gaining the veteran's trust, the therapist may wish to consider using a veteran co-therapist—someone who has "been there" and can easily relate to the veteran's circumstances.

2) It is important for the therapist to create an environment in which the veteran feels comfortable sharing and expressing his emotions. It is not uncommon for families to reinforce traditional masculine stereotypes of nonemotionality (which the veteran himself may support). If the family can adopt an attitude of "It's OK if you cry; it's OK to let go," the veteran will feel more confident in sharing his feelings (Figley & Sprenkle, 1978).

3) The therapist must recognize that the veteran is not dealing with his combat-related stress in a vacuum; that is, he is attempting to cope with normal life stressors simultaneously. Typical transitions which occur for the family over the life cycle (e.g., birth of a child, economic hardships, illness, death of a family member) will produce added tension to the war-related problems already present. The therapist cannot ignore these other stressors in his therapy approach, but will need to create a balance between both.

4) The therapist will need to gain an understanding of the family's normal patterns of interaction. As Stanton and Figley (1978) note, family behavior and communication styles developed over a period of time

become predictable. The therapist, therefore, may need to modify certain habits and introduce new strategies for resolving familial conflict.

CONCLUSION

Of all the catastrophes that befall mankind, perhaps none so dramatically affects a majority of society as war. War exacts a heavy toll in lives, injuries and destruction, and often leaves permanent scars on the psyche of its combatants. The family of the veteran also suffers from the crisis of war. The stressful experiences during the war, combined with the difficulties encountered upon reintegration of the veteran into civilian life, all impact on the family system to disrupt normal functioning.

Overall, the families who endeavor to understand the veteran's military experiences, who can openly and safely communicate, who have a flexible family structure and take advantage of available outside support services will be most successful during the healing process. Professionals can also play a significant role during the readjustment period by creating a safe and nonjudgmental environment in which the veteran and his family can work through the combat-related problems affecting the family.

Despite the lessons learned from previous wars, we would probably be naive to assume that no more Americans will march off to war. It is therefore important that we be aware of the consequences of such a commitment, for both the combatants *and* their families.

CHAPTER

10

Captivity: The Family in Waiting

EDNA J. HUNTER

I came rushing into the house in time to catch the telephone on the fifth ring. A voice on the other end identified himself as being with the State Department. He was terribly sorry to inform me that only a few hours ago the American Embassy in Tehran had been taken over by student radicals and my husband was among the hostages. Yes, to the best of their knowledge, he was unharmed. No, they had no idea yet what the radicals wanted. No, those were all the details he had. Yes, he would keep me informed.

During the Iranian hostage crisis in 1979, similar scenarios were repeated in 62 homes across the United States, and the families and friends—indeed the entire nation—held its breath to see what would happen next. What happened was a dramatic 444-day siege during which we worried not only for the welfare of the hostages, but for their families as well, who were also victims of this traumatic event.

One might hastily conclude that wartime captivity or hostage incidents touch the lives of few individuals. On the contrary, there were over 130,000 American service personnel known to be captured during World War II; over 7,000 taken POW during the Korean War; 82 in the Pueblo incident; 600 returned to U.S. control in the Spring of 1973 from Vietnam;

and 63 involved in the Embassy takeover in Iran recently. As a result of terroristic attacks, during the 10-year period from 1968 through 1978, there were 1,017 deaths and 2,509 persons injured. Add to those figures the loved ones of the captives, and it is obvious that many thousands of individuals have been called upon to cope with this kind of crisis. These figures do not include persons who remain in the missing in action status, or their families (Hunter, in press).

A captivity or hostage-taking experience can significantly impact families in two ways. They are affected directly through the long-term problems of the ex-captive, and indirectly through the resulting adjustment difficulties within the family. This chapter focuses on the unique stressors associated with a captivity situation. Specifically, our discussion focuses on the circumstances of prisoners of war (POWs) and servicemen missing in action (MIAs) and their families during the Vietnam War, as well as the experiences of the hostages recently held in Iran and their families. The chapter addresses both the similarities and differences between the various captivity situations, with special attention paid to their effects on the family members. It also presents recommendations, based on past research,* for professionals and government agencies often called upon to work with and assist these families.

Although captivity experiences are similar in some aspects to other major catastrophes, they differ significantly in that the resulting stress for the family members is both *prolonged* and *indefinite*. Moreover, the situation is ambiguous and often holds the threat of death or permanent loss of the captive family member, but often without immediate confirmation. The threat is ongoing; it does not end in one hour, one week, one month, perhaps even one year. The family cannot "accept" the loss of their missing member, nor can the captive totally reconcile the loss of his freedom. As a result, the family experiences both prolonged and intermittent feelings of helplessness, hopelessness, powerlessness, anger, guilt, and rage which combine to prevent rapid and effective coping strategies from developing within the family system.

Some of the earliest studies focusing on captivity stress derive from World War II investigations of wartime stress (Duvall, 1945; Hill, 1945,

---

*This chapter primarily draws on the findings of a seven-year longitudinal study of the families of POWs and MIAs in Southeast Asia during the Vietnam conflict from 1964 to 1973, as conducted by the Center for POW Studies in San Diego, California (Hunter, 1980). Moreover, the Iranian crisis will be discussed in terms of the observations and recommendations of a multidisciplinary group of scholars, the Task Force on Families of Catastrophe, who developed a report which focused on the captive situation as it affects the families of the hostages.

1949; Stolz, 1952, 1954). More recently, the Yom Kippur War in Israel resulted in substantial attention by psychologists and sociologists to family members' efforts to cope with wartime stress (Spielberger, Sarason & Milgram, 1981). The bulk of the literature focusing primarily on the effects of captivity on families comes from studies conducted at the Center for POW Studies (Hunter, 1977; Plag, 1974). Most recently, an interdisciplinary group of scholars (Task Force on Families of Catastrophe) extended the work of the Center for POW Studies and other research on victimology to make timely and relevant observations about the families of the American hostages in Iran (Figley, 1980a).

What accounts for this increased interest in captivity stress? First, the U.S. military has recorded significant increases of *married* military personnel since the advent of the all-volunteer forces in 1973 (Hunter, Den Dulk, and Williams, 1980). When they are deployed, these service personnel leave behind families who must cope with extreme and prolonged stress should the service person be taken prisoner of war, become missing in action, or be taken hostage. Second, with worldwide terrorist activity on the rise, the risk of capture by radicals necessarily draws attention to this stressor and its effects on family members (as evidenced by the Iran hostage crisis and the kidnapping of military and diplomatic officials). The knowledge gleaned by the studies conducted at the Center for POW Studies, as well as the work of the Task Force and other scholarly groups, remain of interest today to military planners, to service delivery professionals, the State Department, and other government agencies, as well as large international corporations who send employees and their families into developing nations where the risk of terrorism is high (Figley, 1980a; Hunter, 1981a).

UNDERSTANDING THE STRESSORS OF CAPTIVITY

Although any particular captivity experience is unique with regard to treatment by the captor, responses of the captive, effects on family members, processes of coping and later effects of the experience which reverberate within the family system (Hunter, 1977; Segal, Hunter & Segal, 1976), there are similarities for both the captive and the family. This section discusses the elements of captivity which are stressful for the captive and his family, using examples from the Vietnam POW experience and the 1979 Iran hostage crisis.

For the Captive

As stated above, every captive situation is different and the degree of stress experienced by the captive will be dependent on a number of factors.

Duration. The length of captivity will affect the degree of experienced stress. For example, the average confinement for the POWs in Vietnam was five years in comparison to a "short" 14 months for the hostages held in Iran.

Treatment. Treatment by captors varied in these two situations. The POWs held in Vietnam were methodically tortured for the first months of captivity (especially those captured from 1964-1969) (Berg & Richlin, 1977). The Vietnamese offered little or no medical treatment, leaving injuries untreated and broken bones unset. (Vietnam POWs with open head wounds—resulting from surviving an air crash immediately prior to capture—usually died in prisons.) Although some of the hostages in Iran reported incidences of physical, verbal, and mental abuse and being subjected to life-threatening situations, overall there was minimal mistreatment. Indeed, the hostages in Iran were kept in good physical condition and permitted brief periods of exercise after the initial few weeks subsequent to the takeover. Moreover, as evidenced by Richard Queen's early release, the Iranian students were concerned for the overall physical health of their captives and provided medical attention when needed.

Diets differed as well. In Southeast Asia, the food consisted mainly of pumpkin soup and a bit of wormy rice, month after month, year after year. Although not up to the standards of a normal American diet, the food served the hostages in Iran was sufficient to maintain the health of the hostages (Hunter, 1981a).

Group Support. The two captivity situations also differed with respect to the amount of group support. In Southeast Asia, communication between prisoners was forbidden, and no paper, pencils, radios, or other diversionary activities were routinely provided, beyond the normal captor-captive interactions and interrogations seeking to obtain propaganda. This almost total lack of communication in the early years of the Vietnam conflict did not occur in Iran except for the few hostages who were segregated from the others, or those who were held in solitary for periods of time. The hostages were permitted to interact with each other and were allowed to engage in recreational activities.

Contact with Families. With regard to communications with families, there was absolutely no contact for as much as three years following capture for some families of POWs in Vietnam, if then. Indeed, for many MIA families, there has yet to be confirmation of death or imprisonment (Hunter, 1980). In contrast, many letters passed between the hostages in Iran and their families, although with little consistency.

Homecoming and Reintegration. For those former POWs in Southeast Asia who spent so many years in strict isolation, the time-killing mechanisms they employed to cope with that isolation, the degree to which they slowed down ("geared down"), the routines or rituals they developed while prisoners, and the fantasizing they engaged in because of the lack of other diversions all became deeply ingrained (Deaton, 1975). Thus, upon return, those men isolated longest took longer to "gear up," to handle confusion, and to retrieve their minds from the world in which they had lived so long. After release, they tended to view life and freedom as more important than anything else in the world, perhaps even to the exclusion of the needs of their families. Similarly, the Iranian hostages who had been inactive, coping with boredom and idleness and limited in their ability to be physically active, were anxious to capitalize on their freedom and came home full of energy to get on with life. Unfortunately, for some of the families of the captives, the separation had been extremely busy and nonstop. As one wife commented, "We needed different types of recuperation."

The captive also returned with guilt feelings which persisted into the post-release period and affected family functioning. These guilt feelings occurred as a result of a combination of factors: the captor's verbal barrage; the powerlessness and loss of self-esteem ("I'm being punished, thus I must be guilty"); guilt over the family's being left alone to cope; guilt over not behaving up to one's own standards, or of capitulating under duress and signing a confession or propaganda statement; guilt over returning with the thought that perhaps others did not live because they had resisted harder, or even had died trying to effect *your* rescue (Hunter, 1981a).

The Center's POW studies indicated that the ex-captives expected, despite their prolonged absences, that the family would have changed little during the hiatus. Many were totally unprepared for the "new," mature, highly independent wives who awaited their return. Ironically, the wives, fully anticipating that their husbands had changed drastically as a result of their traumatic experiences, found little change, according to their reports. Captivity, however much it had solidified the men's basic personality traits, had not actually changed them (Hunter, 1981c; McCubbin et al., 1974). This held equally true for the returned American hostages from Iran.

For the Families

Separation. When a family member is lost, either temporarily or permanently, the family is profoundly affected. The elements of the captivity experience which are particularly upsetting for family members include the ambiguity of the situation and the indeterminate duration of the stressor, which result in feelings of helplessness and hopelessness, disrupting normal functioning. A primary emotion experienced by family members, especially during the initial months, is fear—fear not only for the captive but for themselves and their eventual fate as well. As time passes, feelings of isolation, alienation, anger, guilt, hostility, and depression develop, as do psychophysiological stressors arising from forced role changes within the family structure and the requirement for one parent to fill the dual mother/father role. These feelings will be experienced in a type of emotional rollercoaster pattern which finds family-member reactions ranging from hope to despair to rage and remorse (Figley, 1980a). The wife of a serviceman missing in action in Vietnam, commenting on the plight of the waiting Iranian hostage families, made the following observations based on her own personal experiences:

> The families of the hostages are probably experiencing all of Kübler-Ross's steps of the grief cycle, on a "temporary" basis. They are bouncing back and forth within that cycle. . . . They are experiencing a sense of helplessness; they cannot control their own lives . . . their once-secure family now rests on the whims or fickleness of captors who are highly suspect. . . . They cannot take charge of the issue that has disrupted their lives; it is far too big. . . . Wives will experience intense fear for their husband's safety. They will also be angry, because they have been left alone, and then they will feel guilty because they are angry. . . . The final outcome is uncertain; the "limbo" could end tomorrow or next year. . . . Some wives may be able to reach decisions, based only

on their husband's pre-stated wishes. . . . Others may be able to
demonstrate more independence or autonomy. Some may be par-
alyzed (Foley, 1980).

After these emotional ups and downs continued month after month and
year after year, both the captive and the family tended to level out their
emotions and develop what has been termed "psychological numbing"
or blunted affect (Hunter, 1981a).

Continuing ambiguity is extremely stress-producing. Moreover, stress
is often related to actual physical illness, as well as to family dysfunctioning (Boss, 1980a; Holmes & Rahe, 1967; Lewis, Beavers, Gossett &
Phillips, 1976;). Based upon the factor of ambiguity, the Center's studies
of the Vietnam POW/MIA wives predicted that personal, psychological
and physical adjustment would *decrease*, going from comparison group
wives (wives of military men who had not been taken POW), to POW
wives whose husbands had returned, to wives of men killed in action
(KIA), and, lastly, to the MIA wives, who would be expected to manifest
the *greatest* number of psychological and health problems. These four
categories of wives were compared on an index derived from a health
inventory completed four years after the POWs' release, and the hypothesis was supported. The MIA wives, as a group, reported significantly poorer physical and emotional health than the KIA wives, the
POW wives, and the comparison group wives (Hunter, 1980). Similarly,
family members of the Iranian hostages reported physical ailments
throughout their ordeal, ranging from sleeplessness, irritability, depression and lack of concentration.

Because ambiguity and indefiniteness characterize any captivity experience, the family members find it difficult to take positive actions to
resolve their dilemma; yet they discover they are forced to make changes
because of the sudden gap in the family system. The family may want
to leave that gap open, but as time passes, the missing member's role
is likely to be reduced in order for the family system to function effectively. Either way, the roles which the captured person filled previously
must be assumed by family members remaining within the system or
by others from outside it, if the family is to achieve some balance of
family homeostasis and continue functioning (Boss, Hunter & Lester,
1977).

Homecoming. Although the period of family disruption following the
capture is extremely difficult, in contrast with the popular view homecoming can be equally stressful, since at that time family members must

once again make shifts in family role structures in addition to adjusting to other changes which have occurred during the period of captivity (Stratton, 1978). Typically, neither the released captive nor his family anticipate the many adjustment problems associated with the reunion/reintegration process.

Both the captive and the family members begin the family reintegration process with misconceptions and incongruent "fantasies set in concrete," as one former POW wife expressed the marital discrepancy. For example, prior to homecoming, many wives expressed strong fears about the possibility of lingering exotic illness, acute psychosis, or homosexual behaviors in their husbands. Fortunately, anticipatory fears were usually worse than reality. Few of these dire predictions materialized, and where problems did exist, the wives found they could adjust to the "known" more easily than to unknowns.

During the Iran crisis, some of the fears of the family members were fueled by "experts" who predicted drastic changes in the mental health of the hostages upon repatriation. As one wife noted, "We were constantly bombarded with 'horror stories' from the doctors about all the dreadful things that were going to become evident when our people came home" (Morefield, 1982). As history now shows, these prognoses never came true; however, they caused an additional burden of stress for some families.

COPING

Dysfunctional Coping

The uncertainty inherent in a captivity situation can result in a breakdown of the family's coping ability, leaving family members with dysfunctional strategies for handling the stress.

Stagnation. Perhaps most common is the family's inability to act and move on with life. Many families are hesitant to make shifts in the family structure to compensate for the missing member's absence, and thus they attempt to operate as if the absent member were still present (Boss, 1980a). Often this situation results in unclear, undefined lines of responsibility and authority and a lack of leadership. Decisions are postponed or never made. This was particularly true for those families where the missing member was MIA in Vietnam. Because of the government's policy which kept the wives in an ambiguous marital status for years after the end of the conflict, it has been impossible for some families to resolve their loss, to grieve, and then proceed with life (Hunter, 1981b).

Self-enforced Isolation. Many families, both during the Vietnam war and the Iran hostage siege, felt stigmatized or "singled out." For example, during the Iran crisis some families felt they were the center of attention whenever they were out in public. They were often the recipients of prolonged stares from strangers and the object of curiosity. Moreover, many were constantly beset by the media. For the families of the POW/MIAs, many of the women discovered there really was no acceptable social role for women in an ambiguous marital status. They often reported feeling like a "fifth wheel," useless and superfluous (Hunter, 1980). As a result of this unusual attention, many families isolated themselves from friends and community, preferring to keep to themselves rather than be objects of watchfulness. Moreover, they often felt no one understood what they were going through, so why bother to socialize.

Blaming. For captive families, there is an initial tendency to blame someone, and at first the wife is likely to blame herself. There is much guilt, both for the parents of the captured person, as well as for wives and children. There are ruminations about what could have been: "We could have done so many things together"; "Perhaps I didn't raise him to be strong enough to survive."

Later the blame shifts from self to the captive: "He shouldn't have left us"; "He could have asked for a different duty assignment." Still later, the blame, anger and hostility shift to the government organization: "The war is wrong"; "He shouldn't even be over there"; "They aren't trying hard enough to find/release him." Most families eventually discovered the need to overcome the extreme guilt and anger in order to survive and to function effectively once again (Hunter, 1981b).

Parental Pressure/Neglect. Research shows that the ability of children to cope with extreme stress is a reflection of their mothers' ability to cope effectively (Hunter & Hickman, 1981; McCubbin et al., 1974, 1977). The Center's studies of the Vietnam POW/MIA families showed that the mother often did not want to discuss the missing father because it was too painful for her. Often she was so involved with her own ambiguous situation that children were closed out; she had no time to listen to them. Sometimes the children felt as though they had been abandoned by *both* parents. Very young children, who did not really understand the situation, tended to accept only what they could handle emotionally at that point in their development. At first, many were adamant that their father was alive; they rejected his death completely, even when the mother had finally accepted it. In some instances mothers tended to place too much responsibility on the child, especially firstborn sons. They were now the "head of the household," and they were expected to "take care of mother" (Hunter, 1980).

Younger brothers and sisters of MIAs were also affected deleteriously. Parents were sometimes so overwhelmed with grief for the lost child that they neglected the living children. As one young adolescent boy remarked, "My parents always talk about my dead older brother, but I'm alive! I guess I'll have to commit suicide to get them to care about what I do."

Functional Coping

What are the characteristics of those individuals and families best able to cope with the stress of captivity? Research shows that older, more highly educated and mature individuals with firmly ingrained values, a sense of humor, and a commitment to a cause appear more likely to function well with the stresses of captivity (Hunter, 1977; Nardini, 1973; Spaulding, 1975). Long-established marriages with open communication, high achievement, religious-moral orientations, families with children, and flexibility of family role structure are those that appear to cope more effectively with stressful family disruption (Hunter, 1977; McCubbin, 1979; Nice, 1978; Nice, McDonald & McMillan, 1981). Specific actions which appear directly related to functional families include taking positive actions, structuring time, maintaining family routines/rituals, actively seeking group support, and maintaining an active social life.

Preparation. Studies indicate that where couples have been able to discuss, prior to the crisis, the possibility of something happening which would prevent the return of the husband, those wives were better able to handle the ambiguous separation resulting from the captive situation. In other words, where the couple faced the possibility of the man being killed, taken prisoner, or being declared missing in action during war or being held hostage in a foreign country, the wife was more likely to have taken preventative measures such as arranging for housing, power of attorney, or sufficient finances to reduce potential problems for the family during the separation (Hunter, in press). To prepare for minimizing the stress during the repatriation process, the family should attempt to be fully informed about the details of the captivity experience in particular and, if possible, be educated about "typical" captivity situations in general. Stress can be significantly reduced if both parties are given sufficient information about long-term stress disorders. Family members will then come to recognize their feelings and reactions as normal responses and feel more at ease during the transition.

Positive Action. By taking positive actions and looking to the future, family members can counteract some of their feelings of helplessness and powerlessness. Maintaining normal family routines and functioning (e.g., celebrating birthdays and holidays, taking vacations) will help promote a feeling of power or control even when little exists. For the Vietnam POW/MIA wives, as well as the wives separated from spouses during the Iranian hostage crisis, necessity bred independence. These wives learned to make legal and financial decisions, buy and sell family property and goods, make family decisions and discipline the children, even though that had been the husband's role in the past. But these abilities were not developed immediately. Personal in-depth interviews by the Center's staff in 1972, prior to the POWs' release, indicated that after the initial shock, numbness, anger and rage, the depressed stage set in, and it usually ended sometime between the second or third year following casualty. At that point, the wives typically made a conscious decision that in order to cope with their marital limbo, they had to quit "marking time in place" and get on with living. However, coping effectively with the captivity of the husband to some extent meant closing out his role within the family system (Boss, Hunter & Lester, 1977; Hunter, 1980, 1981b).

Interestingly, during separation, POW wives who had closed out the husband's role (that is, made all decisions and took actions as if the husband were no longer in the family system) actually coped better than those who did not, as measured by fewer personal and emotional adjustment problems, children's problems, and so forth.

The Special Case of Wives and Parents of MIAs. In the special case of MIA families, most wives were finally able to accept the fact that the husband was dead once the other POWs returned and their husbands did not. Memorial services held at that time were helpful for these wives since the ritual aided them in completing the grief cycle and reaching the final stage of acceptance (Hunter, 1981b).

But what about the parents? Their response to such a crisis, in many ways, was even more difficult. Many of the wives have commented that they truly believed not only that the parents suffered more, but also that their grief appeared more prolonged. The difficulties the parents encountered and their ability and inability to cope deserved more attention than was forthcoming either during the Vietnam conflict or the Iranian hostage situation. The spotlight was primarily on wives and children. Parents were often ignored, not only by governmental support services and officials, but also by the media (Morefield, 1982).

The Vietnam studies showed that parents suffered differently from wives and children. Parents were more likely to express doubt about their sons' abilities to withstand the difficult incarceration. They questioned whether they themselves had prepared their "child" to cope with imprisonment. They recalled childhood incidents which proved, at least in their own minds, that their child could not possibly cope with isolation, strange diets, or lack of exercise within a prison environment. They then blamed themselves for such deficiencies in training, and whether real or imagined, their guilt about their own deficient parental performance had to be dealt with, and their fears had to be eased if they were to resolve their grief (Foley, 1980).

The plight of the parents of those missing in action in Vietnam was particularly poignant. Still suffering even today are those elderly parents who will probably *never* be convinced that their sons are dead. As one mother said, "You wives can still have another life; he was my only son; I shall never have another. I shall always hope that some day he will come walking through that door."

Studies also found that fathers of MIAs reacted differently to their loss than did the mothers (McCubbin & Metres, 1974). During a series of religious retreats held for families in the summer of 1973 shortly after the return of the POWs from Southeast Asia, attention was focused on these parents' grief. Mothers especially showed a need to talk about their experience, their grief, frustrations, and aspirations, whereas fathers appeared to seek help in expressing their feelings and in getting in touch with their anger and frustrations that lay hidden beneath a façade of understanding silence.

Parents too went through the stages of grief as wives did, and they suffered physical symptoms such as anorexia, insomnia, and fatigue, as well as psychological reactions such as preoccupation with the images and memories of the missing son. Some parents felt that the Vietnam war was totally unjustified and therefore their sons' casualty could not be reconciled by reference to the "traditions of our country" and "the price of freedom." For others, however, the tragedy could be explained by reaffirmation of their beliefs in these patriotic values. Unlike the mothers, most fathers did not appear willing to express their feelings openly or to discuss the personal meaning of their sons' casualty (McCubbin & Metres, 1974).

Parents, it seems, attended these religious retreats for reasons which differed, at least with respect to focus, from those of the wives of POW/MIAs. For the wife of the ex-captive or MIA wife, attendance at the retreat merely for the "opportunity for a vacation" appeared to be much more important than it was for the parents. Perhaps wives who had to cope with the practicalities of raising children, pursuing careers, or establishing new lifestyles, had already "come to terms" with themselves and their future plans, while mothers were still struggling to come to terms with their feelings about their loss. In other words, wives were asking *"How* do I cope," while mothers still asked, *"Why* did it happen and what are the chances he will still return?" (Hunter, McCubbin & Benson, 1974).

Some parents emphasized the importance of looking at the entire situation through their sons' eyes: "He loved the military and wouldn't have been happy doing anything else"; "He knew the risks and was willing to accept them because he believed in what he was doing, even if it meant the possibility that he would die in combat." Despite such reasoning, parents nonetheless found it difficult to accept their loss. Most parents, more so than the wives, reported that religion had helped them cope with their situations. For some parents, their beliefs and religious teachings were the only possible way to explain the casualty and the hardships and pain they had endured over the months and years. Through prayer they sustained hope: through their beliefs they gained understanding.

At the time of the retreats, these parents still faced dilemmas and had to work out equitable and personally satisfying balances between conflicting sets of tasks:

1) between acknowledging and accepting the ultimate loss of a son and yet maintaining hope for his eventual return;
2) between concentrating on commitments to other family members and devoting greater energy toward reconciliation of the MIA situation;
3) between pursuing a personal, active, and unrelenting cause for obtaining a full acounting and demanding more from government agencies; and
4) between moving forward with their lives and remaining committed to a life centered around their absent sons.

As some parents slowly began to realize their sons probably were not coming home, they repressed the thoughts because of the guilt which they aroused. A few parents implicitly believed that their constant and never-ending preoccupation with thoughts of their sons' survival was, in fact, the very force which kept them alive. One mother said, "I have often felt guilty for not having thought about my son every moment." (McCubbin and Metres, 1974).

Parents, like the wives, felt helpless and powerless. To gain some control over the situation some had virtually let it become a way of life. They were totally involved in local and national POW/MIA activities, such as letter writing, campaigning, and talking to local civic groups. After many years, however, by 1973 some were asking, "When do I stop?"

Nonetheless, most parents, mothers in particular, as well as wives, felt they had changed and grown personally as a result of the total experience. Most believed they had gained self-confidence and matured in their ability to relate to the public and to stand up for what they believed in.

Short-term Coping. It is noteworthy that wives, as well as captives, found it effective to cope in six-month segments: "He'll be home by Christmas."; "He'll be home by June." Many wives have said, "Had I known what I had to cope with in the very beginning, I would have said, 'There is no way I can do it,' and I might have killed myself." Thus, analogous to the philosophy of Alcoholics Anonymous, the goal appears to be to cope one day at a time, or even one hour at a time when necessary (Hunter, 1981b). Even captives found that in their prayers, after many months passed, they ceased praying for freedom; instead they thanked God for having given them the strength to get through the day.

Communication. Open communication can explain and thus alleviate many problems which might arise because of the changes in family roles, the wife's past feelings about having been "deserted," or the ex-captive's expressed need for moments of solitude. The ex-captive and the wife should both realize that discipline of the children may be a difficult issue after the long absence. The wife may feel defensive if the long-absent husband comments on the children's misbehavior, because she feels his remarks reflect on how she has performed her dual role during his captivity. And the returning husband may interpret his wife's new-found independence and competency as evidence that he is no longer "needed"—that he no longer has a role within the family. Only when feelings are shared can family reintegration proceed. As time passes, family members will discover they have unexpected strengths and abilities to survive, of which they were previously unaware (Hunter, 1981c),

Support from Other Families

Interactions with other families who are experiencing or have experienced similar situations will provide needed support and reassurance and give insights to family members about the predictable processes of separation and adaptation. Wives interviewed by the Center's staff indicated frequently that other POW/MIA wives offered the greatest amount of support to them. Those who had been in limbo longer were of tremendous assistance to the others in the early stages of waiting and grieving. When the loss first occurred, these wives reported they thought they would never be able to survive, but when they were afforded the opportunity of talking with others in the same situation who had survived, they were able to recognize that it was possible to shed their depressions, laugh and enjoy themselves once again (Hunter, 1977, 1980, 1981b, 1981c, in press).

The families of the Iran hostages also discovered the benefit of support by the other families. The opportunities afforded the families to get together (e.g., State Department briefings, the flag ceremonies in Hermitage, Pennsylvania, the efforts of the Family Liaison Action Group (FLAG), an organization that was established specifically for the families of the hostages by the families themselves, or the West Point connection for the homecoming) were helpful for sharing experiences, talking through problems, legitimizing fears and doubts, etc. The support of the group is very crucial for survival for both the captive and the family members (McCubbin, Hunter & Dahl, 1975).

INTERVENTION IMPLICATIONS

The preceding sections of this chapter examined the unique aspects of captivity as a family stressor and presented some of the functional and dysfunctional responses of families to that stressor. Now let us turn to some of the strategies or programs for preventing or attenuating problems associated with captivity, based upon past research findings. These strategies fall into two major categories: 1) recommended behaviors for effective professional assistance; and 2) suggestions for governmental policies and programs which should be implemented in future wartime POW/hostage crises.

Effective Professional Assistance

The professional who will be most effective in helping the family cope is one who is an informed, empathic listener. The professional's first task may simply be one of educating the family members about typical stress reactions. Family members should be assured their behaviors are "normal" reactions under the circumstances. The professional should be nonjudgmental. Family members should be encouraged to share their feelings without their being labeled as "good" or "bad." Indeed, they may need, at times, to ventilate their anger and hostility upon the counsellor. Above all, the therapist should not "feel sorry" for them; he or she must allow them to face the reality of loss. The effective therapist realizes that each individual must find his/her own unique coping mechanisms. What assists one family may present added problems for another. For example, contact with the news media may be welcomed by one person, but abhorred by another as an added stressor.

Those families who shun social activities or are geographically isolated will be particularly in need of professional help. Empathic, well-informed counsellors who understand what the families are going through can be very helpful to those who must cope with the stressors associated with a captivity experience.

Suggested Governmental Policies and Programs

Based upon the Vietnam POW/MIA experience and the Iranian hostage crisis, a number of suggestions have been made which can perhaps help families who find themselves in similar situations in future years (Figley, 1980a; Hunter, in press). First and foremost, there should be an outreach program from the very beginning because that is when the need for support from others is greatest for these families. For example, when the Center for POW Studies' staff first contacted the wives in 1972, many of the husbands had already been missing or POWs for five, six, or even seven years. The wives asked, "Where were you when I *really* needed you?" (Hunter & Plag, 1973).

Of primary importance is the need for each family to be assigned a "point of contact." This individual would be able to coordinate information flow both to and from the family, run interference and provide general services (e.g., legal, medical, financial, and emotional) to the family upon request. This person should be a trained professional, experienced in working with families undergoing a captivity situation, sensitive to the individual needs of the family and available night or day (Figley, 1980a; Hunter, in press). A liaison would be a buffer between the family and the outside world and could potentially reduce a large amount of the stress experienced by the family. The government should also encourage and provide opportunities for families to meet together. These family interactions will decrease feelings of isolation and that no one cares or understands what they are going through. A forum should be provided in which they can vent their frustrations (Foley, 1980).

The appropriate government agency should keep close contact with the families on a regular basis, even when there are no new facts to report. Those facts which are available should be shared with family members, especially if they are not particularly encouraging. Immediate updates are of critical importance when there has been a change in the captivity situation. It is imperative that the families be informed as quickly as possible to avoid their receiving the information from other sources (e.g., media, rumor) which could possibly distort the facts.

With regard to treating *parents* of captives or hostages who have been classified as missing in action or possibly dead, the clinician must remember that helping parents understand and accept such an outcome may simultaneously *increase* their feelings of guilt and frustration. After months or years of maintaining hope in the face of overwhelming odds, and keeping alive the active search for some answer, any inclination towards "giving up" will bring on feelings of guilt and self-condemnation. Nonetheless, during the period when the parents await word from governmental agencies about the fate of their sons, the clinician can play a valuable role by assisting in the alleviation of these anxieties and feelings of guilt—feelings normally associated with the process of "acceptance" of an outcome of possible non-return.

It is also recommended that an ad hoc group of advisors be established from the outset of the crisis to work with selected national organizations to develop a tailor-made intervention program for both the captives and their families, to assist in planning the homecoming and setting up needed programs for assistance to the families during the reintegration period (Figley, 1980a). All assistance groups should work with family members in organizing mental health programs and interventions to deal with the crisis. The government should work *with* the families, not *around* them; in this way, some of the feelings of helplessness and powerlessness of the families would be removed.

A moratorium period following repatriation is needed both to celebrate the ex-captives' return as well as to allow for adjustment to the new-gained freedom. Families should be thoroughly briefed on the details of the returned captives' experience, and the returnees should likewise be briefed on any major changes which have taken place in society or within their own families. Since the families have also experienced extreme stress during the crisis and have undergone changes, the returnee also must be made aware of them if adjustment is to proceed efficaciously.

Finally, in any future MIA situation, wives should not be kept in an ambiguous marital status indefinitely and indiscriminately by governmental edict. After a reasonable period of time with no indication that the missing person is alive, his status should routinely be changed to "presumed dead."

CONCLUSIONS

Although traumatic situations such as captivity experience are stressful, crises also offer many individuals an opportunity for personal growth, and often individuals, as well as families, become stronger as a result of the adversity. Because of the long separation, wives discover they really are capable, well-functioning, mature individuals who are able to make intelligent decisions for the family (Hunter, 1980, 1981b, 1981c, in press). Even the ex-captive attests to benefits from the experience.

A POW or hostage has months or years to contemplate who he is, what he has done, and what he would like to accomplish in the future. Many ex-captives indicated that they now know who they really are and what is important in life (Segal, Hunter & Segal, 1976). Moreover, the families who survived (and most mature, well-established ones did) also look back and perceive some benefits. They report that their marriages are more mature with more open communication between the marital dyad, and that their children are more responsible than they would have been, had not the long stressful separation intervened (Hunter, 1977, 1980, 1981b, 1981c). Many of the children also believe that they are more mature, more responsible individuals than they might have been. These families indeed have a "personal history" of successful coping. We have learned from their experiences, and perhaps what we have learned can help other families who face this trauma in future years.

FUTURE IMPLICATIONS

Based on the foregoing discussion it seems obvious that governmental planners who must respond to crises such as a prisoner of war or hostage emergency should act *before* the event occurs, rather than reacting after it occurs. Support systems should be in place at the time they are needed, and adequate, trained personnel who can respond *immediately* should be available without unnecessary delay. Prompt attention to victims of sudden extreme stress is needed to attenuate or alleviate the immediate and long-term effects of trauma to family members which have been shown to occur following crises such as a hostage or POW experience.

CHAPTER

11

Looking to the Future: Research, Education, Treatment, and Policy

CHARLES R. FIGLEY and

HAMILTON I. McCUBBIN

The "power and vitality of the family," we trust, were obvious throughout the chapters in this volume, focusing on the struggles of the families of catastrophe. The powerful catastrophes which rocked these families have left lasting memories, though often subtle and indirect. As you considered each of the special cases of these families and the millions they represent who are caught in similar catastrophes, we hope that you came to recognize the remarkable similarities among families in crisis. For although the sources of stress may be different—emerging from inside the boundaries of the family or imposed from outside—the characteristic patterns of family reactions to stress are detectable across situations, family structures, and time. Especially for those of you who have read both volumes in this *Stress and the Family* series, the generic elements of stress and coping within families should be obvious.

The purpose of this final chapter is to bring into focus both volumes, by emphasizing and illustrating the major points of convergence with special concern for the future. In other words, given what we know about stress and the family, where do we go from here? Or, to put it more bluntly: So what? We will attempt to address the implications of our understanding about families and stress by focusing on four distinct areas which are most often viewed as the by-products of scholarly inquiry: future directions in research, education, clinical treatment, and social policy. More than simply a summation of this volume and volume I, we hope that this exercise will, at least in part, serve as a springboard for you to learn more about how each of us copes with the stress of life within the context of the family.

RESEARCH: TOWARD A GENERIC THEORY

The enterprise of research is the systematic development of empirically-based theories. A useful theory will not only help us understand a particular phenomenon, such as family violence, but more importantly it will help us to predict the occurrence and impact of the phenomenon. As more and more scholars turn their attention to the areas of human stress in general and family stress in particular, it is vitally important that theory development be an integral part of any programmatic research effort. We believe this for at least four reasons:

1) Unlike many areas of social science research, stress is a general label for a rather abstract conceptualization which not only transcends human perception, behavior, and physiology but is also multidisciplinary. Thus, it is a generic term (Lazarus, 1966) which requires precise operationalization in order to effectively bridge so many areas and applications. A theory of stress requires similar precision in definitions.

2) In addition to requiring precision in conceptualization, theory building and the concept of stress *also* both require multivariate parameters (i.e., many factors to explain variations in stress reactions) which are associated in some way to account for a specific stress-related response. Such causal models (cf., Schumm, Southerly & Figley, 1980) in the family stress area would be especially compatible with similar models in medical research focusing on stress (Ellertson, Johnsen & Ursin, 1978).

3) Because the area of family stress and coping is so new, it is susceptible to non-programmatic, one-shot, incidental research efforts so characteristic of research areas temporarily in vogue in the social sciences. With theory building as an important goal of family stress research from the beginning, there is greater likelihood of cooperation and col-

laboration among scientists and, as a result, breakthroughs in the area will come about much more quickly.

4) Stress research has the potential of yielding enormously useful information on the prevention and effective management of stress, but such knowledge will be useless unless and until the findings can be coalesced into a predictive model. In other words, isolated findings of a relationship between two variables (e.g., married heart attack patients cope better than unmarried ones) among a homogeneous sample (white, middle-aged men) at a single point in time do not provide sufficient basis for developing a treatment program impacting either variable, even among the limited population studied.

In this volume and the previous one it is clear that the family reacts with some degree of predictability to life stressors, be they normative or catastrophic, or emerging inside or outside the family. The models proposed in the initial chapters of each of our volumes reflect these generic patterns. Thus, we would urge that future research in the area of family stress be especially interested in the continuous revisions of both our theories and those of others. Most of the chapters in both volumes discussed the need for future research. In Chapter 7 (Volume I) by Ahrons, for example, it is suggested that ". . . coping strategies and rule construction processes must be made much more theoretically explicit" (p. 115).

Beyond the concerns of theory building, our researchers have urged efforts to understand the special circumstances of families and the unique stressors which affect their lives. Hogan, Buehler, and Robinson Volume I, Chapter 8, for example, suggest that research should investigate both the strengths and weaknesses of co-parenting arrangements, but especially their function as a *source* of stress and a mitigator of stress. McAdoo (Chapter 12, Volume I) calls for more research in the area of stress and functional coping within the family-kin network, ". . . with the expectation that such knowledge can be used to strengthen Black families now and in the future," and cautions researchers not to approach the Black family with preconceived ideas about their perceptions of stress. Coward and Jackson (Chapter 13, Volume I) issue similar cautions to researchers studying the stress of rural life, so that they do not conceptually confuse levels of satisfaction with levels of stress. And, of course, Chapter 1 (McCubbin & Patterson) and Chapter 10 (Melson), in Volume I, provide the richest source of direction for researchers, since both are devoted to a thorough discussion of the theoretical parameters of family stress.

The first chapter (Figley) in this volume provides a similar contribution regarding the nature of catastrophe and, as you have seen, numerous chapters here have discussed research directions. Certainly Sprenkle and Cyrus (Chapter 4) provide an important set of hypotheses to be operationalized and tested in terms of the stressful facets of the divorcing process, especially for those who are emotionally abandoned (e.g., "Stress will also be greater if a person does not believe he or she has alternative sources of intimacy.") Burge (Chapter 7) calls for an increased empirical base regarding the victims of rape: coping strategy; the factors affecting recovery of the victim, ". . . as well as those who live and work with her." Similarly, Smith (Chapter 8) cites 11 questions which would lead to the development of programmatic research efforts in the area of disaster (e.g., How does government policy affect family coping and recovery after disasters?).

Thus, in both volumes, specialists on various family stressors urge their colleagues to focus more attention on the family stress area in general and their special area of interest in particular. By doing so, they are suggesting, we will someday to able to understand and be able to do something about how and why families react as they do. If a generic model of family stress is possible, as the initial chapters in this and the previous volume demonstrate, then, guided by theory, research programs focusing on various issues (e.g., child abuse and neglect) and contexts (e.g., Black families, POW families) may be applicable to families affected by *other* sets of stressors in *other* contexts. Models which make such generalizing possible, we believe, would be a major breakthrough in the social sciences. With sufficient empirically-based information about the family as a stress absorber, stress producer and stress reactor—as demonstrated throughout this series—education, treatment, and policy can be developed to help families cope with stress in the future.

EDUCATION: GENERAL, CURRICULAR AND TRAINING INITIATIVES

Public Education Programs

Knowing more about family stress, its origin and impact, can be important to the general welfare of the public. Public education programs sponsored by public (government-funded programs such as through the Veterans Administration, the military, and the National Institute of

Mental Health) and private (e.g., the Red Cross, YMCA, YWCA, religious institutions) entities through various media, including television, can help the general public become more aware of the sources of stress and how families cope effectively. In this volume, for example, Smith (Chapter 8) notes the importance and effectiveness of educating families about emergency preparedness for avoiding the negative impact of natural disasters. Burge (Chapter 7) notes the utility of educating the general public, and especially the family, of the characteristic symptoms of rape-related stress reactions. In Volume I, public education programs in the area of stress are uged by most of the chapter authors with regard to such sources of stress as human sexuality (Chapter 3 by Zuengler & Neubeck), childbirth (Chapter 4 by Miller & Myers-Walls), stepfamilies (Chapter 9 by Visher & Visher), and financial management (Chapter 14 by Noecker Guadagno).

Certainly our children should be educated about stress within the family context. Curricular innovations which incorporate the concepts and principles of human stress and coping are already taking place, as is the incorporation of modern computer technology and its applications. These additions will equip our youth to anticipate and manage more effectively future sources of stress.

Undergraduate Curricula

Education about the family in our nation's colleges and universities is found within one of several departments: sociology, where the emphasis is on social roles; psychology, with an emphasis on individual development and behavior; interdisciplinary, such as child development and family studies, and family social science and social work, with an emphasis on the family as a system and intervention; and other departments which only recently have focused on the family. The emphasis on family stress could easily bridge all of these departments, as we believe the volumes in this series are appropriate textbooks for courses in these departments. Certainly the multidisciplinary authorship of chapters throughout the series demonstrates the wide-ranging appeal of the family stress concept.* Curricula could be arranged by major sources of stress, for example, very similar to the topics of the 26 chapters in these two volumes.

---

*For example, Miller (sociology), Melson (psychology), Myers-Walls (child development and family studies), Noecker Guadagno (home economics), J. Visher (psychiatry), Needle (public health), and Jose (health education).

Graduate Curricula

Similar innovations at an advanced level could be developed in graduate programs which focus on the family, especially those which train family practitioners. There is considerable potential for shifting the emphasis in family therapy, for example, from its current emphasis on pathology to more behaviorally-based models (cf., Guerney, 1978) with family stress as the central focus. Certainly, master's and doctoral research focusing on the numerous issues and questions surrounding family stress would be useful to both the development of the field as well as the general welfare of the family and its members.

In-service Education and Training

Finally, if the family stress concept is important enough to justify renovation in secondary, post-secondary, and graduate education programs, and programs for the general public, what about professionals who should have an understanding of the family and reciprocal influence on individuals?

Medical specialists, especially nurses, for example, would benefit from an understanding not only of the special sources of stress for the hospitalized child (cf., Chapter 2), but also of the predictable ramifications for the family's effective and ineffective methods of coping. These professionals should be able to utilize specific methods to facilitate family coping and adaptation.

Similarly, professionals working with military veterans (cf., Chapter 9) and POWs (cf., Chapter 10) and their families would be trained to look for various symptoms of stress and help mitigate further stress by helping the families utilize, for example, their natural coping methods and resources. As noted in Chapter 9, such programs are now being promulgated by the government, especially within the Veterans Administration.

Personnel managers in particular and corporate executives in general should be aware of the work-family stress interface and be trained to recognize and handle the emotional fallout. Poor family stress coping, as noted in several Chapters (Volume I, Chapters 6,8, and 11), may result in countless hours of lost work time and low productivity.

Most important of all, however, are the thousands of professionals who work directly with families: educators, counselors, clergy, therapists, medical specialists, emergency assistance specialists, Red Cross workers, and others. They are in key roles to help mitigate the predicatable fallout of unmanaged family stress. Their guidance to families struggling to cope with stress could be invaluable. Training them and others in the basics of family stress management would create important resources for the families who contact them.

TREATMENT: SERVING AS COPING CONSULTANTS

What specifically would be taught in these in-service training programs and in family intervention programs at the graduate level? The family stress approach would, of course, include many of the principles discussed in these two volumes. Every chapter presents the special professional intervention needs of the family, as well as insights and guidelines for providing these services. For example, in this volume Patterson and McCubbin (Chapter 2) stress the importance of "interventionists to promote family well-being . . . (by using) the family situation as an opportunity to improve its problem-solving skills, coping repertoire, and overall interpersonal relationships" (p. 34). They recommend that intervention programs promote prevention and focus on current functioning, and help families understand the medical realities of the disability, and "develop a range of coping strategies." Needle, Glynn and Needle (Chapter 3) also emphasize the importance of prevention programs and working within the context of the family —especially viewing adolescent drug abuse problems within a family systems perspective.

Sprenkle and Cyrus (Chapter 4) devote considerable attention to the philosophy, strategy, and specifics of intervention. They discuss in detail the new area of divorce therapy in efforts to reduce or prevent family stress. For example, they emphasize the importance of being supportive, directive, didactic, and confrontive. They outline in some detail a strategy for helping the families—and especially the mate abandoned—affected by sudden divorce. Crosby and Jose (Chapter 5) suggest that intervention programs following a death should promote grief resolution and help establish independence and self-sufficiency. They go on to outline in some detail a strategy for doing this. Voydanoff, in Chapter 6, suggests that programs which help the unemployed family should emphasize self-sufficiency and the utilization of community and social supports.

In Chapter 7, Burge notes two critical tasks for working with rape victims and their families. Her advice would be applicable to working with any one of a number of victims of catastrophe and their families.

She suggests attempting to help the victim "get back to normal" and to prepare the family for supporting the victim by helping the family members express their feelings about the catastrophe, educating them about the rape experience and recovery, and helping and encouraging them to be receptive to the victim's concerns and feelings. The victim should be allowed and encouraged to reestablish the autonomy the rape has partially removed. Smith (Chapter 8) emphasizes more of a community approach to intervention, including prevention and preparedness related to disaster-related catastrophic stress. She divides her suggestions among emergency services professionals, disaster relief professionals, and mental health professionals. Hogancamp and Figley (Chapter 9) note the advantages of working with veterans within a family context. They suggest that clinicians become educated about war-related stress reactions of both veterans and their families, create a supportive clinical environment for the free expression of feelings, and facilitate "rejoining" the family following the purging of any emotional conflicts related to their military experience; they are then able to be more effective in dealing with the daily stressors of life within and outside the family. In the next chapter Hunter (Chapter 10) gives similar advice, cautioning the clinician to distinguish between giving former captives and their families sympathy versus empathy. She devotes considerable attention to suggested governmental policies and programs which, if carried out effectively, may mitigate the need for clinical intervention.

Volume I includes an equal amount of advice to interventionists — educators, counselors, policy makers, program planners—on the use of information on family stress in various problemmatic contexts. Examples from each chapter are presented here only as illustrations: Chapter 3 (Zuengler & Neubeck) emphasizes the importance of clinicians serving as supplemental sex educators. In Chapter 4, Miller and Myers-Walls are cautious about professionals' interventions which further alienate parents, reinforcing their basic insecurities of parental competence. On a similar note, Kidwell et al. in the next chapter emphasize the importance of prevention programs for mitigating family stress. In Chapter 6, Skinner bypasses the professional and speaks directly to the reader in an effort to help prospective dual-careerists think through the central issues in the decision to seek such a highly stressful albeit rewarding lifestyle. In the next chapter, Ahrons urges counselors to help families affected by the stress of divorce redefine the boundaries of their bifurcating family and the new roles, rules, and regulations which inevitably must follow. Hogan et al. (Chapter 8) emphasize that programs should be developed by counselors and educators which include comprehensive management skills; while Visher and Visher in the next chapter focus on the provision of "realistic expectations about the challenges and rewards of stepfamily life." Portner (Chapter 11) notes the utility of educational programs and support groups in coping with work-related family stressors. McAdoo (Chapter 12) notes with equal enthusiasm the importance of extended kinship and social support networks for Black families and the need for social service programs to facilitate the maintenance and use of these support networks. Coward and Jackson in the next chapter caution ethnocentric clinicians to approach the stress of rural families with sensitivity to local customs and values. Guadagno (Chapter 14) notes how family stress can be reduced significantly by preventive educational and counseling programs in financial planning assistance.

Thus, the concept of family stress, as illustrated by the contributions in these two volumes, has considerable potential for improving our understanding of and effectiveness in helping the family and the members within it. Within a short time, no doubt, a companionate volume will focus on effective and innovative methods of intervention for family management of stress. For now, however, the challenges herein are exciting and inviting.

POLICY: HELPING FAMILIES HELP THEMSELVES

The activities of research and scholarship, education and treatment are important to the future growth and efficacy of the concept of family stress. Moreover, they are the enterprise of the students of the family, who include the authors and editors of these volumes. But there is one additional area which has not yet been addressed which may be the most important context for understanding and applying the precepts of stress and the family: the public policy arena.

Not long ago the federal government sponsored a national White House Conference on Families. Similar to other such conferences before it, the purpose was to provide an opportunity for those most interested in the issues—professionals, laymen, policymakers, and implementors—to meet together to set priorities which would, at least in theory, eventuate in governmental initiatives in the form of revised or new programs, procedures, or activities most appropriate for bringing about the changes urged by the conference. After nearly a year of debate, struggle, and political maneuvering, three separate meetings took place

(Baltimore, Minneapolis, and Los Angeles) in 1980. It is interesting to note that, despite the divisiveness of the conferees (e.g., split on such issues as the Equal Rights Amendment, reproductive freedom, abortion, and the definition of the family), among the top five priorities at all three conferences were issues related to family stress and an urgent call for public policy reform.

Many of the chapters throughout Volumes I and II focus on important policy issues and several specific recommendations. Several chapters (Volume I, Chapters 6, 8, and 11) discuss the importance of quality child care, the equality of men and women, maternity and paternity leaves, and flexible work schedules, which would relieve considerable pressures on the working woman with a concomitant reduction in family stress. Hogan et al. (Volume I, Chapter 8) believe the evidence for modifying existing child custody laws are obvious, given the normative stress that divorcing parents endure. Visher and Visher (Volume I, Chapter 9) suggest that policies formulated with intact families in mind must be reconsidered as the percentage of stepfamilies increases steadily and complicates the issues of child custody and AFDC payments, which parent gets the child's report card, and other related issues. McAdoo (Volume I, Chapter 12) and Coward and Jackson (Volume I, Chapter 13) note that current policies in the United States are biased toward white people living in urban areas and provide specific suggestions for correcting this situation.

The second volume provides even more directions to policymakers regarding the families of catastrophe and their special stressors. Patterson and McCubbin (Chapter 2) caution against further reductions in funding for programs for families of the chronically ill child and the increasing need for prevention of family stress. Voydanoff (Chapter 6) points out the importance of advance notice of plant closings to help the family prepare for the shock of resulting unemployment, as well as providing sufficient and extended unemployment compensation. Similar prevention-oriented suggestions are found in another chapter (Smith, Chapter 8) to mitigate the predictable emotional upheaval following a devastating natural disaster by developing a "partnership among federal, state, and local emergency services personnel, and the private sector like the Red Cross and Salvation Army, emergency medical professionals, and mental health workers . . ." (p. 142). The final two chapters suggest that veterans (Chapter 9) and returning prisoners of war and others held captive in the service of their country (Chapter 10) deserve policies and programs which appreciate not only the sacrifices of those who are returning, but the family members to whom they return.

Consistent with these recommendations, and especially the research they are based on, a hefty report was sent to the U.S. State Department (Figley, 1980a) which recommended a set of policy and program options for the management of a very special group of families. The families were those who had at least one of their members held hostage in Iran. For 444 days 52 Americans were held against their will while the two countries negotiated their release. The report was compiled by a dozen of the most respected scholars on stress and the family who met at Purdue University in February of 1980 to consider the plight of the families of these Americans held hostage in Iran. What emerged from their deliberation was a compendium of scholarly reprints of previously published work in the area of stress and the family; position statements which discussed the current and future stressors the "hostage families" would face during the captivity period; specific recommendations for policies and programs to mitigate as much pain and suffering as possible; and a summary of these observations along with a specific plan for an assistance program for these special "families of catastrophe." The final Report of the Task Force is reprinted in the appendix of this volume and is an illustration of the utility of collaboration among scholars from various disciplines, professional positions, and regions of the country who have a common interest in stress and the family and a willingness to apply their knowledge to help families in need.

All of the recommendations made to the State Department in February 1980 were actually carried out, including a reunion of the hostages and their families within six months following their return to the United States. The normative stress endured by these families, plus the catastrophic stress imposed on them by unfolding and capricious international events, provide an important model not only for the demonstration of the impact of normative and catastrophic stress pileup, but also the need for and importance of policies and programs which are sensitive to the needs of these families throughout their ordeal. It was not a surprise to anyone who has studied the stress of these and other families like them (e.g., families of war veterans and POWs) to hear the hostages admit upon return that: "The families are the true heroes. We knew what was happening to us and the families did not" (Dougherty, 1981).

CONCLUSION

As American families face the future with ever-increasing sources of stress from within and outside their boundaries, those who are dedicated to the enterprise of family studies—either as creators or appliers of information—must make important choices. These choices will involve the priorities they assign to various issues and interests which abound in this most intriguing and relevant field. We believe that the explication and management of family stress are among the most promising directions in family scholarship and intervention. It is promising because the subject matter is rich in interest, the axioms heuristic for *both* intellectual and practical results, and the time lag between the two quite small compared to other lines of research inside and outside the social sciences.

Thus we end these two volumes on *Stress and the Family* very much as we began in the preface to the series: with enthusiasm and hope for this new and burgeoning area of research in the social sciences—family stress and coping. The measure of progress in any field is the frequency with which the concepts emerging progress from being uncommon and indigenous to being universally adopted. We hope that these are merely the first in a long series of textbooks in the area of stress and the family; that the utility of this area of scholarship will continue to grow; and that its concepts, principles, and lessons will gain popularity not only with students of the family, but also with families themselves.

APPENDIX

Final Report of the Task Force on Families of Catastrophe

Editors' note. The following summary comprises the final report of the Emergency Meeting of the Task Force on Families of Catastrophe, sponsored by the Family Research Institute at Purdue University, which was held on February 4 and 5, 1980. This was the first mobilization of the Task Force which recommended a set of policy and program options for the management of the families of the 52 Americans held hostage in Iran.

PREFACE

It has now been nearly four months since 53 Americans have been held hostage in Iran. At a point in December when it appeared that this crisis would not end quickly, I began to explore the possibility of organizing a task force of colleagues knowledgeable about families caught in catastrophes to provide some insights into this particular crisis. As interest grew among those I contacted, the Task Force on Families of Catastrophe emerged—a permanent group of scholars and practitioners with special interest and expertise in the area of immediate and long-term family reactions to catastrophe. By definition, the Task Force could be mobilized in a relatively short time following a major crisis to provide cogent and timely observations and suggestions for helping families caught in the catastrophe. This crisis in Iran provided the first catastrophe for our consideration, and 12 of the Task Force members* met at Purdue University, February 4-5, 1980. The report that follows is a condensation of the deliberations of that meeting and is an amplification of the oral report presented to the State Department on February 11, 1980 by Drs. Figley, McCubbin, and Spanier of the Task Force.

We gratefully acknowledge the David Warfield Fund, administered by The New York Community Trust, and Welfare Research Inc.'s Social Services Research Institute, administered by the Department of Health, Education and Welfare's Administration for Public Services, which provided funds to support the emergency meeting at Purdue University and the compilation of this report. The Task Force would also like to acknowledge the extraordinary efforts of Vicki Hogancamp of the Family Research Institute, who coordinated the meeting and the preparation of the report, and the encouragement and support of Dr. Norma Compton, Dean of the School of Consumer and Family Sciences, and Dr. Donald Felker, Head of the Department of Child Development and Family Studies.

Charles R. Figley, Ph.D.
Coordinator of the Task Force

MATERIALS REVIEWED BY THE TASK FORCE

As noted in our briefing, the Task Force is a multidisciplinary group of scholars and clinicians with special expertise in a variety of scientific fields within the social and intervention sciences: psychology, psychiatry, sociology, marital and family therapy, and nursing. The Task Force carefully reviewed and focused their deliberations on five scientific, clinical, and case study materials:

Family reactions to catastrophe is a growing field of specialization which is at the core of the conceptual rationale for the Task Force. The contributions to this area span all the disciplines noted previously and focus on major traumatic events which affect families either indirectly,

---

*The initial members of the Task Force who were present at the Purdue meeting included: Pauline G. Boss, Ph.D., Ann Wolbert Burgess, D.N.Sc., Raymond T. Coward, Ph.D., Park Elliott Dietz, M.D., Charles R. Figley, Ph.D., Charlan Graff, Ph.D., Edna J. Hunter, Ph.D., Hamilton I. McCubbin, Ph.D., Frank M. Ochberg, M.D., Virginia H. Sibbison, Ph.D., Graham B. Spanier, Ph.D., and Douglas H. Sprenkle, Ph.D. Special Guests at the Emergency Meeting were Betty Foley, Ann Griffith, William T. Southerly, M.S., and Steven McVey.

through only one of its members, or directly, through all or a large portion of the family system. Such events include, for example, natural and man-made disasters such as the 1972 Buffalo Creek Dam Disaster (West Virginia), the Three-Mile Island Emergency, the 1955 Yuba City (California) flood, and the 1979 rock concert tragedy in Cincinnati; rape, terrorism, and other violent acts against individuals; war-related catastrophes (e.g., as a military combatant, prisoner of war, concentration camp survivor); and other sudden, highly traumatic events which impact the family system. For example, the Center for POW Studies has been responsible for a significant research effort which detailed the immediate and long-term adjustments not only of the returned POWs but of their families and the families of those missing and killed in action as well.

Family stress theory and research, apart from the narrower focus on traumatic effects, center on the family system and its ability to prevent, absorb, and produce stress reactions. Sources of stress may evolve from within the family as a function of the natural development and maintenance of the family system (e.g., parent-child conflict, children being born into or becoming emancipated from the nuclear family unit, sibling relationship conflicts), dealing with stress from outside the family (e.g., impact of television, job-related stressors, contacts with kin and other outsiders), and their cumulative and interactive, direct or indirect, effects on the family system and its members.

General family studies in the social sciences is another significant and growing area of inquiry which incorporates not only the above areas but focuses on general role structure and function within the family, family relationships and mutual/counteracting support systems within the family, communication patterns, rituals, boundary and moral maintenance mechanisms, as well as a host of issues of interest to family historians, anthropologists, economists and various child development and family studies specialists.

Family intervention literature covers the clinical and educational contributions which discuss strategies found to be effective in either preventing or ameliorating problems through various counseling, enhancement, or enrichment programs. Most of these programs are family-centered, suggesting that the entire family system is the client, not just one family member with a problem. These intervention programs, together with reviews of more individually oriented programs which could be transformed into family-centered programs, most frequently have wide application in helping families suffering from a wide variety of pathologies.

AXIOMS EMERGING FROM THE LITERATURE

As noted in our briefing, through the presentation of individual précis (see appendices*) and open discussions during the emergency meeting, several axioms or overarching principles derived from the scientific literature emerged which focused on the family system and its reactions to catastrophe in general and to coping with a family member held hostage in particular. Following is the identification and brief explication of each of the axioms.

1) *The family is a living system.* Miller's theory (1978) suggests that a system like the family is a set of units with relationships among them. This overriding principle of viewing the family as an open, living, constantly shifting, adapting and readjusting system serves as the cornerstone for appreciating the impact of catastrophe on the family and its members. When a family member is lost—either temporarily or permanently, due to violent or non-violent circumstances—the family is profoundly affected. Depending upon the circumstances (e.g., who, what, where, when, why), the family quickly adopts various temporary methods for coping with the crisis. This may include, for example, shifts in patterns of family functioning, changes in role responsibilities, "filling in" for the absent member, developing temporary methods for handling the imposed, crisis-related tasks. For the hostage-member family, for example, considerable information and energy must be coordinated due to the crisis, which, in turn, causes considerable strain on extant intrafamilial relationships (e.g., anxiety over the danger to their family member, dealing with strangers, including the media representatives, and monitoring new information).

2) *Family and family-member reactions to trauma are both complex and predictable.* As a system, when the family is exposed to a catastrophic experience it reacts much like individuals react, in a way which either neutralizes or controls the dangerousness of the stressful stimuli. The classic traumatic and post-traumatic stress responses are evident, for example, among various family members either directly (in harm's way) or indirectly (through one's kin) affected by the catastrophe. The degree of susceptibility to this kind of stress appears to be a function of several factors, including, but not limited to, the position within the family (e.g., mother, father, spouse), relationship to the victim(s) directly affected by

---

*Not included here.

the catastrophe, temperament and personality factors, experience with similar kinds of emergencies, and other factors. Individual reactions to trauma include sleep disorders, startle responses, violent mood shifts, hypertension, lack of concentration, psychosomatic disorders, and other stress-related behaviors. Collectively, the family develops patterns of behaviors and rituals to handle the emergency, which include assignments of various members to collect additional information and provide updates on new developments. In general, in times of crisis the family tends to draw inward for strength, cutting off superficial social ties, and, at least temporarily, suspending superficial bickering.

3) *Family-member reactions to prolonged catastrophe follows a roller-coaster pattern ranging from hope to despair to rage to remorse.* This particular axiom suggests that the hostage-member families will become increasingly impatient as time passes and will experience hope when events appear to be leading to release of the hostages and despair when those events do not lead to the release of their kindred. Eventually the families may find themselves wishing for an end to the situation, regardless of the outcome, and will feel guilt and remorse about experiencing a normal reaction to a stressful situation. The most difficult feeling these families must cope with is their sense of helplessness and lack of control over the danger to their family member—helplessness to control their own family functioning and lack of control over the larger political situation.

4) *Frequently families of catastrophe feel stigmatized and partially ostracized by the community.* Families identified with various catastrophic events often become isolated from their community either by their own doing, as noted in the axioms above, or because the community no longer knows how to treat them. Many have suggested that this ostracism is due to outsiders' irrational fears that contact with those touched by catastrophe will somehow infect them with the catastrophe as well. In any case, the families affected sense a change in the way others relate to them and conclude (often incorrectly) that they are being shunned. For example, after being interviewed by the media, hostage-member families become more readily recognized by the public and therefore are the recipients of prolonged stares by strangers. Unfamiliar with this reaction, the family members often conclude that public sentiment is at best pity and at worst ghoulish curiosity. As a result, these hostage-member families turn to each other for mutual support and sharing of a common experience in an attempt to lessen the gap between themselves and the general public.

5) *The return of the endangered family member is proportionately as traumatic as the initial effects of the removal or endangerment.* This axiom suggests that violent shifts in the status of the family (either from the safe to the danger mode or from the danger mode to the safe mode) are traumatic in themselves and requires homeostatic shifts within the family. As a result, a moratorium period is needed to both celebrate the absent member's return as well as to adjust to the stressful changes his/her return brings about. It is important to study the reactions of the family and its members at the introduction of the catastrophe in order to predict its reaction to the termination of the catastrophe. Often the families' reactions to reintegration are directly related to the families' success in coping prior to the resolution. The reintegration process will vary considerably from family to family depending upon the variability of the family and its coping capabilities.

6) *The returned family member, after prolonged separation under dangerous conditions, benefits by mutual exchange of information with the family about their separate experiences during the separation.* In order to feel a part of the family again, the homecomer is encouraged by the family to disclose all pertinent information which would be useful to the family in understanding what has taken place during the absence and in order to neutralize the dangerousness perceived by the family. Similarly, the homecomer needs to know what changes took place in the family during his/her absence in order to be fully reintegrated within the family. Often both the family and the endangered member develop many erroneous perceptions of what happened to each other during the separation, which in turn lead to internal conflict and unfair criticism and accusations (e.g., blaming the victims for changes the family had to undergo during his/her absence). In general, neither the returning family member nor the family anticipate many adjustment problems associated with the homecoming and when they experience them it adds to their confusion and detracts from the growing family morale.

INTERVENTION OPTIONS EMERGING FROM THE AXIOMS

As noted in the oral briefing, the Task Force members, in addition to explicating what the research and clinical literature states about families of catastrophe, offered a considerable number of suggestions for assisting the hostages' families now and following the release of the hostages.

The overriding sentiment was the development of a comprehensive, family-centered program which included the families' direct input in the planning, characterized by considerable interfamily contact as well as contact with the government. Following are the major axioms abstracted from the précis and the deliberations of the Task Force.

1) *Keep the families as well informed as possible with immediate updates in information.* It is apparent that the State Department is trying very hard to make sure the families involved in the crisis are among the first to know about the latest developments in the crisis. These communication systems should be improved, however, as the days of captivity mount, to avoid any loss of faith on the part of the families that the government is doing everything possible to secure the hostages' release. Thus, it might be useful to establish a regular, daily telephone briefing for each family, unless the family prefers less frequent calls or is satisfied with the present system. The major purpose of the frequent updates is to offset the predictable sense of uncertainty and generalized fear being experienced by many of the family members. If they can be assured that they will receive information on all new developments quickly as they become available, they will not jump at every phone call or fear missing every newscast.

2) *Encourage families to function normally, relying on their own natural networks and resources.* The families should be encouraged to rely on their natural strengths and support systems in times of crisis. The stronger those natural helping networks, the better prognosis for enduring the terror-filled weeks without major family dysfunctioning and being more of a resource to the family member being held hostage once he/she is returned to the U.S. Thus, during this period, public and private services should be viewed both as supplemental and temporary.

3) *Encourage and enable families to interact with fellow hostage-member families and the released hostages.* The concept which has emerged recently from the catastrophe treatment literature is the notion of defusing the trauma through "contact with fellow survivors," or people who have survived the same catastrophe or one quite similar to it. This contact provides reassurance that what survivors are experiencing—as well as what they felt during the emergency—is quite normal and predictable and provides insight into what the survivor can expect in the future. Thus, families affected by the crisis will gain immeasurable benefits by talking with family members of other families to discuss mutual concerns

such as public notoriety, relations with the press, the government, and the general public, physical and emotional reactions to the crisis, family adjustments, and decisions made in the absence of the family member held hostage. Moreover, those hostages who were released or escaped should be united with the families of those still held. This will provide extremely important opportunities for both parties to share common concerns and may be quite effective in purging any unresolved guilt felt by the ex-hostages about their being free while their colleagues are still held in Iran.

4) *Assign an individual to each family to coordinate information flow, both to and from the family, and provide general services to the family at the direct request of the family.* A highly trained, sensitive, and well-informed co-ordinator should be assigned to each hostage-member family, if requested by the family, to "run interference" as well as provide guidelines and assistance in dealing with outsiders. The coordinator would be available to screen telephone calls and letters, filter information from and to the State Department, prepare press releases for media representatives and monitor media interviews, and assist the family with all legal, medical, financial and emotional needs appropriate for the government to provide. This individual should have access to all pertinent information about the crisis and be able to intercede with the government in order to get immediate action for the families.

5) *Form an ad hoc group of advisors to work with selected national organizations to develop a tailor-made intervention program for both hostages and their families to assist in the return and reintegration of the hostages into mainstream society.* Mental health professionals and associations should be consulted to help develop intervention programs for the hostages and their families. These cooperative efforts between government and private sector will not only benefit the individuals directly affected by the crisis, but will establish a strong, functional operation which can be mobilized for future catastrophes.

6) *Families should be fully informed about what to expect when their relative is released from Iran and throughout the repatriation process.* A majority of the stresses these families are encountering may be due to a lack of information about long-term reactions to trauma and stress disorders. The government, in conjunction with experts in the field, should brief the families about stress reactions in general and long-term psychosocial readjustment problems in particular. It should be emphasized to the

families that the feelings they are experiencing are normal, considering the circumstances. If at all possible, the families should be alerted to all the details of their family member's captivity, so that the hostage need not endlessly repeat describing the events, and the families will not be shocked by the hostages' appearance or reactions upon repatriation. In addition, the families should be informed about the dynamics of a "typical" hostage situation (e.g., the captive identifying with the captor and espousing his philosophies; the captive becoming dependent on his captor, displaying "childlike" behavior, etc.). The families need to be made aware of these possible responses and not be surprised by statements the hostages make about their captivity and captors.

7) Hostage members should also be fully informed about their families and what they have endured during captivity. Hostages should be given a week-by-week capsule summary of what was happening at home during captivity. This might include, for example, a journal, scrapbook or diary account of the days the hostage was held and the events at home that took place during that time. The hostages should appreciate the stress that was placed on the families during his/her time of captivity and not be shocked that the family underwent changes in functioning and structure to compensate for his/her absence. The hostage should expect the family to be demanding in terms of time and attention because the families are reassuring themselves that their kindred is alive and well.

Upon release of the hostages and their subsequent return to the U.S., families should be encouraged to celebrate being reunited with their loved ones. These celebrations should reflect the individual families' uniqueness and past history of family gatherings and should be protected from outside interference. In addition, the government should maintain close contact with the families and provide any and all services requested if the needs relate to the catastrophe.

The Iranian hostage situation provides an excellent "jumping off" point to explore the long-term psychosocial readjustment problems of families and individuals caught in catastrophe. Therefore, in conjunction with the families, hostages and the government, a long-term, nonthreatening research and evaluation program should be developed to assist family scholars in future program planning for catastrophe survivors and their families. In the case of the Iranian hostage crisis, the government should maintain a support staff to assist families for at least two years post-repatriation.

It is critically important to emphasize that at no time should the government bypass the family in organizing mental health programs and interventions to deal with this crisis situation. The government should work *with* the families, not *around* them. During all stages families should be consulted on all major service delivery programs to insure program flexibility and applicability to individual families as well as to provide the families with some sense of control to counteract their feelings of helplessness.

OPERATION WELCOME HOME AMERICANS

Although the Task Force did not recommend a specific program of intervention, the following model program reflects much of their thinking and is a representative application of their deliberations.

Phase I: Reentry preparation. At least three weeks prior to the release of the hostages, family members should be alerted to and given the opportunity for input into the development of a reentry program for the hostages and their families. During this period families could be asked to arrange a homecoming celebration for their returning family member by 1) preparing a "care package" of materials which would be given to their hostage family member soon after release including letters, cards and notes from family and friends, hometown newspapers, photos, and various other items which will help bridge the gap in time and space that has occurred; 2) identifying a family member to serve as spokesperson for the family to help in developing a plan for a community celebration upon return of the hostage member, scheduling contacts with media, friends, and others, and be responsible for the logistical matters associated with getting the family to the U.S. entry point to meet the hostages upon their return; 3) encouraging them to develop their own family celebration and method of caring for their returned family member; and 4) preparing the family for what to expect in terms of their own readjustment as well as the readjustment process their returning family member will go through. During this period the family should be kept well informed about any and all new developments affecting the hostage situation and encouraged to promote and maintain contact with other hostage-member families and ex-hostages.

Phase II: Reentry decompression (Week 1, post release). During this first week the hostages will be hospitalized in Germany in an isolated and protected environment, where, we assume, the following tasks will be performed: 1) complete medical and psychological examinations; 2) debriefing for information about their captivity (useful for intelligence purposes, in developing a therapeutic groundwork for assessing the catastrophic impact and appropriate intervention (prevention/treatment) program, and also communications to the family for their information and edification); 3) any necessary crisis intervention counseling; 4) briefing on traumatic and post-traumatic stress reactions (noting normal reactions of survivors and steps to take if less common reactions emerge); 5) contacts with family and selected friends via telephone and/or closed-circuit television or taped messages; 6) distribution of the "care packages" prepared by the family; 7) news updates on world, national, and local events. In addition, we recommend that the hostages be alerted to the nation's need for celebration of their return and the need to treat the hostages as heroes. Moreover, the hostages should be alerted to the family's ordeal during the period of captivity—how each family member has suffered, how they will want to spend a great deal of time with the hostage upon return, how the return may be stressful for everyone and effective methods to be taken in helping the family recover from this catastrophe.

During this interim period of waiting for the return of the hostages to the U.S., we recommend that the government provide a decompression program for the families as well. The families should be called to Washington (or wherever the hostages will return to the U.S.) for a seminar a few days in advance of the hostages' return, during which they should be: 1) briefed on any and all information about the captive experience—including specific bits of information on each individual hostage—collected since release; 2) given an opportunity to talk with their hostage family member each day (preferably via closed circuit television so they can interact visually as well as by voice); 3) informed about the normal adjustments to a catastrophe such as this, both short- and long-term, for both the hostage and family; 4) briefed on all the details of the reentry program, providing another opportunity to fine-tune the program to the individual needs of each family. Overall, this will be a time for these families to shift from a family of waiting and worry to a family of welcoming and celebration.

Phase III: Homecoming (Weeks 2-4, post release). Because the nation has suffered through this long ordeal along with their fellow Americans and because of the ferment experienced by almost all citizens, it is very important that the nation be treated to an opportunity to celebrate the homecoming. A period of time should be set aside (no longer than 24 hours) when the hostages return to the U.S. for a formal, national celebration marking the end of the crisis. A similar period of community celebration could take place immediately upon the family's return with their hostage member, during which the news media, well-wishers, and community leaders could welcome home the hostages. After these two public opportunities to celebrate the return, the families should then be left completely alone and provided any requested assistance to insure that all their needs are met.

Phase IV: Reunion (during Week 4, post release). We recommend a pleasant and private location be found to accommodate all of the hostages and their families for a reunion. Following various comments from key government officials, seminars would be offered which focus on the various normal and expected adjustments of the hostages and their families. Sessions would follow a "rap group" format, designed to provide the hostages with the opportunity to talk through any annoying problems they have faced since release and to discuss what their immediate and long-term plans are. Parallel sessions could be planned for parents, wives, other significant adults, and children. The goal of the retreat should be to provide the hostages and their families a final chance for celebration in a protected environment and to bring closure to the emergency.

Phase V: Long-term recovery. It is important that the families and the hostages be reassured that they will not be forgotten and that all requested assistance relevent to the crisis will be provided. Contacts among the families and the hostages should continue to be encouraged and, if necessary, supported financially.

CONCLUSION

Catastrophes, such as the Iranian hostage crisis, have a significant impact on the individuals directly involved as well as their families. It is critical to note that the families of the hostages are the "unsung heroes" and are suffering as much as, if not more than, the hostages themselves in their attempts to deal with the ambiguities and unknowns of the situation. In response to this concern for the families, the Task Force focused its attention on identifying the specific problems facing the hostage families as well as exploring possible alternatives for assisting these families through the crisis.

The Task Force will reconvene in Gatlinburg, Tennessee at the Groves Conference on Marriage and the Family at the end of May at which time members will discuss issues pertaining to the effects of prolonged separation on personal and family relationships. Thus, our deliberations will continue and will focus as needed on the long-term adjustments of the hostage-member families and their returned kindred and how they are linked with the emerging area of family adjustment to catastrophe.

References

Adler, A. Neuropsychiatric complications in victims of Boston's Coconut Grove disaster. *Journal of the American Medical Association*, 1943, *123*, 1098-1101.

Administrator of Veterans Affairs. 1980 Annual Report. Washington, D.C.: Superintendent of Documents, U.S. Government Printing Office, 1980, pp. 6-7.

Albrecht, S.L. Reactions and adjustments to divorce: Differences in the experiences of males and females. *Family Relations*, 1980, *29*, 59-68.

American Psychiatric Association. *Diagnostic and statistical manual of mental disorders*, 3rd edition. Washington, D.C.: American Psychiatric Association, 1980, pp. 236-237.

Anderson, R.N. Rural plant closures: The coping behavior of Filipinos in Hawaii. *Family Relations*, 1980, *29*, 511-516.

Anderson, W.A. *Some observations on a disaster subculture.* Columbus, OH: The Disaster Research Center, 1965.

Angell, R.C. *The family encounters the depression.* New York: Charles Scribner's Sons, 1936.

Anspach, D. Kinship and divorce. *Journal of Marriage and the Family*, 1976, *38*, 323-330.

Arnold, G. Problems of the cerebral palsy child and his family. *Virginia Medical Monthly*, 1976, *103*, 225-227.

Attardo, N. Psychodynamic factors in the mother-child relationship in adolescent drug addiction: A comparison of mothers of schizophrenics and mothers of normal adolescent sons. *Psychotherapy and Psychosomatics*, 1965, *13*, 249-255.

Auerswald, E.H. Drug use and families—in the context of twentieth century science. In B.G. Ellis (Ed.), *Drug abuse from the family perspective.* Rockville, MD: National Institute on Drug Abuse, 1980.

Baker, L. *The transition to divorce: Discrepancies between husbands and wives.* Unpublished doctoral dissertation. Purdue University, 1981.

Bakke, E.W. *Citizens without work.* New Haven: Yale University Press, 1940.

Bane, M.J. Marital disruption and the lives of children. In G. Levinger & O.C. Moles (Eds.), *Divorce and separation: Context, causes and consequences.* New York: Basic Books, 1979.

Bartlett, D., The use of multiple family therapy groups with adolescent drug addicts. In M. Sugar (Ed.), *The adolescent in group and family therapy.* New York: Brunner/Mazel, 1975.

Barton, A. *Communities in disaster: A sociological analysis of collective stress situations.* New York: Anchor, Doubleday Books, 1970.

Bateson, G., Jackson, D.D., Haley, J., & Weakland, J. Toward a theory of schizophrenia. *Behaviorial Science*, 1956, *1*, 251-264.

Bell, B.D., Kara, G., & Batterson, C. Service utilization and adjustment patterns of elderly tornado victims in an American disaster. *Mass Emergencies*, 1978, *3*, 71-81.

Bennet, G. Bristol floods 1968. Controlled survey of effects on health of local community disaster. *British Medical Journal*, 1970, *3*, 454-458.

Berg, S.W., & Richlin, M. Injuries and Illnesses of Vietnam war POWs: 1. Navy POWs. *Military Medicine*, July 1977, *141*, 7.

Berman, W.H., & Turk, D.C. Adaptation to divorce: Problems and coping strategies. *Journal of Marriage and the Family*, 1981, *43*, 11-39.

Bernard, J. The good-provider role: Its rise and fall. *American Psycholigist*, 1981, *36*, 1-12.

Bitzer, R. Caught in the middle: Mentally disabled Vietnam veterans and the Veterans Administration. In C.R. Figley & S. Leventman (Eds.), *Strangers at home: Vietnam Veterans since the war*. New York: Praeger, 1980, pp. 305-324.

Black, K.N. What about the child from a one-parent home? *Teacher*, 1959, *5*, 24-28.

Blaufarb, H., & Levine, J. Crisis intervention in an earthquake. *Social Work*, 1972, *17*, 16-19.

Bloom, B.L., Asher, S.J., & White, S.E. Marital disruption as a stressor: A review and analysis. *Psychological Bulletin*, 1978, *85*, 867-894.

Bohannon, P. (Ed.) *Divorce and after*. New York: Anchor Books, 1971.

Bolin, R. Family recovery from natural disasters. *Mass Emergencies*, 1976, *1*, 267-277.

Bolin, R., & Trainer, P. Conceptual model of family recovery. In E. Quarantelli (Ed.), *Disasters: Theory and research*. Beverly Hills, CA: Sage Publications, 1978, pp. 234-247.

Booth, G.V. *Kinship and the crisis of divorce*. Unpublished doctoral dissertation. Southern Illinois University at Carbondale, 1979.

Boss, P. The relationship of psychological father presence, wife's personal qualities and wife/family dysfunction in families of missing fathers. *Journal of Marriage and the Family*, August 1980, 541-549. (a)

Boss, P. Normative family stress: Family boundary changes across the life-span. *Family Relations*, October 1980, 445-450. (b)

Boss, P., Hunter, E., & Lester, G. Wife's androgyny, psychological husband/father presence and functioning in a one-parent military family-system: A report of research in progress. Paper presented at the Military Family Research Conference, Naval Health Research Center, San Diego, CA, September 1977.

Brandwein, R., Brown, C., & Fox. E. Women and children last: Social situation of divorced mothers and their families. *Journal of Marriage and the Family*, 1974, *36*, 498-514.

Brenner, M.H. *Mental illness and the economy*. Cambridge: Harvard University Press, 1973.

Brenner, M.H. *Estimating the social costs of national economic policy*. Washington, D.C.: Government Printing Office, 1976.

Brenner, M.H. Personal stability and economic security. *Social Policy*, 1977, *8*, 2-4.

Briar, K.H. *The effect of long-term unemployment on workers and their families*. Palo Alto: R and E Research Associates, 1978.

Brodsky, C.M. Rape at work. In M.J. Walker & S.L. Brodsky (Eds.), *Sexual assault*. Lexington, MA: Lexington Books, 1976.

Brown, G.W., & Harris, T. *Social origins of depression: A study of psychiatric disorder in women*. New York: Free Press, 1978.

Brown, P., Felton, B.J., Munela, R., & Whiteman, V. Attachment in adults: The special case of recently separated marital partners. *Journal of Divorce*, 1980, *3*, 303-317.

Brownmiller, S. *Against our will*. New York: Bantam Books, 1975.

Burge, S., & Figley, C.R. *The social support scale*. Unpublished manuscript, Purdue University, 1982.

Burgess, A.W., & Baldwin, B.A. *Crisis intervention theory and practice: A clinical handbook*. Englewood Cliffs, NJ: Prentice-Hall, 1981.

Burgess, A.W., & Holmstrom, L.L. *Rape: Crisis and recovery*. Bowie, MD: Brady, 1979. (a)

Burgess, A.W., & Holmstrom, L.L. Rape: Sexual disruption and recovery. *American Journal of Orthopsychiatry*, 1979, *49*(4), 648-657. (b)

Burr, W.R. *Theory construction and sociology of the family*. New York: Wiley, 1973.

Burton, I., Kates, R.W., & White, G.F. *The environment as hazard*. New York: Oxford University Press, 1978.

Calavita, K. *Unemployed men and kinship interaction*. Paper presented at the annual meeting of the American Sociological Association, San Francisco, August 1977.

Cannon, W.B. *Bodily changes in pain, hunger, fear, and rage*. 2nd ed. New York: Appleton, 1929.

Canzoneri, V., & Simon, F. Frank: A Vietnam veteran. In *A matter of life and death special*. Boston: WGBH Education Foundation, 1981.

Cardwell, V. *Cerebral palsy: Advances in understanding and care*. New York: Association for the Aid of Crippled Children, 1956.

Cavan, R.S. Unemployment—crisis of the common man. *Marriage and Family Living*, 1959, *21*, 139-146.

Cavan, R.S., & Ranck, K.H. *The family and the depression*. Chicago: University of Chicago Press, 1938.

Cazenave, N.A. Middle-income Black fathers. *The Family Coordinator*, 1979, *28*, 583-593.

Chamberlain, B.C. The psychological aftermath of disaster. Mayo Seminars in Psychiatry, in *Journal of Clinical Psychiatry*, 1980, *41*(7), 238-244.

Chodoff, P., Friedman, S., & Hamburg, D. Stress, defenses and six coping behaviors: Observations in parents of children with malignant disease. *American Journal of Psychiatry*, 1964, *120*(8), 734-749.

Clayton, R.R. The family and federal drug abuse policies—programs: Toward making the invisible family visible. *Journal of Marriage and the family*, 1979, *41*, 637-647.

Cobb, S. Social support as a moderator of life stress. *Psychosomatic Medicine*, 1976, *38*, 300-314.

Cobb, S., & Kasl, S. *Termination: The consequences of job loss*. Cincinnati: NIOSH, 1977.

Cohn, R.M. The effect of unemployment status change on self-attitudes. *Social Psychology*, 1978, *41*, 81-93.

Coleman, S.B. Cross-cultural approaches to addict families. *Journal of Drug Education*, 1979, *9*, 293-299.

Coleman, S.B. Incomplete mourning in substance abusing families: Theory, research and practice. In L. Wolberg & M. Aronson (Eds.), *Group and family therapy, 1981*. New York: Brunner/Mazel, 1981.

Coleman, S.B., & Davis, D.I. Family therapy and drug abuse: A national survey. *Family Process*, 1978, *17*, 21-29.

Coleman, S.B., & Stanton, M.D. The role of death in the addict family. *Journal of Marriage and Family Counseling*, 1978, *4*, 79-91.

Compton, B., & Gallaway, B. *Social work processes*. Homewood IL: Dorsey Press, 1974.

Cornell, J., *The great international disaster book*. New York: Charles Scribner's Sons, 1976.

Cotroneo, M., & Krasner, B.R. Addiction, alienation, and parenting. *Nursing Clinics of North America*, 1976, *11*, 517-525.

Crosby, J. Taking the fifth: Resistance in dealing with negative feelings about parents. *The Personnel and Guidance Journal*, May 1982, 331-335.

Cuber, J.F. Family readjustment of veterans. *Marriage and Family Living*, 1945, *7*, 28-30.

Darling, R. *Families against society: A study of reaction to children with birth defects*. Beverly Hills, CA: Sage Publications, 1979.

Dean, A., & Lin, N. The stress-buffering role of social support. *Journal of Nervous and Mental Disease*, 1977, *165*, 403-417.

Deaton, J.E. *Coping strategies of Vietnam POWs in solitary confinement*. Unpublished Master's Thesis, San Diego State University, San Diego, CA, 1975.

Department of Health, Education and Welfare. *Healthy people: The Surgeon General's report on health promotion and disease prevention*. Washington, D.C.: U.S. Public Health Service, 1979.

Dodge, P. Neurological disorders of school-age children. *Journal of School Health*, 1976, *46*, 338-343.

Dohrenwend, B.S., & Dohrenwend, B.P. (Eds.). *Stressful life events: Their nature and effects*. New York: Wiley, 1974.

Dougherty, W. Verbatim statement made at a national press conference at West Point Military Academy, New York, January 1981.

Drabek, T.E. Social processes in disaster: Family evacuation. *Social Problems*, 1969, *16*, 336-349.

Drabek, T.E. Personal correspondence, 1981.

Drabek, T.E., & Key, W.H. *Meeting the challenge of disaster: Family responses and long-term consequences.* Paper presented at the Japanese-United States Research Conference on Organizational and Community Responses to Disaster, Columbus, Ohio, September 1972.

Drabek, T.E., & Key, W.H. The impact of disaster on primary group linkages. *Mass Emergencies,* 1976, *1,* 89-105.

Drabek, T.E., Key, W.H., Erickson, P.E., & Crowe, J.L. *Longitudinal impact of disaster on family functioning.* Denver, CO: University of Denver, Department of Sociology, 1973.

Drabek, T.E., & Stephenson, J.S. When disaster strikes. *Journal of Applied Social Psychology,* 1971, *1* (2), 187-203.

Duncan, D.F. Family stress and the initiation of adolescent drug abuse: A retrospective study. *Corrective and Social Psychiatry and Journal of Applied Behavior Therapy,* 1978, *24,* 111-114.

Duvall, E. Loneliness and the serviceman's wife. *Marriage and Family Living,* 1945, *7,* 77-81.

Dworkin, J. *Global trends in natural disasters, 1947-1973.* Natural Hazard Research Working Paper # 26. Boulder, CO: Institute of Behavioral Science, University of Colorado, 1974.

Dynes, R. *Organized behavior in disaster.* Lexington, MA: D.C. Heath, 1970.

Eaton, W.W. Life events, social supports, and psychiatric symptoms: A re-analysis of the New Haven data. *Journal of Health and Social Behavior,* 1978, *19,* 230-234.

Eisenberg, P., & Lazarsfeld, P. The psychological effects of unemployment. *Psychological Bulletin,* 1938, *35,* 358-390.

Elder, G.H., Jr. *Children of the great depression.* Chicago: University of Chicago, 1974.

Ellertson, B., Johnsen, T.B., & Ursin, H. Relationship between the hormonal responses to activation and coping. In H. Ursin, E. Baade, & S. Levine, (Eds.), *Psychobiology of stress: A study of coping men.* New York: Academic Press, 1978.

Ellis, B.G. (Ed). Report on a workshop on reinforcing the family system as the major resource in primary prevention of drug abuse. In *Drug abuse from the family perspective.* Rockville, MD: National Institute on Drug Abuse, 1980.

Erickson, P.E., Drabek, T.E., Key, W.H., & Crowe, J.L. Families in disaster: Patterns of Recovery. *Mass Emergencies,* 1976, *1,* 203-216.

Erikson, K.T. *Everything in its path: Destruction of community in the Buffalo Creek flood.* New York: Simon and Schuster, 1976.

Farberow, N.L. *Training manual for human service workers in major disasters.* Rockville, MD: National Institute of Mental Health, 1978.

Federico, J. The marital termination period of the divorce adjustment process. *Journal of Divorce,* 1979, *3,* 93-106.

Ferman, L.A., & Gardner, J. Economic deprivation, social mobility, and mental health. In L.A. Ferman & J.P. Gordus (Eds.), *Mental health and the economy.* Kalamazoo: W.E. Upjohn Institute, 1979.

Figley, C.R. Child density and the marital relationship. *Journal of Marriage and the Family,* 1973, *35*(2), 272-282.

Figley, C.R. (Ed.). *Stress disorders among Vietnam veterans: Theory, research and treatment.* New York: Brunner/Mazel, 1978.

Figley, C.R. Combat as disaster: Treating combat veterans as survivors. Invited presentation at the annual meeting of the American Psychiatric Association, Chicago, May 14, 1979.

Figley, C.R. (Ed.). *Mobilization I: The Iranian crisis: Final report of the Task Force on Families of Catastrophe.* W. Lafayette: Purdue University, 1980.(a)

Figley, C.R. Conceptualization and diagnosis of traumatic and post-traumatic stress disorders. Veterans Administration Seminar, Coon Rapids, Minnesota, November, 1980. (b)

Figley, C.R. *Traumatization and comfort: Close relationships may be hazardous to your health.*

Featured presentation at the conference, "Families and Close Relationships: Individuals in Social Interaction," Texas Tech. University, Lubbock, Texas, February, 1982.

Figley, C.R., & Leventman, S. Introduction: Estrangement and victimization. In C.R. Figley & S. Leventman (Eds.), *Strangers at home: Vietnam veterans since the war*. New York: Praeger, 1980.

Figley, C.R., & Salison, S. Treating Vietnam veterans as survivors. *Evaluation and Change*: Special Issue, "Services for Survivors," 1980, 137-139.

Figley, C.R., & Southerly, W.T. Psychosocial adjustment of veterans. In C.R. Figley & S. Leventman (Eds.), *Strangers at home: Vietman veterans since the war*. New York: Praeger, 1980, p. 172.

Figley, C.R., & Sprenkle, D.H. Delayed stress response syndrome: Family therapy indications. *Journal of Marriage and Family Counseling*, July 1978, 4, 53-60.

Fisher, B. *When your relationship ends: The divorce process rebuilding blocks*. Boulder, CO: The Family Relations Learning Center, 1979.

Foley, B. *Reflections of an MIA wife*. Paper presented at a meeting of the Task Force on Families of Catastrophe, Purdue University, West Lafayette, IN, February 4-5, 1980.

Frankl, V. *Man's search for meaning*. New York: Washington Square Press, 1963.

Frears, L.H., & Schneider, J.M. Exploring loss and grief within a holistic framework. *The Personnel and Guidance Journal*, 1981, 22, 341-345.

Freedman, T.G., & Finnegan, L.P. Triads and the drug-dependent mother. *Social Work*, 1976, 21, 402-404.

Friesema, H.P., Caporoso, J., Goldstein, G., Lineberry, R., & McCleary, R. *Aftermath: Communities after natural disasters*. Beverly Hills, CA: Sage Publications, 1979.

Fritz, C.E. Disasters compared in six American communities. *Human Organization*, 1957, 16 (2), 6-9.

Fritz, C.E. Disaster. In R. Merton & R. Nisbet (Eds.)., *Social problems*. New York: Harcourt, Brace and World, 1961.

Fritz, C.E., & Marks, E.S. The NORC studies of human behavior in disasters: A problem in social control. *Journal of Social Issues*, 1954, 10, 26-41.

Furstenberg, F.F., Jr. Work experience and family life. In J. O'Toole (Ed.), *Work and the quality of life*. Cambridge: MIT Press, 1974.

Gal, R., & Lazarus, R.S. The role of activity in anticipating and confronting stressful situations. *Journal of Human Stress*, 1975, 1 (4), 4-20.

Garber, J., & Seligman, M.E.P. (Eds.). *Human helplessness: Theory and applications*. New York: Academic Press, 1980.

Gibbs, P. *Now it can be told*. New York: Harper, 1920.

Glasser, P., & Navarre, E. Structural problems of the one-parent family. *Journal of Social Issues*, 1965, 211, 98-109.

Gleser, G.C., Green, L., & Winget, C. *Prolonged psychosocial effects of disaster: A study of Buffalo Creek*. New York: Academic Press, 1981.

Glicken, M.D. The child's view of death. *Journal of Marriage and Family Counseling*, 1978, 4, 2.

Glynn, T.J. (Ed.). *Drugs and the family*. Washington, D.C.: U.S. Government Printing Office (National Institute on Drug Abuse Research Issues Series Volume 29, DHHS Publication No. (ADM) 81-1151), 1981. (a)

Glynn, T.J. From family to peer: A review of transitions of influence among drug-using youth. *Journal of Youth and Adolescence*, 1981, 10, 363-384. (b)

Goetting, A. *The effects of divorce on adults and children in contemporary American society: A review of research*. Paper presented at the Annual Meeting of the National Council on Family Relations, 1980.

Golan, N. *The influence of developmental and transactional crises of victims of disasters*. Paper presented at the Second International Conference on Psychological Stress and Adjustment in Time of War and Peace, Jerusalem, Israel, 1978.

Goldman, P. What Vietnam did to us. *Newsweek*, December 14, 1981, 82.

Goode, W.J. *Women in divorce*. New York: Free Press, 1956.

Gore, S. *Social supports and unemployment stress*. Paper presented at the Annual Meeting of the American Sociological Association, San Francisco, August, 1977.

Gore, S. The effect of social support in moderating the health consequences of unemployment. *Journal of Health and Social Behavior*, 1978, *19*, 157-165.

Green, B.L. *Prediction of long-term psychosocial functioning following the Beverly Hills fire*. Doctoral dissertation, University of Cincinnati, 1980.

Greenwald, H.P. Politics and the new insecurity. *Social Forces*, 1978, *57*, 103-118.

Grinker, R.R., & Spiegel, J.P. *Men under stress*. Philadelphia: Blakiston, 1945.

Groth, A.N., Burgess, A.W., & Holmstrom, L.L. Rape: Power, anger, and sexuality. *American Journal of Psychiatry*, 1977, *134*(11), 1239-1243.

Guerney, B. *Relationship enhancement*. San Francisco: Jossey-Bass, 1977.

Guerney, L.F. Filial therapy program. In Olson, D.H. (Ed.), *Treatment relationships*. Minneapolis: Graphics Publishing, 1976.

Haas, J.E., & Drabek, T.E. Community disaster and system stress: A sociological perspective. In J.E. McGrath (Ed.), *Social and psychological factors in stress*. New York: Holt, Rinehart, and Winston, Inc., 1970, pp. 264-286.

Haas, J.E., Kates, R.W., & Bowden, M.J. (Eds.). *Reconstruction following disaster*. Cambridge, MA: MIT Press, 1977.

Haas, J.E., & Mileti, D.S. Socioeconomic impact of earthquake prediction on government, business, and community. *California Geology*, July 1977, 148-157.

Haley, J. *Uncommon therapy*. New York: W.W. Norton, 1973.

Hansen, D.A., & Johnson, V.A. Rethinking family stress theory. In W. Burr, R. Hill, I. Reiss, & F.I. Nye (Eds.), *Contemporary theories about the family* (Vol. 1). New York: Free Press, 1979, pp. 582-603.

Harbin, H., & Maziar, H. The families of drug abusers: A literature review. *Family Process*, 1975, *14*, 411-431.

Hare-Mustin, R.T. Family therapy following the death of a child. *Journal of Marital and Family Therapy*, April 1979, *5*, 2.

Hetherington, E.M., Cox, M., & Cox, R. Divorced fathers. *The Family Coordinator*, 1976, *25*, 417-428.

Hetherington, E.M., Cox, M., & Cox, R. The aftermath of divorce. In J.H. Stevens & M. Matthews (Eds.), *Mother-child, father-child relations*. Washington, D.C.: NAEYC, 1977.

Hill, R. The returning father and his family. *Marriage and Family Living*, 1945, *7*, 31-34.

Hill, R. *Families under stress, adjustment to the crisis of war, separation and reunion*. New York: Harper, 1949.

Hill, R. Generic features of families under stress. *Social Casework*, 1958, *39*, 139-150.

Hill, R., & Hansen, D. Families in disaster. In G. Baker & D. Chapman (Eds.), *Man and society in disaster*. New York: Basic Books, 1962, pp. 185-221.

Hirsch, B.J. Natural support systems and coping with major life changes. *American Journal of Community Psychology*, 1980, *8*, 159-171.

Hirsch, R. Group therapy with parents of adolescent drug addicts. *Psychiatric Quarterly*, 1961, *35*, 702-710.

Hoff, L. *People in crisis: Understanding and helping*. Menlo Park, CA: Addison-Wesley, 1978.

Holmes, T.S., & Rahe, R.H. The social adjustment rating scale. *Psychosomatic Research*, 1967, *11*, 213-218.

Holmstrom, L.L., & Burgess, A.W. Rape: The husband's and boyfriend's initial reactions. *The Family Coordinator*, 1979, *28*(3), 321-330.

Horowitz, M.J. Stress response syndromes: Character style and brief psychotherapy. *Archives of General Psychiatry*, 1974, *31*, 768-781.

Horowitz, M.J. *Stress response syndromes*. New York: Aronson, 1976.

Horowitz, M.J. Psychological responses to serious life events. In V. Hamilton & D.M. Warburton (Eds.), *Human stress and cognition*. New York: Wiley, 1979.

Huberty, D.J. Treating the adolescent drug abuser: A family affair. *Contemporary Drug Problems*, 1975, *4*, 179-194.

Huerta, F., & Horton, R. Coping behavior of elderly flood victims. *The Gerontologist*, 1978, *18*, 541-546.

Hunt, M. *Sudden divorce.* Presentation at the Annual Meeting of the Groves Conference on Marriage and the Family, Gatlinburg, Tennessee, May 1980.

Hunter, E.J. (Ed.). *Prolonged separation: The prisoner of war and his family* (DTIC No. A051-325). San Diego, CA: Center for Prisoner of War Studies, Naval Health Research Center, 1977.

Hunter, E.J. Combat casualties who remain at home. *Military Review*, January 1980, 28-36.

Hunter, E.J. *Coercive persuasion: The myth of free will?* Paper presented at the 89th annual American Psychological Association Convention, Los Angeles, CA, August 24, 1981. (a)

Hunter, E.J. Marriage in limbo. In W. Dumon & C. De Paepe (Eds.), *Proceedings of the XIXth International CFR Seminar on Divorce and Remarriage*. Leuven, Belgium, August 30-September 4, 1981. pp. 21-35. (b)

Hunter, E.J. *Wartime stress: Family adjustment to loss* (Technical Report No. USIU-TR-07). San Diego, CA: United States International University, 1981. (c)

Hunter, E.J. Treating the military captive's family. In F. Kaslow & R. Ridenour (Eds.), *Treating military families*. New York: Guilford Press, in press.

Hunter, E.J., Den Dulk D., & Williams, J.W. *The literature on military families—1980: An annotated bibliography* (DTIC No. AD-A093-3811). United States Air Force Academy, CO, August 1980.

Hunter, E.J., & Hickman, R.A. *As parents go, so go the children: The adjustment and development of military children* (Technical Report No. USIU-TR-01). San Deigo, CA: United States International University, 1981.

Hunter, E.J., McCubbin, H.I., & Benson, D. Differential viewpoints: The MIA wife versus the MIA mother. In H.I. McCubbin et al. (Eds.), *Family separation and reunion.* Washington, DC: Superintendent of Documents, U.S. Government Printing Office (Cat. No. D-206-21), 1974, pp. 74-80.

Hunter, E.J., & Plag, J.A. *An assessment of the needs of POW/MIA wives residing in the San Diego metropolitan area: A proposal for the establishment of family services* (Technical Report No. 73-39). San Diego: Navy Medical Neuropsychiatric Research Unit (Naval Health Research Center), 1973.

Hynes, W.J. *Single parent mothers and distress: Relationship between selected social and psychological factors and distress in low-income single parent mothers.* Unpublished doctoral dissertation, The Catholic University of America, 1979.

Irving, H.H. *Divorce mediation: A rational alternative to the adversary system.* New York: Universe Books, 1981.

Jackson, D.D. The question of family homeostasis. *Psychiatric Quarterly Supplement*, 1957, Part 1, *31*, 79-90.

Jacobson, D.S. The impact of marital separation/divorce on children: Parent child separation and child adjustment. *Journal of Divorce*, 1978, *1*, 341-360.

Janis, I.L. *Stress and frustration.* New York: Harcourt Brace Jovanovich, 1969.

Janis, I.L. *Stress and frustration. Personality variables in social behavior.* New York: Harcourt Brace Jovanovich, 1971.

Jessor, R., & Jessor, S.C. *Problem behavior and psychosocial development: A longitudinal study of youth.* New York: Academic Press, 1977.

Johnson, L. Scars of war: Alienation and estrangement among wounded Vietnam veterans. In C.R. Figley & S. Leventman (Eds.), *Strangers at home: Vietnam Veterans since the war.* New York: Praeger, 1980, pp. 213-228.

Johnson, S. *First person singular: Living the good life alone.* Philadelphia: Lippincott, 1977.

Johnston, L., Bachman, J.G., & O'Malley, P.M. *Drugs and the nation's high school students: Five year national trends, 1979 highlights.* National Institute on Drug Abuse, Washington, D.C.: U.S. Government Printing Office, 1979.

Kalinowsky, L.B. Problems of war neuroses in light of experience in other countries. *American Journal of Psychiatry*, 1950, *107*, 340-346.

Kalish, R.A. Chapter twelve. In H. Feifel (Ed.), *New meanings of death*. New York: A Blakiston Publication, McGraw-Hill, 1977, pp. 217, 228, 230.

Kalish, R. *Death, grief and caring relationships*. Monterey, CA: Brooks/Cole, 1981.

Kandel, D. Convergences in prospective longtitudinal surveys of drug use in normal populations. In D. Kandel (Ed.), *Longitudinal research in drug use: Empirical findings and methodological issues*. Washington, D.C.: Hemisphere-John Wiley, 1978.

Kandel, D. Kessler, R., & Margulies, R. Antecedents of adolescent initiation into stages of drug use: A developmental analysis. *Journal of Youth and Adolescence*, 1978, *7*, 13-40.

Kasl, S.V., & Cobb, S. Some mental health consequences of plant closing and job loss. In L.A. Ferman & J.P. Gordus (Eds.), *Mental Health and the economy*. Kalamazoo: W.E. Upjohn Institute, 1979, pp. 255-299.

Kaslow, F.W. Divorce and divorce therapy. In A.S. Gurman & D.P. Kniskern (Eds.), *Handbook of family therapy*. New York: Burnner/Mazel, 1981, pp. 662-696.

Kates, R.W., Haas, J.E., Amaral, D.J., Olson, R.A., Ramos, R., & Olson, R. Human impact of the Managua earthquake. *Science*, 1973, *182*, 981-990.

Katz, S., & Mazur, M.A. *Understanding the rape victim: A synthesis of research findings*. New York: John Wiley, 1979.

Kaufman, E. Family structures of narcotic addicts. *International Journal of the Addictions*, 1981, *16*, 273-282.

Kempler, H., & Mackenna, P. Drug abusing adolescents and their families: A structural view and treatment approach. *American Journal of Orthopsychiatry*, 1975, *42*, 223-224.

Kerlinger, F.N. *Foundations of behavioral research*. New York: Holt, Rinehart, & Winston, 1973.

Kessler, R.C., & Essex, M. Marital status and depression: The role of coping resources. *Social Forces*, in press.

Kessler, S. *The American way of divorce: Prescription for change*. Chicago: Nelson-Hall, 1975.

Kilijanek, T.S., & Drabek, T.W. Assessing long-term impacts of a natural disaster: A focus on the elderly. *The Gerontologist*, 1979, *19*, 555-556.

Killian, L. The significance of multiple-group membership in disaster. *American Journal of Sociology*, 1952, *57*, 309-314.

Kilpatrick, D.G., Veronen, L.J., & Resick, P.A. Assessment of the aftermath of rape: Changing patterns of fear. *Journal of Behavioral Assessment*, 1979, *1*(2), 133-148.

Kirsten, G., & Robertiello, R. *Big you, little you*. New York: Pocket Books, 1978.

Kitson, G., & Raschke, H. Divorce research: What we know; what we need to know. *Journal of Divorce*, 1981, *4*, 1-37.

Klagsbrun, M., & Davis, D. Substance abuse and family interaction. *Family Process*, 1977, *16*, 149-174.

Komarovsky, M. *The unemployed man and his family*. New York: Dryden, 1940.

Kopp, S. *If you meet the Buddha on the road, kill him*. Palo Alto: Science and Behavior Books, 1972.

Kormos, H.W. The nature of combat stress. In C.R. Figley (Ed.), *Stress disorders among Vietnam veterans: Theory, research and treatment*. New York: Brunner/Mazel, 1978, p. 4.

Kovacs, J. An approach to treating adolescent drug abusers. In E. Senay, V. Shorty, & H. Alksne (Eds.), *Developments in the field of drug abuse*. Cambridge, MA: Schenkman, 1975.

Krantzler, M. *Creative divorce*. New York: M. Evans, 1974.

Krause, N., & Stryker, S. *Job-related stress, economic stress, and psychophysiological well-being*. Paper presented at the annual meeting of the North Central Sociological Association, May 1980.

Kressel, K., & Deutsch, M. Divorce therapy: An in-depth survey of therapists views. *Family Process*, 1977, *16*, 413-444.

Kressel, K., Jaffee, N., Tuchman, B., Watson, C., & Deutsch, M. A typology of divorcing couples: Implications for mediation and the divorce process. *Family process*, 1980, *19*, 101-116.

Kübler-Ross, E. *On death and dying*. New York: Macmillan, 1969.

Kunreuther, H. *Disaster insurance protection: Public policy lessons*. New York: Wiley, 1978.

Lafferty, L., Paine, H., & Smith, S.M. *How to survive an earthquake: Home and family preparedness*. Downey, CA: CHEC Publications, 1979.

Lander, J.F., Alexander, R.H., & Downing, T.W. *Inventory of natural hazards data resources in the federal government*. Washington, D.C.: U.S. Department of Commerce and U.S. Department of the Interior, 1979.

Lazarus, R. *Psychological stress and the coping process*. New York: McGraw-Hill, 1966.

Lein, L. Male participation in home life. *The Family Coordinator*, 1979, *28*, 489-495.

LeMasters, E.E. *Blue-collar aristocrats*. Madison: University of Wisconsin, 1975.

Leopold, R.L., & Dillon, H. Psycho-anatomy of a disaster: A long-term study of post-traumatic neuroses in survivors of a marine explosion. *American Journal of Psychiatry*, 1963, *119*, 913-921.

Lewis, J., Beavers, W., Gossett, J., & Phillips, V. *No single thread*. New York: Brunner/Mazel, 1976.

Lewis, R.A., & Spanier, G.B. Theorizing about the quality and stability of marriage. In W.R. Burr, R. Hill, F.I. Nye, and I.L. Reiss (Eds.), *Contemporary theories about the family* (Vol. 1). New York: Free Press, 1979, pp. 268-294.

Lieberman, E.J. American families and the Vietnam war. *Journal of Marriage and the Family*, 1971, *714*, 709-721.

Lifton, R.J. Advocacy and corruption in the healing profession. In C.R. Figley (Ed.), *Stress disorders among Vietnam veterans: Theory, research and treatment*. New York: Brunner/Mazel, 1978, pp. 209-230.

Lifton, R.J. *The broken connection*. New York: Simon & Schuster, 1979.

Lifton, R.J., & Olson, E. The human meaning of total disaster: The Buffalo Creek experience. *Psychiatry*, 1976, *39* (1), 1-18.

Lindemann, E., & Kubdenabb, E. (Eds.). *Beyond grief: Studies in crisis intervention*. New York: Jason Aronson, 1979.

Linedecker, C. *Kerry*. New York: St. Martin's Press, 1982.

Little, C.B. Technical-professional unemployment: Middle-class adaptability to personal crisis. *The Sociological Quarterly*, 1976, *17*, 262-274.

Longfellow, C. Divorce in context: Its impact on children. In G. Levinger & O.C. Moles (Eds.), *Divorce and separation: Context, causes and consequences*. New York: Basic Books, 1979.

Lowenthal, M.F., & Haven, C. Interaction and adaptation: Intimacy as a critical variable. *American Sociological Review*, 1968, *33*, 20-30.

Madanes, C. *Strategic family therapy*. San Francisco: Jossey-Bass, 1981.

Madanes, C., Dukes, J., & Harbin, H. Family ties of heroin addicts. *Archives of General Psychiatry*, 1980, *3*, 889-894.

Mann, P. Residential mobility as an adaptive experience. *Journal of Consulting and Clinical Psychology*, 1972, *39*, 37-42.

Margolis, L.H., & Farran, D.C. *Unemployment: The health consequences in children*. Unpublished paper, 1981.

Marroni, E. *Factors influencing the adjustment of separated or divorced Catholics*. Unpublished M.S.W. thesis, Norfolk State College, Norfolk, 1977.

Maslow, A.H. *Motivation and Personality*. New York: Harper and Row, 1954.

Masters, W.H., & Johnson, V.E. The aftermath of rape. *Redbook*, June 1976, 161-162.

Mattsson, A. Long-term physical illness in childhood: A challenge to psychosocial adaptation. *Pediatrics*, 1972, *50*, 801-811.

Maywalt, T.E. *Cooperative Flood Loss Reduction*. Presentation at Natural Hazards Research Applications Workshop, Boulder, Colorado, 1981.

McCubbin, H.I. Integrating coping behavior in family stress theory. *Journal of Marriage and Family*, May 1979, 237-244.

McCubbin, H.I. *Understanding stress*. Seminar presented at the National Extension Family

Specialists Conference, Memphis, Tennessee, March 5, 1981.

McCubbin, H.I., Dahl, B.B., & Hunter, E.J. (Eds.). *Families in the military system.* Beverly Hills, CA: Sage, 1976.

McCubbin, H.I., Dahl, B.B., Lester, G., Benson, D., & Robertson, M. Coping repertoires of families adapting to prolonged war-induced separations. *Journal of Marriage and the Family,* 1976, *38*(3), 461-471.

McCubbin, H.I., Dahl, B.B., Lester, G., & Ross, B. The returned prisoner of war and his children: Evidence for the origin of second generational effects of captivity. *International Journal of Sociology of the Family,* 1977, *7,* 25-36.

McCubbin, H.I., Dahl, B.B., Metres, P., Hunter, E.J., & Plag, J.A. (Eds.). *Family separation and reunion: Families of prisoners of war and servicemen missing in action.* Cat. No. D-206.21:74-70. Washington, DC: U.S. Government Printing Office, 1974.

McCubbin, H.I., Hunter, E.J., & Dahl, B.B. Residuals of war: Families of prisoners of war and servicemen missing in action. *Journal of Social Issues,* 1975, *31,* 4.

McCubbin, H.I., Joy, C.B., Cauble, A.E., Comeau, J.K., Patterson, J.M., & Needle, R.H. Family stress and coping: A decade review. *Journal of Marriage and the Family,* 1980, *42,* 855-871.

McCubbin, H.I., McCubbin, M., Nevin R., & Cauble, E. *CHIP—Coping health inventory for parents.* St. Paul: Family Social Science, 1979.

McCubbin, H.I., McCubbin, M., Patterson, J.M., Cauble, A., Wilson, L., & Warwick, W. CHIP—Coping health inventory for parents: An assessment of parental coping patterns in the care of the chronically ill child. *Journal of Marriage and the Family,* in press.

McCubbin, H.I., & Metres, P.J., Jr. Maintaining hope: The dilemma of parents of sons missing in action. In H.I. McCubbin et al. (Eds.), *Family separation and reunion.* Washington, DC: U.S. Government Printing Office (Cat. No. D-206-21: 74-70), 1974.

McCubbin, H.I., Nevin, R., Larsen, A., Comeau, J., Patterson, J.M. Cauble, E., & Striker, K. *Families coping with cerebral palsy.* St. Paul: Family Social Science, 1981.

McCubbin, H.I. & Olson, D.H. *Beyond family crisis: Family adaptation.* Paper presented at International Conference on Families in Disaster, Uppsala, Sweden, June 1980.

McCubbin, H.I. Patterson, J.M. *Systematic assessment of family stress, resources and coping: Tools for research, education and clinical intervention.* St. Paul: Family Social Science, 1981.(a)

McCubbin, H.I., & Patterson, J.M. *Family stress and adaptation to crisis.* Paper presented at the annual meeting of the National Council on Family Relations, Milwaukee, October 1981.(b)

McCubbin, H.I., & Patterson, J.M. The family stress process: The double ABCX model of family adjustment and adaptation. In H. McCubbin, M. Sussman, & J. Patterson (Eds.), *Advances and developments in family stress theory and research.* New York: Haworth, 1983.

McMurray, L. Emotional stress and driving performance: The effects of divorce. *Behavioral Research in Highway Safety,* 1970, *1,* 100-114.

Mendes, H. Single fatherhood. *Social Work,* 1976, *21,* 308-312.

Meyer, E., & Crothers, B. Psychological and physical evaluation of patients with cerebral palsy studied for periods of ten years or more. *American Journal of Physical Medicine,* 1953, *32,* 153-158.

Mileti, D.S. Human adjustment to the risk of environmental extremes. *Sociology and Social Research,* 1980, *64* (3), 327-347.

Mileti, D.S., Drabek, T.E., & Haas, J.E. *Human systems in extreme environments: A sociological perspective.* Monograph #21. Boulder, CO: Institute of Behavioral Science, University of Colorado, 1975.

Mileti, D.S., Hutton, J.R., & Sorensen, J.H. *Earthquake prediction response and options for public policy.* Boulder, CO: Institute of Behavioral Science, University of Colorado, 1981.

Miller, J.G. *Living systems.* New York: McGraw-Hill, 1978.

Moen, P. Family impacts of the 1975 recession. *Journal of Marriage and the Family*, 1979, *41*, 561-572.

Moen, P. Developing family indicators. *Journal of Family Issues*, 1980, *1*, 5-30.

Monthly Vital Statistics Report. National Center for Health Statistics, *29*, September 17, 1981.

Moore, H. E. *Tornados over Texas*. Austin: University of Texas Press, 1958.

Moos, R.H. (Ed.). *Human adaptation: Coping with life crises*. Lexington, MA: D.C. Heath, 1976.

Morefield, D. Personal communication, February 9, 1982.

Mueller, D.P. Social networks: A promising direction for research on the relationship of the social environment to psychiatric disorder. *Social Science and Medicine*, 1980, *14A*, 147-161.

Nace, E.P., O'Brien, C.P., Mintz, J., Ream, N., & Meyers, A.L. Adjustment among Vietnam veteran drug users two years post service. In C.R. Figley (Ed.), *Stress disorders among Vietnam veterans: Theory, research and treatment*. New York: Brunner/Mazel, 1978.

Nardini, J.E. Readjustment problems of the returned prisoner of war. *Medical Service Digest*, 1973, *24*, 17-19.

National Institute on Drug Abuse. *Drug abuse warning network: 1979 dawn annual report*. Washington, D.C.: U.S. Government Printing Office, 1980.

Needle, R.H., & Carlaw, G. *Adolescent family education project*. Unpublished manuscript, University of Minnesota, 1981.

Nevin, R. Parental coping in raising children who have spina bifida cystica. *Dissertation Abstracts International*, 1979, *39* (2), (7912057).

Nevin, R., McCubbin, H.I., Comeau, J., Cauble, E., Patterson, J.M., & Schoonmaker, L. *Families coping with myelomeningocele*. St. Paul: Family Social Science, 1981.

NIAAA. U.S. Department of Health and Human Services, Fourth Special Report to the U.S. Congress on Alcohol and Health (DHS Publication No. [ADM]80-1080), January 1981.

Nice, D.S. *An overview of the family studies program at the center for prisoner of war studies*. Paper presented at the Fifth annual Joint Medical Meeting Concerning POW/MIA Matters, Brooks Air Force Base, San Antonio, Texas, September 1978.

Nice, D.S., McDonald, B., & McMillian, T. The families of U.S. Navy prisoners of war from Vietnam five years after reunion. *Journal of Marriage and the Family*, 1981, *43*, 2, 431-437.

Nicholson, W., & Corson, W. *A longitudinal study of unemployment insurance exhaustees*. Princeton: Mathematica, 1976.

Noone, R.J., & Reddig, R.L. Case studies in the family treatment of drug abuse. *Family Process*, 1976, *15*, 325-332.

Norsigian, J. Rape. In The Boston Women's Health Book Collective, *Our bodies and ourselves*. New York: Simon & Schuster, 1979.

Notman, M.T., & Nadelson, C.C. The rape victim: Psychodynamic considerations. *American Journal of Psychiatry*, 1976, *133* (4), 408-412.

Nye, F.I. Emerging and declining family roles. *Journal of Marriage and the Family*, 1974, *36*, 238-245.

Ochberg, F.M. The victim of terrorism. *The Practitioner*, 1978, *220*, 293-302.

Olson, D.H., Sprenkle, D.H., & Russell, C.S. Marital and family therapy: A decade review. *Journal of Marriage and the Family*, 1980, *42*, 973-994.

Osterweis, M., Bush, P.J., & Zuckerman, A.E. Family context as a predictor of individual medicine use. *Social Science and Medicine*, 1979, *13*, 287-291.

Palm, R. *Real estate agents and special studies zone disclosure: The response of California home buyers to earthquake hazards information*. Boulder, CO: Institute of Behavioral Science, University of Colorado, 1981.

Parad, H. *Crisis intervention: Selected readings*. New York: Family Service Association of America, 1966.

Patterson, J.M., & McCubbin, H.I. The impact of family life events and changes on the health of a chronically ill child. *Family Relations*, April 1983.

Pattison, E.M. *The experience of dying*. Englewood Cliffs, N.J.: Prentice-Hall, 1977.

Perrucci, C., & Targ, D. (Eds.). *Marriage and the family, a critical analysis and proposals for change*. New York: David McKay Company, 1974.

Perry, H.S., & Perry S. *The schoolhouse disasters: Family and community as determinants of the child's response to disaster*. Washington, D.C.: Disaster Research Group, National Academy of Sciences, 1959.

Perry, J.B., Jr., & Pugh, M.D. *Collective behavior: Response to social stress*. St. Paul, MN: West Publishing Company, 1978.

Perry R.W. Evacuation decision-making in natural disasters. *Mass Emergencies*, 1979, *4*, 25-38.

Perry R.W., Greene, M., & Lindell, M.K. *Human response to volcanic eruption: Mt. St. Helens, May 18, 1980* (Report BHARC - 400/80/032). Seattle, WA: Battelle Human Affairs Research Centers, December 1980.

Perry, R.W., & Lindell, M.K. The psychological consequences of natural disaster: A review of research on American communities. *Mass Emergencies*, 1978, *3*, 105-115.

Petersen, R.C. *Marijuana research findings: 1980*. Rockville, MD: National Institute on Drug Abuse Research Monograph Series Number 31, 1980.

Phillips. D.K. The case for veteran's preference. In C.R. Figley & S. Leventman (Eds.), *Strangers at home: Vietnam veterans since the war*. New York: Praeger, 1980, p. 344.

Plag, J.A. *Proposal for the long-term follow-up of returned prisoners of war, their families, and the families of servicemen missing in action: A basis for the delivery of health care services*. Paper presented at the POW Research Consultants' Conference, San Diego, CA, April 1974.

Pollin, W. Health and education effects of marijuana on youth. Statement before the Subcommittee on Alcoholism and Drug Abuse Committee on Labor and Human Resources. U.S. Senate, Washington, D.C., October 21, 1981.

Powell, D.H., & Driscoll, P.F. Middle-class professionals face unemployment. *Society*, 1973, *10*, 18-26.

President's Commission on Mental Health, Report of the Special Working Group. *Mental health problems of Vietnam era veterans*, Vol. 111. Washington, D.C.: Superintendent of Documents, U.S. Government Printing Office, 1979, pp. 1321-1357.

President's Commission on Veteran's Pensions. *Veterans benefits in United States*, Vol. 1, 1956.

Price-Bonham, S., & Balswick, J.O. The noninstitutions: Divorce, desertion, and remarriage. *Journal of Marriage and the Family*, 1980, *42*, 959-972.

Quarantelli, E.L. A note on the protective function of the family in disasters. *Marriage and Family Living*, 1960, *22*, 263-264.

Quarantelli, E.L., & Dynes, R.R. Response to social crises and disaster. *Annual Review of Sociology*, 1977, *3*, 23-49.

Rabkin, J.G., & Struening, E.L. Life events, stress, and illness. *Science*, 1976, *194*, 1013-1020.

Rainwater, L. Work, well-being, and family life. In J. O'Toole (Ed.), *Work and the quality of life*. Cambridge: MIT Press, 1974, pp. 361-378.

Rapoport, L. The state of crisis: Some theoretical considerations. In H. Parad (Ed.), *Crisis intervention: Selected readings*. New York: Family Service Association of America, 1966. (a)

Rapoport, L. Working with families in crisis: An exploration in preventative intervention. In H. Parad (Ed.), *Crisis intervention: Selected readings*. New York: Family Service Association of America, 1966.(b)

Rapoport, R. Unemployment and the family. Loch Memorial Lecture, Family Welfare Association, London, 1981.

Raschke, H.J. *Social and psychological factors in voluntary postmarital dissolution adjustment*. Unpublished doctoral dissertation, University of Minnesota, Minneapolis, 1974.

Raschke, H.J. The role of social participation in post divorce adjustment. *Journal of Divorce,* 1977, *1,* 129-140.

Rodabough, T. Alternatives to the stages model of the dying process. *Death Education,* April 1980, *4,* 1-19.

Root, K.A. *Workers and their families in a plant shutdown.* Paper presented at the annual meeting of the American Sociological Association, San Francisco, August 1977.

Root, K.A., & Mayland, R.L. *The plant's closing, what are we going to do?* Paper presented at the annual meeting of the National Council on Family Relations, Philadelphia, October 1978.

Rosenberg, H. C. *Atomic soldier.* Boston: Beacon Press, 1980.

Rosenfield, C. Job search of the unemployed, May 1976. *Monthly Labor Review,* 1977, *100,* 39-43.

Rossi, P.H., Wright, J.D., Wright, S.R., & Weber-Burdin, E. Are there long-term effects of American natural disasters. *Mass Emergencies,* 1978, *3,* 117-132.

Saffer, T.H., & Kelly, O. *Count down to zero.* New York: G.P. Putnam's Sons, 1982.

San Fernando Valley Child Guidance Clinic. *Coping with children's reactions to earthquakes and other disasters.* Northridge, CA: San Fernando Valley Child Guidance Clinic, 1972.

Satir, V. *Peoplemaking.* Palo Alto: Science and Behavior Books, 1972, pp. 59, 81-94, 101, 173.

Schanche, D. The emotional aftermath of "the largest tornado ever." In R. Moos (Ed.), *Human adaptation: Coping with life crises.* Lexington, MA: D.C. Heath, 1976, pp. 385-393.

Schlozman, K.L., & Verba, S. The new unemployment: Does it hurt? *Public Policy,* 1978, *26,* 333-358.

Schnabel, R. Disaster preparedness: Report to the Congress. Washington, D.C.: Office of Emergency Preparedness, 1972.

Schneidman, E.S. *Deaths of man.* New York: Quadrangle, The New York Times Book Co., 1973.

Schottland, C.I. Notes for report to the U.S. Senate Committee on Veterans' Affairs and subcommittee on Health and Hospitals, U.S. Senate Committee on Veterans' Affairs, 1973.

Schram, D.D. Rape. In J.R. Chapman & M. Gates (Eds.), *The victimization of women.* Beverly Hills, CA: Sage, 1978.

Schuetz, A. The homecomer. *American Journal of Sociology,* 1944-45, *50,* 369-376.

Schumm, W.R., Southerly, W.T., & Figley, C.R. Stumbling blocks or stepping stones: Path analysis in family studies. *Journal of Marriage and the Family,* 1980, *42*(2), 251-262.

Segal, J., Hunter, E.J., & Segal, Z. Universal consequences of captivity: Stress reactions among divergent populations of prisoners of war and their families. *International Social Sciences Journal,* 1976, *XXVIII,* 593-609. (Revised version in *Evaluation and Change,* Special Issue, 1980.

Seldin, N.E. The family of the addict: A review of the literature. *International Journal of the Addictions,* 1972, *7,* 97-107.

Selvini Palazzoli, M., Boscolo, L., Cecchin, G., & Prata, G. *Paradox and counterparadox.* New York: Aronson, 1978.

Selye, H. *The stress of life.* New York: McGraw-Hill, 1956.

Selye, H. *Stress without distress.* Philadelphia: Lippincott, 1974.

Selye, H. *The Stress of life* (2nd ed.). New York: McGraw-Hill, 1976. (a)

Selye, H. *Stress in health and disease.* Boston: Butterworths, 1976. (b)

Sheppard, H.L., Ferman, L.A., & Faber, S. *Too old to work—too young to retire.* Washington, D.C.: Government Printing Office, 1959.

Shere, M. The social-emotional development of the twin who has cerebral palsy. *Cerebral Palsy Review,* 1957, *17,* 16-18.

Silverman, D.C. Sharing the crisis of rape: Counseling the mates and families of victims.

American Journal of Orthopsychiatry, 1978, *48,* 166-173.

Slote, A. *Termination.* New York: Bobbs-Merrill, 1969.

Smart, R.G., & Fejer, D. Drug use among adolescents and their parents: Closing the generation gap in mood modification. *Journal of Abnormal Psychology,* 1972, *79,* 153-160.

Smith, J. *Free fall.* Valley Forge, PA: Judson Press, 1975.

Solomon, M.S., & Hersch, L.B. Death in the family: Implications for family development. *Journal of Marital and Family Therapy,* April 1979, *5,* 2.

Spanier, G.B., & Casto, R.F. Adjustment to separation and divorce: A qualitative analysis. In G. Levinger & O.C. Moles (Eds.), *Divorce and separation: Context, causes and consequences.* New York: Basic Books, 1979.

Spanier, G.B., & Thompson, L. *The rewards and costs of ending a marriage.* Unpublished manuscript, 1981.

Spaulding, R.C. (Ed.). *Proceedings of the third annual joint medical meeting concerning POW/MIA mmatters.* San Diego, CA: Naval Health Research Center, 1975.

Spielberger, C.D., Sarason, E.G., & Milgram, N.A. *Stress and anxiety, Volume 8.* Washington, DC: Hemisphere Publishing Corporation, 1981.

Spock, A., & Stedman, D. Psychologic characteristics of children with cystic fibrosis. *North Carolina Medical Journal,* 1966, *27,* 426-428.

Sprenkle, D.H., & Storm, C.L. *Divorce therapy: The first decade review of research and implications for practice.* Paper presented at the Annual Meeting of the National Council on Family Relations, Portland, Oregon, 1980.

Stanton, M.D. The addict as savior: Heroin, death, and the family. *Family Process,* 1977, *16,* 191-197.

Stanton, M.D. The family and drug misuse: A bibliography. *American Journal of Drug and Alcohol Abuse,* 1978, *5,* 151-170.

Stanton, M.D. Family treatment of drug problems: A review. In R.L. DuPont, A. Goldstein, & J. O'Donnell (Eds.), *Handbook on drug abuse.* Rockville, MD: National Institute on Drug Abuse, 1979. (a)

Stanton, M.D. Drugs and the family. *Marriage and Family Review,* 1979, *2,* 1-10. (b)

Stanton, M.D. A family theory of drug abuse. In D.J. Lettieri, M. Sayers, & H.W. Pearson (Eds.), *Theories on drug abuse: Selected contemporary perspectives.* Washington, D.C.: U.S. Government Printing Office (DHHS Publication No. [ADM] 80-967), 1980. (a)

Stanton, M.D. The hooked serviceman. In C.R. Figley & S. Leventman (Eds.), *Strangers at home: Vietnam veterans since the war.* New York: Praeger, 1980, p. 288. (b)

Stanton, M.D., & Figley, C.R. Treating veterans within the family system. In C.R. Figley (Ed.), *Stress disorders among Vietnam veterans: Theory, research and treatment.* New York: Brunner/Mazel, 1978, pp. 283-284.

Stanton, M.D., Todd, T.C., Heard, D.B., Kirschner, S., Kleiman, J.I., Mowatt, D.T., Riley, P., Scott, S.M., & Van Deusen, J.M. Heroin addiction as a family phenomenon: A new conceptual model. *American Journal of Drug and Alcohol Abuse,* 1978, *5,* 125-150.

Steele, D.W. The counselor's response to death. *The Personnel and Guidance Journal,* November 1977, *56,* 3.

Stolz, L.M. The effect of mobilization and war on children. *Social Casework,* 1952, *32,* 143-149.

Stolz, L.M. *Father relations of war-born children: The effects of postwar adjustment of fathers on the behavior and personality of first children born while fathers were at war.* Palo Alto: Stanford University Press, 1954.

Stratton, A. The stress of separation. *U.S. Naval Institute Proceedings,* July 1978, 53-58.

Sutherland, S., & Scherl, D. Patterns of response among victims of rape. *American Journal of Orthopsychiatry,* 1970, *40* (3), 503-511.

Symonds, M. Victims of violence. *American Journal of Psychoanalysis,* 1975, *35* (1), 19-26.

Tanner, I.J. *The gift of grief.* New York: Hawthorne Books, 1976.

Taubin, S., & Mudd, E. *The traditional nuclear family.* Paper presented at the Groves Conference on Marriage and the Family, Gatlinburg, Tennessee, May 1981.

Teague, C.H. Easing the pain of plant closure. *Management Review*, 1981, *33*, 23-27.

Tierney, K.J., & Baisden, B. *Crisis intervention programs for disaster victims: A source book and manual for smaller communities*. DHEW Publication #(ADM) 79-675. Washington, D.C.: U.S. Dept. of Health, Education, and Welfare, National Institute of Mental Health, 1979.

Titchener, J.L., & Kapp, F.T. Family and character change at Buffalo Creek. *American Journal of Psychiatry*, 1976, *133*, 295-299.

Todd, D. Warrior's women. *A Matter of Life and Death Special*. Boston: WGBH Education Foundation, 1981.

Travis, G. *Chronic illness in children*. Stanford: Stanford University Press, 1976.

Turner, R.H., Nigg, J.M., Paz, D.H., & Young, B.S. *Earthquake threat: The human response in Southern California*. Los Angeles, CA: Institute for Social Science Research, University of California at Los Angeles, 1979.

Ursin, H., Baade, E. & Levine, S. (Eds.). *Psychobiology of stress: A study of coping men*. New York: Academic Press, 1978.

Vaillant, G. Parent-child disparity and drug addiction. *Journal of Nervous and Mental Disease*, 1966, *142*, 534-539.

Venters, M. *Familial coping with chronic and severe illness: The case of cystic fibrosis*. Unpublished paper, 1980.

Veterans Administration. *POW: Study of former prisoners of war*. Studies and Analysis Service, Office of Planning and Program Evaluation. Washington, D.C.: Superintendent of Documents, U.S. Government Printing Office, May 1980.

Voydanoff, P. *The influence of economic security on morale*. Unpublished thesis, 1963.

Voydanoff, P. Unemployment and the family. In J. Sale (Ed.), *Readings*. Pasadena: The National Consortium for Children and Families, 1978.

Voydanoff, P. Unemployment and family stress. In H. Lopata (Ed.), *Research in the interweave of social roles* (Volume 3), in press.

Waller, W. *The veteran comes back*. New York: Dryden Press, 1944, pp. 106-107, 180-181.

Waller, W. The veteran's attitudes. *Annals of the American Academy of Political and Social Science*, March 1945, *238*, 174-179.

Wallerstein, J., & Kelly, J. *Surviving the breakup: How children and parents cope with divorce*. New York: Basic Books, 1980.

Watriss, W. Agent Orange. *National Vietnam Veterans Review*, December 1981, *1* (5), 270-278.

Watzlawick, P., Beavin J., & Jackson, D.D. *Pragmatics of human communication*. New York: W.W. Norton, 1967.

Webster's new collegiate dictionary. Springfield, MA: G.&C. Merriam Co., 1981.

Weingarten, N. Treating adolescent drug abuse as a symptom of dysfunction in the family. In B.G. Ellis (Ed.), *Drug abuse from the family perspective*. Rockville, MD: National Institute on Drug Abuse, 1980.

Weis, K., & Borges, S.S. Victimology and rape: The case of the legitimate victim. *Issues in Criminology*, 1973, *8*, 71-115.

Weiss, R.J., & Payson, H.E. Gross stress reaction. In A.M. Freedman & H.I. Kaplan (Eds.), *Comprehensive textbook of psychiatry*. Baltimore: Williams & Wilkins, 1967.

Weiss, R.L. *Marital separation*. New York: Basic Books, 1975.

Werner, A. Rape: Interruption of the therapeutic process by external stress. *Psychotherapy: Theory, Research, and Practice*, 1972, *9* (4), 349-351.

White, P.N., & Rollins, J.C. Rape: A family crisis. *Family Relations*, 1981, *30*, 103-109.

White, S.W., & Bloom, B.L. Factors related to the adjustment of divorcing men. *Family Relations*, 1982.

Whiteside, T. *The pendulum and the toxic cloud*. New Haven: Yale University Press, 1979.

Wikler, L. Chronic stresses of families of mentally retarded children. *Family Relations*, 1981, *30*, 281-288.

Williams, T. (Ed.). *Post-traumatic stress disorder of the Vietnam veteran.* Cincinnati: Disabled American Veterans, 1980.

Williamson, D.S. New life at the graveyard: A method of therapy for individuation from a dead former parent. *Journal of Marriage and Family Counseling,* January 1978, 4, 1.

Wilson, J. Conflict, stress and growth: The effects of war on the psychosocial development among Vietnam veterans. In C.R. Figley & S. Leventman (Eds.), *Strangers at home*: *Vietnam veterans since the war.* New York: Praeger, 1980, pp. 123-166.

Wilson, P.R. *The other side of rape.* St. Lucia, Queensland, Australia: University of Queensland Press, 1978.

Wilson, R. Disasters and mental health. In G. Baker and D. Chapman (Eds.), *Man and society.* New York: Basic Books, 1962.

Woodling, B.A., Evans, J.R., & Bradbury, M.D. Sexual assault: Rape and molestation.' *Clinical Obstetrics and Gynecology,* 1977, 20 (3), 509-530.

Zawadzki, B., & Lazarsfeld, P. The psychological consequences of unemployment. *Journal of Social Psychology,* 1935, 6, 224-251.

Zimmering, P. Heroin addiction in adolescent boys. *Journal of Nervous and Mental Disease,* 1951, 114, 19-34.

Name Index, Volumes I and II

Subject Index, Volumes I and II

236